The VINEGAR of SPILAMBERTO

Also by Doris Muscatine

A Cook's Tour of San Francisco

A Cook's Tour of Rome

Old San Francisco: The Biography of a City

The University of California / Sotheby Book of California Wine

Monday Night at Narsai's

The VINEGAR

From left to right:
Charles, Lissa, Jeff, and Doris Muscatine
on the Spanish Steps in Rome

of SPILAMBERTO

And Other Italian

Adventures with Food,

Places and People

Doris Muscatine

Shoemaker Hoard

The chapter "The Vinegar of Spilamberto" originally appeared in
a slightly different form in *Gastronomica*, Summer 2003.
The chapter "Mushkaboola" originally appeared in a slightly
different form in *The Journal of Gastronomy*, Vol. 1, Summer 1984.

Library of Congress Cataloging-in-Publication Data
Muscatine, Doris.
The vinegar of Spilamberto : and other Italian adventures
(food, friends and—) / Doris Muscatine.
p. cm.
Includes bibliographical references and index.
ISBN (10) 1-59376-081-7 (alk. paper)
ISBN (13) 978-1-59376-081-6
1. Cookery, Italian. 2. Italy—Description and travel.
3. Italy—Social life and customs. I. Title.
TX723.M88 2005
394.1'2'0945—dc22   2005010496

Text design by David Bullen
Frontispiece photo by De Antonis
Map by Mike Morgenfeld
Printed in the United States of America

Shoemaker ⟨S⟩ Hoard
An Imprint of Avalon Publishing Group, Inc.
Distributed by Publishers Group West

10 9 8 7 6 5 4 3 2 1

To Ora and the late Carlo Cipolla,
who passed on their love for Italy

and to my grandchildren,
Naomi, Sonia, Sam, Wynne, Cole, and Max,
the next generation of Italian travelers

Contents

Acknowledgments

My infinite thanks to Elena Servi Burgess Friedman for her painstaking reading of the manuscript, in particular her attention to Italian words and phrases; but most important of all, for her being such a dear and precious friend.

Also thanks to Alessandra Cattani; Howard Bern for his fond remembrances of Rossi-Doria; the Istituto Italiano di Cultura, in particular to Gianmaria Mussio, the Information Officer; Tanya Gregory, for her friendship and her knowledge of the most esoteric details; Darrell Corti; Pierre-Jean Averseng of Agri-Truffe France; Molly Moore of The Wine Institute; and Jeff Findley of the Berkeley Public Library. It is in no way possible to thank Robert Lescher, my agent and dear friend, for his time and effort beyond the call of duty. A word about my publishers, Trish Hoard and Jack Shoemaker, a rare breed and getting even rarer. Every author should be so blessed! Also my utmost appreciation to Roxanna Font, their managing editor, for her meticulous attention to all the important details, but most especially for her abundant good cheer.

Last, my very special thanks to my very special husband, Charles, who shared the many Italian adventures, and read every word of the manuscript, offering everything from comma insertions to invaluable suggestions. Most important of all, his enthusiastic support and steadfast appreciation cheered me on and made me believe in the book. It isn't every spouse who genuinely chuckles aloud as he reads his wife's manuscript.

The VINEGAR of SPILAMBERTO

CHAPTER ONE

The Beginnings: Mushkaboola

On Thursdays, the maid's day off, if my mother and father worked late in the store downtown, I would make my own six-year-old version of dinner, a delicious concoction that I named mushkaboola: Take half a leftover baked potato, one leftover loin lamb chop, any amount of leftover canned peas, ditto of leftover cooked spinach, and cut all into chunks. Turn gently in melted butter in a frying pan until warmed through. Turn out onto a dinner plate and douse liberally with ketchup, which should be mixed in before eating. If no loin lamb chop is available, break two eggs over the other ingredients in the pan and cook, stirring gently, until the eggs are set. Serves one, unless your cousin Natalie is there.

That was my start in the kitchen. Until I moved to California some fifteen years later, mushkaboola was probably the most complicated dish I ever ate. Although I was born in New York, I never got to sample the diverse cuisine there until much later. My parents whisked me off to Chicago at six months, and from there to Trenton, New Jersey—in those days hardly a gastronomic pleasure dome. The high point of my mandatory seventh-grade cooking class was creamed chipped beef on toast.

My mother, a businesswoman, did not do the cooking at home, except on the occasions when the maid was ill or it was her day off. But my Russian grandmother was a bona fide member of the food business; maybe I came to my interest in food genetically. Grandmother had started out by making *kwass,* a punch made of water, ice, saccharine, and red coloring that she sold to the peasants who came to peddle their fruit every other weekend in the market in the village of Warshilovka. She had three stands, each manned by one of her young sons, aged six, seven, and eight. She charged a half cent a glass and made enough money to buy flour to bake bread for a week. Soon, she expanded the business in a big way, setting up a regular market-day boarding table in her house. She cooked a large pot of goulash, *rossel flaisch,* rich with gravy, into which the customers dunked generous slabs of rye bread. This was followed by tea, always served in a glass, and home-baked cookies. Since Russians liked vodka with their meals, she also had a quart, concealed in a paper bag, and sold it by the glass, illegally. The state store where she bought it was the only legal seller, and the bottles carried an official government seal. Eventually, she was selling eight or ten bottles on market day, at ten *kopekas* a glass.

One day the excise officer raided the house and found the concealed bottles. Several of the men eating there confessed that they had bought the vodka by the glass. Caught in the act, she admitted her guilt, pleading the extreme financial struggle the family was going through and the fact that she was six months pregnant. Instead of arresting her, the officer summoned her and my grandfather to court in the large town of Vinitza the next week. There my grandfather accepted the transfer of charges, and the presiding judge sentenced him to four months in the Vinitza prison.

From my grandmother, my mother got her sense of robust seasoning, so that when she did cook, the results were always tasty. She believed in high-grade ingredients, garlic, and generous amounts of butter, including a large dab on my morning's soft-boiled egg. The eggs were delivered to the door fresh from the farm. From their trucks, vendors also sold bread, fish (we never bought any), chickens (actually, the chicken man came on a motorcycle), vegetables, and milk in glass bottles of a high-waisted design whose function was to collect the rich heavy cream above the cinch. We had plenty of canned soups, sandwiches on pallid packaged white bread spread with anemic store-bought mayonnaise, but good bagels and corn rye bread from the bakery on Hermitage Avenue or Cohen's on Market Street.

Each night of the week we had a prescribed menu, which never varied: Monday, salmon croquettes and lamb chops; Tuesday, spaghetti and chicken; and so on—like a table d'hôte dinner at a small ethnic restaurant. If it's Wednesday, it must be sweet and sour meatballs. Made of White Rose canned salmon, the croquettes, first dipped in egg, then in crushed corn flakes, were sautéed in butter until golden brown, and served up hot on a leaf of iceberg lettuce: the first composed salad. The spaghetti accompanying the roast chicken was the packaged type topped with canned tomato sauce to which had been added a mince of fresh onion and green bell pepper. No cheese. Not bad. The large roaster was likely to have been a capon. (In 1948, newly arrived in Berkeley, when I asked for one in our chicken parts store, the clerk informed me that capon was an eastern breed.) We never had fresh fish, or any cheese other than Philadelphia cream cheese, except when relatives came visiting from nearby New York. Then we indulged in smoked sturgeon, whitefish, lox, Schweizer cheese, and aromatic sliced meats from the delicatessen.

In spite of the predominance of canned fruits and vegetables in winter, summertime brought the open-air produce market on River Road, which on a much smaller scale was reminiscent of European or Asian markets. The stands displayed white sweet corn in their husks, melons, tree-ripened peaches, fresh-picked berries, and fat beefsteak tomatoes that New Jersey truck farmers produce with such splendid flavor. The huge butter-colored kernels of the new golden bantam corn were exciting, but after the novelty wore off, I preferred the more tender, juicier, sweeter ears of white. We would pick up the ingredients for either of the two salads we had at home: tomatoes, green peppers, green onions, cucumbers, radishes, celery and iceberg lettuce.

Salad one: cut all ingredients into dice, toss with salt, pepper, mayonnaise, ketchup and enough cider vinegar to moisten, and refrigerate for several hours or overnight. (Tastes good left over.)

Salad two: the ubiquitous eastern salad of yore, now making a comeback: cut iceberg lettuce into large wedges and cover with an avalanche of Russian dressing.

The beverage of choice, inherited from my grandparents' European taste for seltzer water, was ginger ale with dinner. Adults drank it mixed with rye or bourbon after meals. It was better than rum and Coca-Cola, another predominant favorite, though as a child I did like cherry cokes. The first time I had wine with dinner was when I was a Bennington sophomore, and a college friend invited me to her New Haven home for the Thanksgiving holidays. Wanting this to be a festive occasion, her father called his local liquor store and asked them to send over a case of wine that was something special. They did. We drank Château d'Yquem with the Thanksgiving turkey.

Although on occasion, my mother cooked such complex dishes as sweet and sour tongue, to which she daringly added raisins, she was not an adventurous cook and even less an adventurous eater. It was from my father, whose experience in the kitchen was entirely limited to scrambling eggs slowly, slowly, in lots of butter—a technique he picked up from a chef at Horn & Hardart's—that I learned to appreciate a broader culinary spectrum. In the summertime, we often made Sunday pilgrimages for a day of swimming and sunning on the sands of Bradley Beach or Atlantic City. I looked forward just as much to the feast Father and I would consume afterwards, starting with a great mound of steamers, kept warm tucked into a giant white linen napkin. Mother would look faintly ill as we plopped them in our mouths, first dunked into and still dripping with warm drawn butter. When we tackled lobsters, she stuck gamely to her boiled chicken. Thanks to the spicy red sauce, which helped mask the sweet taste of the sea, she did occasionally attempt a shrimp cocktail. When she went on her weekly buying trips to New York, Father and I, left to our own devices, were thoroughly wicked. We drove to the Chinese restaurant, in the wrong part of town, climbed up the narrow stairs to the murky, lantern-lit room with its exotic smells, to order barbecued pork with Chinese mustard, chicken chow mein, and pots of steaming green tea.

We could sometimes entice Mother to go along to an Italian restaurant, where one of our favorite dishes was spaghetti and meatballs. She always ate everything, reluctantly, but I think she secretly enjoyed it. Lorenzo's, a bedraggled place down by the railroad station, had wonderful steaks. Only now do I know that it also had—and has always had—sweet and briny clams and oysters on the half shell, and *real* pasta with a sauce made of fresh basil, garlic, parmesan and olive oil, and thick slices of ripe tomatoes with roquefort cheese dressing, and authentic oyster crackers, and good French wine. Long after I had moved to California, and after my mother had died, I went back home for a conference with the family attorney. He took me to Lorenzo's and it was then that I discovered that Trenton had had a first-class restaurant all along.

I first met Charles in a restaurant setting—actually in the dining room of Greenacres Country Club, of which my father was president and where Charles had just gotten a summer job waiting tables. I was still in bobby socks. My parents, being business people and therefore at work six days a week, would go every Sunday, their free day, for their weekly game of golf. To keep me occupied while they played, they enrolled me in an endless series of golf lessons, leaving me with a lifetime distaste for the sport, even though I was quite good at it. The lessons were over long before the golf game, and it was in the restaurant, run by an English couple who happened to be friends of Charles's parents, hence his summer job, that I would find haven. There was music playing over the PA, there were little taste treats always offered, I could help the waiters set up the tables, and the proprietors, Sadie and Sam Levy, were warm and friendly, besides which they had these wonderful cockney accents. Sadie, a tall ample woman with a horsy face, towered over her bald husband. His girth was half that of his wife, and he had the slightly bulging eyes and surprised look of someone who has just been goosed. They were divine. Even more, Sadie was a peerless baker, turning out staggeringly high chocolate cakes, rich, moist, and airy, and phenomenal lemon meringue pies, tall as a skyscraper.

One Sunday when I turned up in the dining room for my usual solace after my golf lesson, it happened to be Charles's first day of work. The band on the PA was playing a lively dance tune, and he was emerging from the swinging door to the kitchen bearing a tray full of glasses. Sadie, fast as a rabbit, took over the tray, whirled Charles and me together, and breathlessly commanded me, "You've got to dance with our handsome new waiter. He's a freshman at

Yale!" And so we met. And so we danced. And one thing led to another.

By the time Charles was finishing his master's degree in English, still at Yale, World War II had broken out. In those days, service in the armed forces, joining the effort to defeat Hitler, seemed to most young men and many women the honorable thing to do. Charles enlisted in the Navy. After a few months of training as a navigator, he was sent to the European front. I was by this time at Bennington College and we corresponded. After two and a half years overseas— Salerno, North Africa, Sicily, Omaha Beach—he came home; shortly thereafter we were married.

When the war ended, a point system determined the date of release from the military, something like a quarter of a point for each month of service, more for being overseas, and a whopping ten points for being married. Having the points, he got out and returned to Yale to get his doctorate. We rented a one-room, shared bath, walk-up apartment on the third floor of an old converted brownstone, and began our two-and-a-half years there as residents of New Haven.

At the end of his studies, among the job offers Charles got was one from Yale and another from the University of California at Berkeley. There was no question in either of our minds that Yale was the offer to take. Charles repaired to the chairman's office to accept. The chairman was busy. Charles waited. And waited. And waited. It grew dark, it was dinner time, Charles was hungry. He decided to come back in the morning. But we talked well into the night and became more and more convinced that this was our chance to break away and try something new, have some adventure. By morning, we had decided to leave the familiar halls of Yale for distant and unknown parts. And thus we came to California.

In spite of Father's and my bravery when I was a child, and my introduction to the dry martini by my husband's graduate school colleagues in New Haven, I must have eaten more new dishes, drunk more wines, become acquainted with more ethnic variations in the first few months in California than in my entire life up until that time. It was not only a culinary education, but a commitment to the cause of good food. I would never again broil a chicken meant for the stew pot, let alone serve it up to a most distinguished professor, who was incidentally my husband's thesis advisor. A kind man, he told me, as he sawed away at the unyielding hen, that his Scandinavian mother, then deceased, had once done the same thing.

In the late fifties, when we spent a year on a Fulbright scholarship in Rome, and on subsequent long stays in that country, the commitment to good eating was taken for granted. In 1969, we were spending the summer in Italy. When I had to return abruptly to the States because my mother had become seriously ill, I had long since absorbed the idea that food was not just nourishment but a philosophical enrichment of one's life. For a month, I stayed in my mother's apartment in Trenton and commuted daily by train to the hospital in Philadelphia, a four- or five-block walk from the Reading Terminal. I took a marvelous Toonerville trolley of a train, two or three wildly swaying cars with no air conditioning, but windows that let in fresh air on a good day. It took half an hour from Yardley, Pennsylvania, a smallish town across the Delaware River from Trenton.

In the evening, before I boarded the train back, I would fill my Italian net shopping bag with the food for my dinner from the stands of the Reading Terminal market. There were stalls offering luscious produce, displays of cheese, and enticing prepared foods. There were real butchers and sausage-makers. When I arrived home, I would open a bottle of Louis Martini Zinfandel—I had had the good fortune to find a case in one of Trenton's liquor stores— and start to cook my dinner, usually a piece of chicken or fish, sometimes a choice piece of meat that had caught my eye, a simple salad, a vegetable that had tempted. Inevitably, just as I would take my first sip of wine, the doorbell would ring.

On the pretext of inquiring about my mother's health, the neighbors would really come to watch me eat. And drink. They were sure that anyone who would drink half a bottle of wine with her dinner must be an alcoholic. Anyone who preferred fruit and cheese instead of pastry for dessert was clearly diabetic as well. What surprised them most, I gathered from the tenor of their questions about my eating habits, was that at nine or ten o'clock at night, after a trying day at the hospital, I would bother to fix myself a dinner made from scratch, drink wine with it, and even put flowers on my solitary table. They didn't understand that this respect for food had become a routine part of my life, absorbed almost by osmosis from living in cosmopolitan California, and from our long stays in Europe. Food was just one important part of it. If California suggested the possibility of different attitudes and lifestyles, Europe, and later Asia, increased the exposure and changed one's own philosophy. If I started out a heathen from the wastelands, I learned that there were other ways out there.

CHAPTER TWO

Rome

During the Second World War, my husband, as the navigator of LST 335, first crossed the Atlantic on the way to the European theater. Separated from the convoy because of a disabling fire in one engine, the ship zigzagged wildly to avoid a nonexistent submarine sighted by a paranoid crew member. My first experience on board a ship, in contrast, was sailing to Rome in the late 1950s. Even for Charles, the old Navy veteran, being aboard a true luxury liner was quite a different voyage. After five days of elaborate meals, midnight buffets, dressing for dinner, and a storm or two, all except the weather courtesy of the Fulbright Foundation, our ship, the *Giulio Cesare*, put into the port of Naples.

The hassle of collecting baggage, going through customs, and changing money, which we assumed our rudimentary Italian would make smoother, instead became a tarantella danced to an indecipherable song and an unfamiliar beat. Our trouble was that our

Italian, mine learned by auditing a class at the university for a semester, was not conversational but literary Italian, a language meant to prepare students for the pursuit of great literature, not to get through customs. The spoken past tenses were different and unknown to us; the conversational "she" was not "*ella*" but "*lei*"; "he" not "*egli*" but "*lui*," and so on. Add to that a rich Neapolitan accent. After a time of this, frazzled and hot, we bought refreshments to soothe us and console our two small kids: twenty-five-cent orange drinks for which we managed to pay thirteen dollars.

Somehow, we got from the harbor to the railway terminal and aboard the right train for Rome—children and baggage intact. Our Rome apartment, in a well-to-do, somewhat faceless section called Parioli, had the year before housed American friends, who put us in touch with the landlord. He was there to greet us. A young, shortish man, Ivo was a lawyer by profession, a warm, charismatic soul who managed to understand our efforts at his language and deliberately spoke slowly enough so that we could get the gist of what he was saying. Which included an invitation to dinner. With some relief, we accepted, and once the apartment tour was over and the lease and inventory signed (it included the light bulbs), headed off on foot for a neighborhood trattoria. Traffic was dazzling, cars hurtling past, lanes not respected, total chaos, or so it seemed to us. I swore I would never, ever drive in Rome, never could drive in Rome. Months later, in our used Fiat on the way to the airport in Fiumicino to pick up our visiting friend Florence, I was comfortably unaware that I was driving just as crazily as the rest of them. I was amazed when my white-knuckled friend, aghast and afraid for her life, told me so. Yet underneath the seeming tangle of vehicles there were rules, which I had unconsciously absorbed, for yielding and right of way. There were no smashed in or dented cars, no traffic reports, few accidents, and no speed limits on the autostrada.

On our stroll to dinner with Ivo, we paused near an intersection, where the cars were slowing for the red light. With one anticipatory foot in the street, Ivo suddenly shrieked. A car had grazed the tip of his shoe. In outrage he pounded with a resounding wallop on the roof of the offending car. The light changed. The driver, although overwhelmed by the resonating clap of thunder, had to accelerate. But he also rolled down his window, turned back to make a menacing gesture, and slammed deliciously full force into the car in front of him. We had a fine dinner.

At the beginning of our year as a Fulbright family, there were three weeks of orientation and language classes at the Università per gli Stranieri in Perugia to which we drove in our just-purchased second-hand Fiat. While the adults were occupied, all of the Fulbright children, including our two, attended the local Montessori school. When the school threw a party at the end of our stay, there were delicious hôrs d'oeuvre and—unheard of on American school grounds—abundant wine served to us by our debauched, proselytized children. We loved our pensione, the embracing people who ran it, and the three full-time students who were also staying there. We learned how to dress a salad and ate the freshly caught trout from the nearby Lago Trasimeno.

After our day of language studies at the university—more intensive ones for the scholars, more user-friendly for the spouses—and after the children's classes had let out for the day, we took to exploring the city of Perugia, made easier because of the well-preserved remembrances of its Etruscan, Roman, Medieval, and Renaissance pasts. On foot, we could follow the old walls and walk through gateways from the sixth century B.C., when Perugia was Etruscan. We could amble in the labyrinth of ancient narrow streets and vaulted passageways past houses from the middle ages. We explored the Piazza 4 Novembre, the main square, which contains many of the major monuments of the town, among them the cathedral (begun in the ninth century, rebuilt in the tenth, and again in the fourteenth and fifteenth centuries); the magisterial thirteenth-century Palazzo dei Priori, which houses on its third floor the National Gallery of Umbria and its large collection of Umbrian artists; and the two-tiered, circular Fontana Maggiore, heavily decorated in the marble and bronze style of the thirteenth century, built to commemorate the completion of an aqueduct that had brought water some five miles to the town. We discovered that we very much liked the works of fifteenth- and sixteenth-century Umbrian artists, particularly the frescoes of Perugino, the teacher of Raphael. On the weekends, thanks to our old Fiat, we could drive to the irresistible hill towns and lakeside villages nearby. But not in any of our explorations nor in any of the many guidebooks we consulted was there a breath of a mention about the city beneath the city. Possibly the excavations were still too rudimentary to be accessible to the general public, but we didn't learn about the subterranean Perugia until years later when our friend Carlo, who knew everything about everything, told us.

We drove back to the town at once to see for ourselves. Once there, we descended to the Via Baglione Sotteranea, under and through the walls of the Rocca Paolina, by a series of long steep escalators landmarked by the Porta Marzia. This second-century B.C. Etruscan gateway we knew from our previous stay. But new to us were the immaculate excavations, remarkably well-lighted, that had uncovered complete roads, archways, and houses of a once heavily populated medieval quarter. Chiseled out of tufa, the karst-like stones, indigenous to many parts of Italy, were cobbles, blocks, and bricks that lined the excavated roads, the high rooms of the houses, and the underpinnings of the Rocca Paolina fortress that was largely destroyed in the mid-nineteenth century. On the same trip, we discovered an underground Etruscan well, dank and eerie, that allowed us to peer into its depths from a footbridge crossing the center. We learned that at the edge of town and in the countryside around it, several excavated burial grounds recorded the prevalence in those parts of a very early Etruscan civilization. Somehow, on our first stay in Perugia, we had missed those, too.

But even though we had not yet discovered the subterranean treasure, everything we had seen and experienced had been a revelation. And that included one serious communal problem: During our stay, Perugia was in the midst of a devastating drought. This meant that, among the other measures that we all used to conserve water, we bathed the whole family in the same full tub, kids first, then the adults one at a time. Baths finished, we threw in the day's laundry. We were facing a common difficulty together, and it made us feel a small part of the community. But not everyone, it turned out, had the same reaction. At the end of our remarkable year in Italy, a couple of our fellow Fulbrighters called a meeting, ostensibly to sum up our stay and exchange experiences. It turned out that they had been simmering the whole year about the drought in Perugia, the audacity of the authorities to have sent us to such a crippled place, and the hardships they had suffered during three weeks of rationed water. They even had a petition of protest ready for their fellow Americans to sign. Nobody did.

Our apartment in Rome, one flight up, was in a building of a certain age—as they say about some middle-aged women—a bit worn, a bit wrinkled, but with a good touch up job, in this case, a coat of paint in the clay-ochre tones so common in Italy. There was a formal living room, whose furnishings—rather elaborate sofas, chairs, and end tables—were covered in sheets; it was a place we never used, except on one occasion. The closed shutters contributed to the dark, eerie feeling. Fortunately, there was also an informal living room, where we usually congregated. There were four bedrooms, one of them tiny for the maid, a dining room, two bathrooms and a workable kitchen with a small balcony overlooking the entry. Each room, set along a long central corridor, had its own opaque glass door that closed it from the passageway.

Ivo advised that to find a maid, which he insisted we had to do at once, we must consult the wife of the *portiere*, the man who guarded the entrance and was a kind of superintendent as well. No self-respecting *signora* like me would ever consider doing maid's work, our first lesson in the cultural phenomenon of presenting a favorable impression, a *bella figura*. (The opposite, the scandalous *brutta figura*, was to be avoided at all costs.) And thus we obtained the first of our two Marias, a street-wise brunette with large furtive eyes, lithe and leggy like a young Juliet Prowse, the famous dancer of my generation, and handsomely dressed in the latest fashion, including high heels. Her working clothes were worn only in the apartment; the high fashion was worn for anything that called for going out, such as the market.

It soon became evident that we were no match for Maria, whose inflated market bills became increasingly bold and whose respect for us increasingly diminished. Our problem was that we didn't know how to be employers. As trusting Americans, we didn't check each *lira*; faced with clearly weighted bills, we preferred to believe the explanations for them. On her advice, we bought *tarocchi*, Sicilian blood oranges, and other citrus from a man who sold his region's fruit door to door. That proved to be Maria's undoing. Splitting the profits, they would weigh the fruit, thumbs included, on the old-fashioned portable scale that he carried along. Caught in the act, Maria haughtily laughed it off, but it was enough for us, and we reluctantly discharged her. Later, it turned out that she and Ivo had been having an affair almost from the beginning.

Maria number two was, in contrast to her predecessor, a naïve country girl from Le Marche, cherubic, plump, fair-skinned, with dimpled cheeks, warm blue eyes and long reddish hair, a warm and fuzzy disposition, and religious honesty. Once in Paris, we found a Picasso lithograph that so reminded us of her that we had to buy it. Over time, she and the *portiere's* wife became staunch friends, and we became her surrogate family. She even confided in me that the *portiere's* wife, trying to find a cure for her husband's impotence, had hocked her wedding ring to raise money for an expensive salve advertised to do the trick when rubbed on the affected part.

One day, Maria reported that a "certain person" had confessed to her that he was madly in love with me. He was my *spasimante*, she explained, or secret admirer. Although she dropped very broad hints that led me to believe that he might be the butcher, I was more convinced that she had invented the lover because she was so eager to please me. Her own lover, middle-aged, portly and balding, the wearer of striped business suits, starched shirts, vests, and ties—and a married man we later learned—asked to call on us. It was on that occasion that we opened the blinds and removed the dust covers from the living room furniture; in Maria's eyes, we could now hold a proper audience. Absent her real family, he was coming to ask our permission to court her, which of course we granted.

At Easter time, when the children were on holiday, we decided to go to Venice. We offered to drop Maria off at her home in Le Marche on the way. Her one-room house stood in the midst of rolling farmland. It had dirt floors and a division down the middle. A curtain in the connecting doorway kept the family's animals on their side of the partition. We met Maria's mother. Although still in her thirties, she could easily have been mistaken for an old woman. Under her black babushka, her bronzed leathery face, beaten by the sun, creased into a hospitable grin that revealed she was toothless. A long black dress nearly covered her black cotton stockings, which emerged from the half clogs-half boots covering her feet.

The room's sparse furnishings included a bed, and a card table, set predominantly in the middle, surrounded by four haphazard chairs. Our visit, it turned out, was an unprecedented occasion, an honor which Mamma had gone to great lengths to make successful. After beckoning us to sit on the ramshackle chairs, mother and daughter insisted on serving us lunch: country bread, a delicious gamy, home-made salami, orange-yolked fried eggs from the chickens on the other side of the curtain, horrifyingly costly bananas for the children. The *piece de resistance* was a golden brown chicken, which Mamma had taken to town to be roasted in the bakery's oven because there was none such at home. While we consumed this bounty, Maria wound up the Victrola and proudly put on her one American record. We ate to the strains of "You Are My Sunshine." The two women, who resisted all of our attempts to make them join us— it was an unthinkable intimacy for them to eat with the *signori*— hovered over us to make sure that we enjoyed and finished everything they had set before us.

Italian bakery ovens, it turned out, were frequently called on for purposes other than baking breads and pastries. The chicken roasted in the bakery hadn't been our first encounter with the practice. In the fall, after the grape harvest, Ivo had invited us to join him for the wine festival in Marino, one of the hill towns near Rome. As we were driving to the celebration, a sudden downpour immersed us. As we made our way up the windy, narrow roads to the village, it got worse. Suddenly, the road was a giant lake, which submerged a good part of the car. The engine sputtered. We stalled. No resuscitation was possible. Ivo, coat over head, ran to fetch the mechanic. He came running and examined the engine. The spark plugs were wet.

He promptly took them to the bakery and put them in the oven to dry. The rain was abating, the roasted spark plugs were re-installed, and carefully, carefully we proceeded to park the car and join the festivities.

Roasting spark plugs was not our only discovery. Beside the miscellaneous uses of bakery ovens, there were also more subtle customs that made traditional Italian and American cultures different. Little by little our more or less typical American family—mother, father, son, and daughter (the dog and cat being taken care of by the tenants of our house in Berkeley)—embraced Italian ways, sometimes without even knowing it. Charles, pipe-smoking, tweed jacketed, dutifully professorial in Berkeley, where he was teaching English literature, gave up tobacco and martinis in favor of espresso and wine. Whereas at home we were accustomed to a more complex style of cooking when we ate out, in Italy there was an emphasis on simplicity and freshness of ingredients. Years later, in the United States, that was to become the focus of restaurants that followed the lead of the not-yet-born Chez Panisse. The simple bounties of the Italian table were seductive. I have never seen Charles happier than in a tiny, nondescript trattoria on the way to the Vatican, when he lunched on a plateful of anchovies, a great slab of butter, a crusty country loaf of bread, and his half-liter of ordinary red wine (the obvious reason for the siesta). Sartorially, well-worn tweed jackets and casually fitting slacks gave way on most occasions to the handsome materials and smooth tailoring of custom-made Italian clothes.

I, who had arrived with the short, flat, cropped haircut then peculiar to a number of co-op shopping matrons and Berkeley faculty wives, metamorphosed on my first visit to Sergio, a hairdresser employed by Eve of Rome. My hair was gently pouffed, casually tousled, with a chic, flattering, windblown, run-your-fingers-through-it look. At the same time, I got a free makeup session, ridding me forever of never-plucked brows and a lipstick-only approach. The change was subtle, but it transformed me from the plainer, more severe look of an ex–nursery school teacher who had turned to full-time politics and also wrote on the side.

When we first arrived in California, I had taken a job as a nursery school teacher, the obvious thing that related to my major in psychology when I was at Bennington. My course work had included children's clinics and teaching in a campus nursery school. At the same time, inspired by Adlai Stevenson when he ran for president, I was involved with the grassroots club movement in California, after which I was part of a caucus that helped develop potential candidates. I gave up teaching nursery school to have a baby and run a state assemblyman's campaign full time. I finally ended up a member of the Democratic State Central Committee, but I quit in order to spend more time with our son and devote increased hours to writing. The high point of my political career was when, during a particularly close election, my neighborhood political club got out one hundred percent of the Democratic vote in our precinct. Aghast, the Republican woman in whose garage we voted swore that never again would her premises be used in an election. And they weren't.

In Italy, I went in for manicures and pedicures, bought eye liner, and rouge that was imperceptible because it was brown and looked natural on my olive complexion. On occasion, I treated myself to Italian designer clothes. It was magic. It lifted my spirits, even enough to survive my visit to a rather prominent *signora*, to whom I had been given an introduction by one of her distant American relatives. Wearing my best red suit, my silver-gray mink stole (a gift from my mother), white gloves, and a black net veil in place of a hat over my Sergio coiffure, I thought I looked appropriately well-dressed for my audience. The *signora*, all the while smiling gently, and in the impeccable English of the well-educated European, inquired whether in the United States these days it was *di moda* to wear veils instead of hats.

Sergio was twenty-two when he first transformed my hair, and I have been going to him ever since: continuously that first year and on every occasion when we have returned to Rome. The last time I was there, in the English that he has learned over the years, he happily confided as he snipped away, "You are my oldest customer." Probably true on both counts. He has long since left Eve, opened his own shop in the Piazza Mignanelli with clients who are mostly *contessas* and *principessas*, has for years now made seasonal forays to Paris where he does the models for the great designers' shows and was for a long time a partner to one of the most famous of Parisian hairdressers. I have been there to bless him on his engagement, on his marriage, and on the births of his two daughters (one of whom is now working in the shop alongside him, as her mother did when she ran the front desk). The other noticeable difference is that over the years we have both turned gray.

It was during our first year in Rome that Lissa, my four-year-old daughter, had her first haircut. Each time we shampooed her long hair, she beseeched us to cut it to avoid the impossible tangles that resulted before the days of Jungle Care and other detanglers. I made an appointment with Sergio. He obligingly cut her hair short, with whimsical layers like an artichoke. As we were about to leave, he presented Lissa with a small package wrapped in gift paper, for her Daddy. In it were her shorn locks, shampooed, dried, and combed. He knew that in spite of the fact that she looked entirely beguiling, her Daddy was going to have a hard time with the loss of the long, silken tresses.

Jeff, our son, four years older than his sister, was a great bicycle enthusiast. Planning to buy one in Italy, we didn't bring his bike from home. Don't go to a bicycle store, Italian friends advised us;

the best place to look for one is at the Porta Portese flea market in Trastevere. And thus we were introduced to the institution of the European flea market: The best of them display acres of stuff, new, old, and antique, and are practically self-contained villages. By comparison, the American version is akin to a giant garage sale. Wading through sections devoted to every conceivable kind of merchandise, we came upon the extensive collection of Porta Portese cycles, and with Jeff's help, settled on a gorgeously colorful red and blue one, with the requisite amount of chrome, bells, and whistles. Jeff was enormously pleased, but Lissa was not. She begged to upgrade from a tricycle, which we were going to buy for her, to a two-wheeler. When we discovered that there was a size small enough to accommodate her four-year-old physique, and added training wheels to help balance it, it became feasible. We took home movies of the two of them riding in the park, Jeff swift and skillful, Lissa at first tentative and slow. But after weeks had passed, "Speedy" wanted those training wheels off, and no amount of argument would persuade her that without them she would wobble and crash. Finally, we decided that the only way to convince her was to let her try without them. Charles unscrewed the simple attachment and off the wheels came. Lissa mounted. Then, without the slightest wobble or crash, off she went. We have a movie of that, too.

With their Roman razor-cut haircuts, Charles and Jeff looked more and more Italian. Both kids were learning the language, their accents purer than the adults'. But in spite of the gradual assimilation that was taking place, we were still obviously American. One day, on our way from the Piazza di Spagna, a notable tourist attraction, to a spot near the Vatican, we decided to be extravagant and take a horse cart because it would be such fun for the kids. As we climbed up, my husband, an inveterate map-reader and consistently suspicious of taxi-drivers, and by now the old Roman—although no true Roman would ever set foot in a horse cart—admonished the driver to take the most direct route because we were *not* sight-seeing. The driver clucked, the horse trotted off, but it quickly became apparent that we were heading for the Piazza Barberini, in the opposite direction. My husband protested. The driver argued and kept going. With some indignation, Charles demanded that the carriage stop at once and ordered us all to climb down. We did. My husband began to remonstrate with the driver. A crowd gathered. A policeman arrived. By this time tempers were sizzling, everyone was gesticulating, and the crowd, vociferously on the side of the driver, joined in. Charles explained to the officer that he had specifically instructed the driver to take the shortest route and that instead we were being given the grand tour. The officer then patiently explained that because horse carriages were only allowed to go on certain streets and definitely not on others, the driver was indeed taking the most direct route. Charles apologetically ordered us all to climb back aboard, politely thanked the policeman, courteously asked the driver to proceed, and as the crowd murmured its loud approval, we drove indirectly to our destination. The forgiving driver was now our friend. And he got a big tip.

As fall turned to winter, we thought to try a ski trip to nearby Terminillo. This was the first time for any of us, and Jeff took to skiing with unbounded enthusiasm. Lissa and I soon gave up the cumbersome skis in favor of sledding, mostly my pulling her up the slope so that she could swoosh down. Charles skied with Jeff, who was fearless and insatiable. At the end of the day, while the kids and I returned our rental equipment, Charles decided to try the more advanced slope. It grew darker as he ascended the lift. By the time he got to the end of it, the attendant jumped on his skis and disappeared and Charles realized that he was the sole remaining skier on the mountain. He had no choice but to start down the steep slope.

Knowing neither how to stop nor how to slow down, he crouched, thus discovering that his backside served well as a brake. And so, in that semi-sitting position, he came down hundreds of feet, arriving at the bottom safe but somewhat bedraggled.

By this time, we were understandably famished. We headed for the nearest trattoria, its smells of tomato sauce and garlic beckoning. Before a blazing fire, casually dressed skiers were tucking into great platters of grilled chickens, *insalata mista*, and mounds of pasta. After we had ordered and Charles and I had poured ourselves some wine, Jeff put his head down on the table. His face was flushed brilliantly red. He's overdone it, I thought, not unusual for that particular eight-year-old boy, and he's gotten sunburned besides. When the food arrived, tasting as delicious as it looked, Jeff seemed to lack his usual enthusiasm. He was clearly exhausted and slept all the way home.

Once there, alarmed by his listlessness and still feverish color, we decided to take his temperature. It was well over 103. We phoned the doctor, an elderly Viennese emigrant, previously recommended by friends when I had become violently ill after dinner at a famous restaurant. "*Intossicata*," he had diagnosed on that occasion, and I was terribly insulted. Intoxicated, indeed! I later learned that "*intossicare*" means "to poison" and that what he had been telling me was that, famous restaurant or not, I had food poisoning. This time, he needed to examine Jeff only briefly before he pronounced *sotto voce* that our son had scarlet fever. He whispered this so that the maid wouldn't hear. It turned out that scarlet fever was a disease that demanded a two-week quarantine, meaning that none of us, including Maria, could leave the house for sixteen days. As in the time of the plague, the door had to be posted, drastically shrinking our chances of convincing anyone to bring supplies. The doctor sagely proposed calling it the flu and keeping the real diagnosis among ourselves.

On the *Giulio Cesare* coming over, among the friends that we made was a family from Oregon. Their son, Chris, was one year older than Jeff, and they had hit it off immediately. After the crossing, we continued to see each other and have remained friends ever since. At some point, we discovered that Chris's and Jeff's birthdays were only days apart and thought it would be marvelous fun to celebrate together. With the advice of Sandro, another shipmate who turned out to live a block away from us in Rome and with whom we all kept in touch (and still do), we booked into a *pensione* in Forte dei Marmi, just across from the beach, the warm weather making it a most desirable destination. Whether it was Sandro's Italian presence or the genuine hospitality of our hosts—or perhaps both—we had one of the best birthdays ever. On the day of the celebration, the staff carted a huge table across the sand, just far enough from the sparkling blue water so that the lapping and ebbing provided background music for the occasion. A white linen cloth covered the table set with fine china, silverware, and crystal goblets. Once we were seated, waiters bearing trays laden with food made a continual procession from the *pensione*. Across the sand, they carted platters of antipasti: salami, ham, olives, pepperoncini, stuffed hard-boiled eggs, little meat balls, tuna salad, stuffed peppers, broiled tomatoes topped with cheese, oil, herbs, and breadcrumbs, and a dish of garlicky braised baby artichokes. It was hard not to make a meal of it. When we could eat no more and the dishes had been cleared, there was a proper restorative interval, allowing us to regain momentum and them to cook the pasta. It arrived steaming: *bucatini all'amatriciana*, "macaroni" with a sauce of smoky Italian-style bacon, tomatoes, and cheese; and *gnocchi di patate*, little potato dumplings bubbling with butter and grated pecorino. After that, we attacked a main course of *abbacchio arrosto*, browned and crisped roast suckling lamb infused with garlic, oil, and rosemary. It came with crackling wedges of potatoes that had colored in the same pan. The birthday cake, served as the twilight and shadows descended, was glorious: lavish layers of puff pastry with a custardy filling, swirled in whipped cream and dotted with profiterolles-like garnishes. There were bowls of fruit and bowls of water to wash it in and glasses of Prosecco to toast the birthday boys. When we departed a day or two later, we discovered that our humble Fiat was now spanking clean, washed, polished, and gleaming like new, courtesy of the *pensione*. It was altogether a splendid birthday.

Birthdays, saint's days, and *onomastici*, or namedays, were all causes for celebrations in Italy. In fact, even the most casual events seemed to be excuses for elaborate festivities. Some of the most famous festivals draw crowds of participants. One of the best known is the *palio* in Siena, where riders in medieval costumes representing the *contrade*, or parishes, furiously race their horses bareback around the Piazza del Campo, the huge scallop-shaped main square. Another is the *Carnevale* in Venice, whose elaborately masked and costumed revelers take to the water for endless processions. The *Partita a Scacchi*, a chess game using costumed people as the pieces, and the main square, the Piazza Castello, as the chessboard, is typical of a thousand festivals in a thousand towns, this one taking place in even years in September in the medieval village of Marostica. On the frequent feast days and fairs that celebrate saints, the marchers usually bear a statue of the saint on a kind of open palanquin, the crowds lining the route affixing money to the passing saint's garments. Sometimes, instead of a saint, they honor the Virgin Mary. When we saw this in Italy, it seemed entirely appropriate; such a parade in Middletown, Connecticut, which we witnessed in the early fifties, had come as a total surprise. It turned out that there was a large contingent of Middletown residents whose families had come from the same village in Sicily. To celebrate their heritage, they had adopted the tradition of parading their ancestors' patron saint on the saint's day, using dollar bills instead of *lire*.

My favorite saint of all is Sebastian, who suffered martyrdom in 286 A.D. While serving as an officer of the imperial bodyguards, he committed acts of Christian charity, a no-no. The Emperor Diocletian forthwith impeached him and turned him over to Mauritanian archers. Pierced with their arrows, he was left for dead. In the act of burying him, Irene, the widow of St. Castulus, whoever he was, discovered him to be barely alive, removed him to her quarters and nursed him back to health. When the astonished emperor discovered that the enemy still lived, he ordered him seized and clubbed to death with cudgels. This time it took. Over the centuries, many artists have painted Sebastian, always pierced with arrows in the throes of martyrdom. Some very irreverent friends of mine once founded the St. Sebastian Dart Board Club. His bones reside in reliquaries in France, Spain, Germany, and Belgium and his head in Luxembourg, but nowhere that I know of do any parts of him rest in Italy.

In the churches of Italy, however, relics of other saints and martyrs abound. During our first year in Rome, I read in a guide book that downtown in the church of San Silvestro in Capite, in the Piazza San Silvestro, was the finger of Doubting Thomas. My friend Florence was visiting at the time, and we agreed that this was worth looking into. The church of San Silvestro is relatively small, with columns set into the façade on both sides of heavy double wooden doors that lead to a paved red brick courtyard. Several palm trees seek the light, casting shadows on fragments of old columns and grave stones. According to a surviving document dated June 2, 761, Paolo I had San Silvestro built to house the relics of Christian martyrs who had been buried in the catacombs outside the city walls. In the church courtyard near the entrance, two eighth-century marble

tablets record their names. Over the centuries, there have been mod-
ifications, enlargements, additions, and decorations, many of them
baroque, but San Silvestro has remained a comparatively simple
structure.

When Florence and I searched the chapels, we found statuary,
paintings, and frescoes, mostly by lesser known artists, but not a sign
of Doubting Thomas's finger. Disappointed, but undaunted, we
sought out a custodian, and guidebook in hand, explained what we
were searching for. "Oh," he replied, "we don't have the finger of
Doubting Thomas," but then, in an effort to console us, he added
brightly, "but we do have the head of John the Baptist. Would you
like to see that?" He led us to a chapel to the left of the entrance,
where indeed, in a thirteenth-century reliquary, rested John's head.
We should have known by the name of the church, "In Capite,"
which refers to that head, one of the most precious of all the
Church's treasures. I recently have it on excellent authority, an official licensed guide, that the finger of St. Thomas actually is in
Rome, but at the church of Santa Croce in Gerusalemme.

One further word on Rome's San Silvestro in Capite. From early
days, there was a monastery adjacent to the church, first housing
monks, and finally in 1285 an order of nuns, who followed the dic-
tates of Santa Clara. When the Italian state appropriated the building in 1870 and the nuns were forced to abandon the premises, it
became the central office of the postal service in Rome. It was in that
capacity that we became acquainted with that infinitely mysterious
organization, now unrecognizably modernized from its ways in the
fifties. If you tried to mail a package in those days, the postal
employees played a kind of game to conceal the fact that this was the
hiding place of the parcel post division. Since there was then no such
formation as a line in Italy, just to get to the window to ask directions
took the strategy of a quarterback and the stamina of a Marine.

Once there, and under the contemptuous stares of all those still behind you, the clerk would unceremoniously dismiss you because you were in the wrong place, and worse, your package was not wrapped in the approved fashion. Acceptable rewrapping could be accomplished, fortunately, in a little store in front of the post office proper, by forking over the appropriate payment to two young women who held court behind a desk cluttered with shears, cord, scraps of brown paper, and globs of sealing wax. The writhing crowd of untouchables who needed proper wrapping would beseech, whine, wheedle, shout, poke, and jostle—having not the slightest effect on the women's studied slow motion. When your turn finally came, you had to tell the wrapping clerk whether this was special delivery, insured, or (and this lost you considerable face) a simple mailing. The first two categories commanded respect, with wrapping procedures that were consequently much more demanding. The "insured, special delivery" was the monarch of packages. It demanded numerous folds and counterfolds held by a complex of knots that would have been the envy of many a sailor. Next came a lighted candle and sealing wax to guarantee that every overlap and seam would remain inviolate. The final precaution was a series of lead seals attached through the rigging. With a properly wrapped package in tow, it was only a matter of attacking the post office proper again to find out where and how to mail it. The nuns of Santa Clara would never have believed it.

My Italian training in, and fascination with, saints stayed with me beyond Italy. In fact, when I went to France several years later, to get background for a booklet, "The Heritage and Pleasures of Cognac," I had yet another adventure in trying to locate a relic, this time the heart of the Baron Jean Antoine Otard de la Grange, in the village church of Cognac. The firm for whom I was writing the booklet, Cognac Otard, wanted me to learn about and observe first-hand the history, processes, and not least, the comparative tastes of cognac. It was in the course of these researches that I discovered that the heart of the highly respected Baron Otard was in the local church. Besides having founded the firm in 1795, he had also served as the town's mayor and as its representative in parliament. According to the history I was reading, his home, in the town's center, is now the town hall; and—this was the part that most piqued my interest—upon his death, the town council had directed that his heart repose under the family coat of arms in the church, with the following inscription: "Here lies Sir Otard de la Grange's heart. Chevalier of the Legion of Honour, Mayor of this town, Member of Parliament in 1820 and 1824. Born in Brives in 1763, Died in Cognac in 1824."

Of course, to someone who has seen the head of John the Baptist, this was comparatively recent history, but I was challenged nonetheless to locate the heart of Baron Otard. The appropriate opportunity soon came. Originally assigned to show me the firm of Robert Pruhlo, who made equipment for the distillery on the outskirts of town, Madame Ludwine Chapeau (her real name, as improbable as it seems), and by now my friend—a visit to her house and a look at the family photo album clinched it—asked me if there was anything else, anything at all, that I wanted to see. I told her. She herself had never seen the heart of Baron Otard; in fact, did not know that it rested in the church. But, intrigued as I, she drove me forthwith to search it out. The church was dark, very dark, and we finally began lighting matches to aide in our hunt. No success. Finally, as we were about to give up, a reluctant Mme Chapeau suggested that if we sought out someone connected to the church, they could surely direct us to the heart. We found a dark-robed, tottering official. He didn't know its location either. With many regrets on both sides, we abandoned the search. Several months later, my friend Jeannette Ferrary went to France to write a story on Cognac Otard for the *New*

York Times. She reported back that the wonderful Mme Chapeau, sorely chagrined to have disappointed me, had spent hours in the church searching for the Baron's heart. And she had finally found it. She ecstatically showed it to Jeannette, and made her promise to tell me when she returned home. Jeannette did, and reported, for the benefit of any future seekers, the fact of its existence in the article appearing in the *Times.*

CHAPTER THREE

New Friends

Among the other blessings that our first year in Rome bestowed was the opportunity to meet remarkable people, with whom we have sustained enduring friendships. One of them was Rita Benazzo, whom we first encountered at the home of some American friends for whom she was working as housekeeper and cook. Many years before, her first job with an American family was for a college president, his wife, and their children. They were so appreciative of her talents that they recommended her services for the following year to a colleague, another visiting university president and his family. They, in turn, were so delighted that they, too, referred her on; and so it went, with a long list of American academics eventually queuing up to employ her. In America, no doubt about it, she would herself have been a college president. When she retired years later, as a small token of their esteem, the families for whom she had worked jointly paid for a trip to America.

It is obligatory in Italy for women to use their maiden names for all legal matters and documents, but it is the common practice to use married names socially. In Rita's case, because she was an independent Italian female, she kept her own name for all purposes after she married. She was, without knowing it, a consummate teacher, pacing her spoken language and every gesture so that you understood what she was saying. Her interpretive powers translated your garbled words into meaning. Somehow she made you feel as if you were speaking fluent Italian. Her corrections were so gentle that they took the form of conversational questions or comments, and yet you were learning a correct word or phrase or meaning. She spoke in a clear, lyric tone, musical yet clearly enunciated like operatic recitative. Listening to her was like hearing beautiful music. One time when my daughter Lissa and some high school chums were traveling in Italy, she phoned Rita. Lissa's Italian dated from nursery school during our first year in Rome and was practiced only when she accompanied us on our return visits. She understood Rita's clear telephone directions to her apartment: which bus to take, where to change lines, where to get off, how to get from the bus stop to Rita's home. They got there without incident, and she and her friends, none of whom spoke a word of Italian, spent an engaging afternoon with Rita.

Rita had a round face which was not prone to wrinkling, so that even in her eighties she remained a beautiful woman. She wore her hair, brown when we first knew her, then silver as age set in, in a short practical cut that emphasized the fine features of her dimpled face. She was not tall, nor slim, her figure reflecting a certain satisfaction with her own cooking, and she favored simple well-pressed clothes in dark colors. Even-tempered, humorous and exceedingly wise, she was a steadying influence on more volatile persons. Her husband, charming and dashingly handsome, had a sunny, unruffled nature, which fit his short-lived calling as a children's barber. Soon after their marriage, he developed a tremor in his hands that prevented him from working. He spent the days with his friends, the neighborhood card players, the *poltroni*. Rita, who adored him, continued, ungrudgingly, to support them for the rest of their lives. After his death, she faithfully traveled every Sunday the arduous distance by bus to the cemetery where he was buried, until arthritis and the frailty of old age prevented her.

They lived for years in a one-room apartment near the Piazza di Spagna, even after their daughter Gianna was born. It was not until later in her life, her daughter herself now married, that she was finally able to move into more suitable quarters, a one-bedroom place in a spanking new apartment house, one with an elevator, just off the Via Marconi. She proudly invited us to see it. When we arrived, she offered us drinks, American-style. She had put in a stock of bourbon, rye, and Scotch, stashed on the top of a rolling trolley along with bottles of sparkling water and a very un-Italian bucket of ice cubes. On the shelf below were hôrs d'oeuvre: home-made pizzettas hot from the oven, mini calzoni, stuffed eggs, cheese and crackers, olives, and roasted peppers. On the wall over the couch hung a striking black and white rendering of the Piazza di Spagna, painted by an artist friend of hers. We rejoiced in her good fortune, admired the apartment and the painting, indulged in the drinks and canapés. Several months later, at the end of our stay in Rome, Rita came to the airport to bid us goodbye. She had a large tube under her arm, a going-away present, she said, that we must not open until after we had boarded the plane. It was, of course, the painting of the Piazza di Spagna.

When Rita helped me test the recipes for my Rome book, she absolutely refused any remuneration, even though we were putting in full days of shopping and cooking. Over our protests, she continued working, even though she had developed a serious cough and didn't look well at all. And then one day she nearly collapsed. Pneumonia, the doctor said; he prescribed medications and ordered her to go to bed at once. When we visited her, she had changed the bedding to her very best linen sheets. We brought her a gift for *Ferragosto*, the August celebration of the Feast of the Assumption, a holiday throughout the country. She delightedly accepted an envelope full of *lire*, the amount she would have earned had friendship not intervened. What she could not accept as payment, she could happily receive as a gift for *Ferragosto*.

Over the years, our friendship with Rita has flourished through visits and correspondence. Gianna and her husband Pino have visited us in America and invited us for the feasts Gianna prepares at home; she obviously inherited a talent for cooking from her mother. Gianluca, their son, a young man now, has come to study in Los Angeles in his pursuit of a career in filmmaking. Sadly, the last time we were in Rome, Rita could no longer come out to dinner with us, so we spent a long visit with her at home. We did not get a card from her for the first time this Christmas.

When we went to Italy in the spring, we learned why. Rita had had to move from her coveted apartment—new laws under the Berlusconi government, we gathered, no longer protected her right to live out her life in the place she had thought was her home. She was so depressed that she couldn't send her usual cards, and she had asked Gianna and Pino not to tell us; she was going to write us herself. Before she did, we were in Italy and her family filled us in. She was now a reluctant resident in the Isituto delle Suore Figlie della Divina Provvidenza on the far outskirts of Rome, a home for the *anziani*, or senior citizens. In short an old-age home for women run by an order of nuns.

When we visited her, she was not happy. Everyone there was

decrepit, hobbling about, half deaf, and certainly not able to sustain much interest in current affairs, let alone hold much of a conversation. Despite her ninety-some years, except for a little arthritis, she was not any of the above. Her eyes did bother her if she read too much or watched the news on TV too long. Although it might once have been stimulating, now she found it less than comforting that most of the residents came from other parts of the country with different customs from those of her native Piemonte. She needed people and things that were familiar. Although she had a small balcony and the convent had a large garden, the weather had been so unseasonably cold as to prevent her from taking advantage of either. There was little room in her new quarters for much in the way of personal things, or for any of her collections. It was a far cry from being surrounded by one's own possessions that lend reassurance.

Although Gianna came to visit her as often as she could, it was very difficult: Getting there was a real deterrent, and the visiting hours were miserably short. But she came. We were all hoping that warm weather would expand her narrow confines, extend Rita's chances to meet more active people wandering about in the gardens, get some joy out of watching the school children at play in the adjacent yard. Meanwhile, we exchanged long letters and occasional photographs. And buffered aspirin, the only small thing that Rita requested.

We were not surprised when a letter from Gianna told us of Rita's death. On our subsequent visits to Rome, we have seen Gianna and Pino, but we all miss Rita. She would have been delighted to know that Gianluca had become a father, Gianna and Pino proud grandparents, and Rita, unbelievable as it seems, a great-grandmother.

Another person whom we met during our early years in Italy, introduced to us by an Italian friend, was Barbara, an Australian who was then working in Rome. She had a quick talent for languages, an

Italian that was both fluent and without accent. Keeping on top of things kept her vibrant. She was a perfect model for the latest fashion, knew the best hairdresser of the moment, all of the museums in Rome and their collections, what the most interesting current art shows were, and which restaurants were the oldest, the newest, had the best cooking, or were currently *di moda.* It was at her home that we had the ultimate bipartisan pasta: spaghetti tossed with melted butter, lemon juice, and osetra caviar. When we were about to go on a trip to Puglia, she told us about a specialty of that region, *burrata,* a round ball of mozzarella that is actually a cheese bag closed with a knot of the same cheese, which contains long fettucine-like strands of curd mixed with cream from the whey, giving it an irresistible buttery flavor. We first ate sea beans at her table, a green vegetable that is jointed, crunchy, and about the diameter of a wooden kitchen match. On rare occasions, I find it in my market in Berkeley. The produce buyer there tells me it grows wild along the Mendocino coast, no doubt the source of its slightly briny flavor.

Barbara's hairdo and makeup changed frequently, as well as her current interests: She was a golfer one season, a swimmer the next. A wine lover, she decided to study it seriously, took a professional training course, and ended up a full-fledged sommelier. She took us to the best establishment at the beach in Ostia Antica, where we could rent a *cabina* for the summer. There we stored our folding chairs and umbrella, changed into our bathing suits (mine, of course, a bikini, worn with the high heeled gold beach clogs that were the uniform of the day because they better flattered your legs). At lunch time, we filled the hollow yeasty rolls called *rosette* with sliced meats and the creamy gorgonzola known as *dolcelatte.* For dessert we washed huge bunches of perfumed Muscat grapes in the splashing waters of small fountains that dotted the beach. Or bought watermelon from a wandering boy who hawked it along the beach front singing, "*coco . . . cocomero.*"

It was Barbara who also introduced us to Da Antonio a San Calisto, a simple trattoria that specialized in fish. Located in a small piazza off the much larger Piazza di Santa Maria in Trastevere, the restaurant defined its outdoor seating area by a barrier of plant boxes. As more guests arrived, the waiters would move the hedges outward, continuously expanding the space to accommodate the increasing volume of diners. Angelino Merletti, the talented cook, prepared such addictive dishes as cold seafood salad marinated in garlicky oil and vinegar dressing; spaghetti with fresh small clams called *vongole veraci;* whole roasted sea bass, *ombrina*, that you could select yourself from among the other catch of the day displayed in a refrigerated case out front; or one of our favorites, scampi, fisherman's style, halved in their shells and baked in an oven hot enough to turn the topping of olive oil and bread crumbs brown and crusty. We became habitués. Our daughter Lissa always began with chicken soup afloat with small pasta, our son Jeff with spaghetti topped with a spicy tomato sauce. Over the years, whenever we would pay a return visit, our waiter Giovanni would immediately recognize us and inquire of our children, "*pastina in brodo e spaghetti alla marinara?*"

When Barbara married Piero, an Italian attorney, they moved into a building owned by his family, who occupied the top floor. When we visited them, we had to deposit ten *lire*, then less than a penny, in order to use the elevator. But it kept the wanderers out. When both parents died, Barbara and Piero, who lived on the floor beneath, eliminated the ten *lire* deposit and remodeled their existing quarters, expanding into the penthouse above.

In good weather, their huge landscaped terrace, with a view of the dome of St. Peter's, accommodated both large crowds and intimate dinner parties. When it got dark, they lit the perimeter with *candeli*, which resembled torches in a pie plate: a wick enclosed in a wire cage, much like a cork for champagne, was embedded in a block of wax that entirely filled an aluminum container shaped like a pie plate. When lit, the wax burned with a dancing flame that resisted blowing out when whipped by rain or wind. Surely, it was the reason that St. Peter's used them to illuminate the church's dome on special occasions. You could buy *candeli* in stores that sold religious paraphernalia. When we went home to California, we shipped a box full. One unusually balmy evening, when we were entertaining old friends from Paris, we decided to eat dinner on our deck overlooking the San Francisco Bay. We lined the *candeli* at intervals along the deck railing, to glorious effect. Midway through dinner, we heard fire engines. They stopped in front of our house. Firemen, in full fire-fighting regalia from their helmets to their boots, rang the doorbell. It seemed that an elderly and nervous lady, looking up through the trees, saw the leaping flames and called the fire department. Inspecting the scene, the firemen suggested that we put the *candeli* at the base of the railing rather than on top of it, preserving the aesthetic effect for us and allaying the nervous fears of our neighbor. Politely, almost apologetically, they bid our guests and us adieu, let themselves out, and roared away. Our Parisian friends were astonished: In America the fire department comes unbidden.

One time, just arrived for a stay in Rome, we called to give our greetings to Barbara and Piero. Barbara instantly invited us to join them for dinner at Pier Luigi, a humble but excellent trattoria just down the street from their apartment near the Farnese Palace. Not the place to get dressed up, she reminded us. We were to come first for some Prosecco on the terrace. That evening, when we entered through the heavy wooden doors to the apartment building courtyard, we passed a large Kawaski motorcycle parked inside on the cobblestones. We ascended. When Barbara opened the door to greet us, she was dressed in leathers, her now long black hair cascading freely to her shoulders. She had taken up motorcycling, she explained animatedly, a marvelous way to beat the congested Rome traffic.

After we had eaten—*pasta d'estate*, *pasta alla gorgonzola*, and *pagliata* (a kind of tripe that the chef had braised in a flavorful brownish tomato sauce)—Barbara told us that we were all invited to a party in a building just across the street from where she and Piero lived. She would go home to check on the children and meet us there. The elevator doors opened directly into our host's apartment. When they parted, they revealed a scene from *La Dolce Vita*. A long table filled the length of the room. The melting wax of half-burned candles ribboned down a half-dozen ceramic candelabra, spaced here and there along the table. The large skeleton of a mostly consumed fish reclined on a silver platter. There were partly eaten bunches of grapes here and there, fruit plates with the remnants of apricots and peaches, half-empty wineglasses, decanters partially filled with red wine, torn hunks and crumbs of bread scattered like confetti, the remains of a *taleggio*, a gorgonzola, and an aged parmesan adrift among them, and rumpled linen napkins randomly discarded on the matching long-skirted tablecloth. The guests were casually draped about, an amorous couple reclining intimately on a sofa, several people still lounging at the table, the women attired in couturier gowns, the men in a variety of open-necked silk shirts and dark, well-tailored slacks.

Suddenly, the elevator doors opened again. Out stepped Barbara, gowned in an exquisite floor-length orange silk. One strap held the sylphlike gown in place. The other shoulder was entirely bare. Her long black hair, swirled up into a sophisticated sculpture, hugged her head, and complemented her long, dangling diamond earrings. She was clearly the star of the film.

Another life-long friend we made early in that first year in Rome was Renato Torti. Like many a fine painter before him, he supported himself largely through another line of work, in his case tailoring, a skill at which he turned out to be exceptionally talented. His selection of extraordinary buttons for the clothes he created was legendary. He worked out of his apartment on the Via Casini, where one room served as a work space. His paintings lined the walls, creating more the effect of an art gallery than a tailor shop. When my husband went for the first of the many suits, trousers, overcoats, and jackets that Renato made for him over the years, we also met his wife Amalia and Rodolfo, their only child.

One could imagine Renato, with his aquiline nose and penetrating black eyes, wearing the crown of laurel leaves and the flowing white toga of a Roman emperor, instead of his meticulously tailored pinstriped gray suit. His empress, Amalia, was dignified in her bearing, lustrous pearl earrings and short black hair framing a face so Roman that it proclaimed its origins in the old section of Rome, across the Tiber, known as Trastevere. But for both, the resemblance to ancient Rome was only physical. Philosophically, Renato and Amalia were the antithesis of their regal ancestors. Seriously concerned with the lot of their fellow humans, they were kind and gentle people, politically strong advocates for a socialistic kind of equality and a basic kind of justice—not even a remote possibility of the machinations, poisonings, and other bloodthirsty proclivities that so delighted the old Romans. This fundamental decency prevailed over any of the national customs or superficial differences that might have proved stumbling blocks to a steadfast and enduring friendship of more than forty years. Before long, when we came around for fittings, Renato would mix up a batch of Negronis, Italian cocktails that classically consist of equal parts of bitter Campari, sweet vermouth, and gin, stirred with ice, and finished off with a peel of lemon. (In hot weather it is customary to serve Negronis in tall glasses with seltzer added, making a cold and refreshing thirst-quencher.) Renato's own variation, the one we always drank, went this way: For every serving, mix two ounces of Cinzano Bianco (Cinzano white vermouth), one-half ounce of Carpano Punt e Mes, and one dash of gin; pour over ice and add a twist of lemon. A beneficial side effect, we soon discovered, was that our burbling imperfect Italian began to flow like a mountain stream.

Unlike English, Italian commonly allows the attachment of diminutives and superlatives to words to create shades of meaning, nuances not possible in our language. One of these, "*accio*," roughly means "wicked." Attached to the base word, "*parlare*," to speak, Parlaccio, the name given to a neighborhood trattoria, means something like "dirty talk." The Tortis one night took us there in an effort to broaden our Roman education. The very good food at Parlaccio took second place to the staff's broad, usually scatological, humor. The first thing you noticed was the lack of place settings on the tables. The waiters tossed the silverware in a heap, instructing the customers to set their own places. A carafe of golden white wine, unerringly resembling urine, was always delivered to coincide with a person's exit from the bathroom. The waiters kept up a constant banter, trumpeted in loud Roman dialect, which we didn't understand, commenting on every possible circumstance that allowed for a double entendre or an off-color remark. The antics were abundantly clear, but the Tortis had to translate the dialect into Italian for us.

There is an earthy, sometimes sexual, connection between food and body that is prevalent in both Italy and France, initially startling to those of us who come from more tight-laced backgrounds. The often descriptive naming of foods—for example, the purple, fleshy plums that are known as "nun's thighs," or the delicate meringues known as "nun's farts"—is commonplace. Once in Paris, a friend took us to a restaurant named "Roger La Grenouille," or "Roger the Frog." There were shenanigans aplenty, but the *piece de resistance* came at the end of the meal. The wall-eyed, froglike proprietor, Roger, insisted that everyone had to have the special dessert, something so fabulous that you simply had to taste it. If you declined, in spite of his admonitions, you got it anyway. It turned out to be two scoops of peach ice cream separated by a three-inch high, inescapably phallic *gaufrette*. The women got no spoons. When the meal was over and the diners ready to depart, Roger always thanked his female customers with a warm French salutation, the familiar air kiss to each cheek. Except Roger, after presenting the first cheek, would turn his head only half way. The unsuspecting victim invariably ended up kissing him solidly on the lips.

Renato was born in Genzano, one among a cluster of towns in the Alban Hills, about twenty miles south and east of Rome. During his years in Rome, he maintained a pied-à-terre in Genzano, and after his retirement he and Amalia made it their permanent address. They moved to a small apartment on the Corso Vecchio in the old part of town. From its high perch on the hillside, it overlooked Lake Nemi, a crater once dedicated to Diana. In fact, Frazer's *Golden Bough* got its inspiration from the battle that decided who should serve as the priest for Diana: a life-and-death fight between the current officeholder and anyone who challenged him for that position. As part of the ritual, the challenger had to present a golden bough from one of Diana's trees. The battle took place in the town of Nemi, two miles from Genzano. Modern-day excavations there have uncovered the ruins of Diana's temple. It isn't the only archeological find. Several hundred years before, explorations unearthed two enormous Roman ships on the lake bottom, probably ancient pleasure ferries. Because the technology to retrieve them did not exist until the 1930s, they remained submerged until then. Finally rescued from their watery grave, they found an appropriate new home in a lakeside museum built especially to house them. It proved to be a short-lived resting place: during World War II, reckless German soldiers set fire to the building, destroying it and its contents. The few charred remains and small-scale models of the originals reside in a new museum, a miniature reminder of the great ships of the past.

Early on the Tortis began taking us to Genzano. We met their friends, became acquainted with the local history, enjoyed the galleries and met the local artists in a community enthusiastically dedicated to the arts. One day, we drove out along the Via Appia Vecchia to the home of Enzo and Gabriella Giannini and their young daughter Elisabetta. We had previously met the parents in the United States when the Tortis wrote that they would be representing Italian products at a trade show in San Francisco. Now we were seeing them on their home turf: a gracious house surrounded by vineyards and rows of garden produce to provide more than enough greens and vegetables for a family. On the table, under the arbor where we sat shielded from the summer sun, the Gianninis poured local red wine, slightly *frizzante*, and used a broad flat knife to break pieces of cheese from a huge hunk of pecorino. Moments before, we had picked the customary Italian accompaniment, young green fava beans fresh from the garden, which now sat in a mountainous pile, ready to be shelled and consumed raw and crunchy.

If we were visiting the Tortis in June, we would sometimes go to Nemi to the strawberry festival celebrating the tiny wild berries, the *fragoline di Nemi*, that were surely the best of them all: special enough so that any restaurant with the luck to obtain them proudly noted it on the menu—and charged accordingly. But the festival that we most looked forward to was in Genzano itself, also an annual June event, the *Infiorata* or flower festival, one of the most remarkable celebrations in the country. On Corpus Christi, the entire main street, gently descending from the church, Santa Maria della Cima, some six hundred feet to the large round fountain at its end, is a solid carpet of fresh flower petals, laid out in a dozen intricate designs and patterns. Sometimes, the themes are religious: the crucifixion, the Virgin Mary, various saints, a scene from the ceiling of the Sistine Chapel. Subjects range from portraits of famous musicians, such as Mozart as infant prodigy, to faithful renditions of a work by Caravaggio, or to breathtakingly complex geometric designs.

The first *Infiorata* took place in the Vatican on June 29, 1625, on the occasion of the celebration of Saints Peter and Paul. A chronicler of those times, Giovan Battista Ferrari, published a description of it in 1633 in Latin under the title *De Florum Cultura*. It gave, among other things, a lengthy description of the flowers used to produce the various colors for the pictorial quadrants: four shades of yellow, for example, obtained from such flowering plants as Scotch broom, carnations, gerber daisies, and roses; similar flowers and leaves produced oranges, reds, sky blue, lavender, purple, brown, chestnut brown, tobacco brown, two shades of white, and five of green. The descriptions could have been written today: same flowers, same colors, nothing changed. As to when and how the *Infiorata* made its way to Genzano, there are no precise records, only miscellaneous written accounts and speculations. Local historians believe that many of the artists who had connections to both the Vatican and homes in Genzano brought the idea with them. At first, a few inhabitants laid floral decorations in front of their homes on the Via Livia (now the Via Belardi), where the solemn procession of the Blessed Sacrament took place. The idea spread to the Via Sforza, where in 1782, for the first time, the designs covered the entire length of the street.

Nowadays, the entire community is involved in the festival. First there is a committee of experts who must choose the twelve or thirteen finalists among the myriad proposals for the designs. Then it is necessary to calculate the collections of flowers: which colors and what quantities are needed for the chosen pictures, which to pick first, which to pick last, to insure their freshness. Over a period of days, dozens of women and girls laboriously separate petals from stems, leaves from branches. Stacked in crates, the five thousand kilograms of flower petals are then stored in the grottos under the town hall. Once used for wine storage, because of their constant cool temperature and humidity, these caves are ideally suited to maintain the freshness of the flowers until the day of the *Infiorata*.

In the late afternoon and evening before the event, the artists chalk in the outlines of their designs on the cobblestone blocks of the street. Beginning at eight the next morning, two hundred people, men, women, and children of all ages, begin the task of transporting the cartons of flower petals from the grottos, coordinating the colors and amounts needed by each artist. At the same time, the artists and their helpers begin to fill in, petal by petal, the outlines of the remarkable pictures emerging, butterfly-like, from their chalked cocoons. As the day progresses, enthusiasts, admirers, and thousands of visitors crowd along the sidewalk edging the meters of running tableaux. Windows and balconies of the houses along the Via Belardi are brimful with onlookers, because the view from on high is far superior to that below.

Inside the town hall, on a table outside the cavernous storage areas, are huge slices of spit-roasted pork, its skin golden and crunchy, the stuffing of herbs and garlic infusing the meat it clings to. It makes the most irresistible sandwiches when it is piled between slabs of the domed loaves of country bread for which Genzano is famous. The bread, dense and chewy inside its browned crust, gets its special flavor from the chestnut logs that fire the ovens in which it is baked. It is so good that it is sold in Rome, and was once baked in New York by the DDL bakery, using the authentic Genzano recipe. For those without access to the feast provided by the communal authorities for the revered officials of the festival, whole roasted pigs, heads and all, and mountains of good country bread to put the slices on, are widely available at street stands in town.

Spit-roasted pigs are a popular addiction in many areas of the country. Ariccia, a hill town nearby, specializes in them, as well as in its own rustic country bread. Norcia, a town in Umbria, has a tradition of pork butchers, *norcini*, and all over the country there are *norcinerie*, shops that specialize in pork products—sausage, bacon, cured prosciutto, cooked ham for sandwiches, head cheese, salami. At the foot of the festival street in Genzano, there is a *norcineria* festooned with dozens of prosciuttos suspended by cords from large silvery meat hooks, hanging salamis in various crinkled stages of aging, boughs and branches of laurel leaves surrounding them in a veritable arbor of greenery. A whole pig rests on its funeral slab of white marble, ready for slicing.

The artists complete their work by late afternoon and the sight of the carpeted street is unbelievably stunning. Toward evening, under a baldacchino, the bishop of the diocese, accompanied by the priest and other high officials, majestically robed in flowing white, red, and gold, begin their descent in the solemn procession of the Holy Sacrament. They are escorted by white-gloved *carabinieri*, red plumed—mile-high toques riding atop their heads—who are wearing double-breasted black uniforms accented with red stripes from waist to ankle, the tight-fitting jackets fringed with white epaulets, and slashed diagonally by white sashes. Because of the earlier wetting and tamping down of the petals, there is little destruction by the marchers, a good thing because the festival continues into the next day. It is officially over when the traditional *spallamento* takes place: at precisely seven in the evening, all of the local children set out full speed from the church, this time with destruction in mind, and race like the wind, scattering petals as they go, until they reach the fountain below.

Renato has for years been one of the primary officials involved in the *Infiorata* as well as a participating artist. A few years back, he authored a huge book on the festival. Leather-bound and profusely illustrated, it has tipped-in full-color photographs of some of the best designs over the years, as well as of the workers collecting flowers, separating petals, chalking the cobblestones, laying the art work, the solemn procession, the children running their *spallamento*. Along with the history and a chronology of the festival, there are archival documents and testimonials by poets and writers who have witnessed the remarkable painting with flowers.

Over the years, Genzano has had requests to reproduce the *Infiorata* in other countries. Renato has taken the whole crew of artists and assistants once to Japan and twice to New York, the first time to Rockefeller Center. Beginning in 1992, representatives of the world of *haute couture* participated in creating quadrants for the festival. The designer Missoni was the first, followed by such notables as Fendi and Versace. If their personal style lent a special contribution to the art of the *Infiorata*, the festival wasn't the only beneficiary: I am among the proud possessors of a commemorative Missoni shawl, a four-foot square fantasy of bright colors.

After viewing the finished floral pictures, we and the Tortis would always go to dinner at Da Palozzo, a trattoria belonging to Renato's boyhood friend Alfredo Ronconi, whom everyone always calls Palozzo. He opened the place in the early sixties, and although the premises have expanded, the food is still in the simply prepared, animated style that comes from the best kitchens. High above the lake, the dining room and breezy summer verandah overlook chestnut woods, fields of flowers under cultivation, vineyards that produce the grapes for that slightly bubbly red wine, and a profusion of hillsides overgrown with wild plants: vivid cyclamen, strawberries, mint, and blackberries.

Palozzo, whose father-in-law before him was a great restaurateur, is never rushed nor distracted. He runs the large establishment as if he were entertaining guests in a cozy country home. The sizable kitchen is brought to intimate dimensions by the ladies manning it, who chat amiably away, here sprinkling a bit of salt with the fingers, there sloshing some wine into a bubbling pot of sauce. Palozzo, always ready to joke, to tease, to engage, has sad eyes that contradict his demeanor. He smokes too much, as his husky voice suggests. But as he ages—more wrinkles, less hair—he still retains the good looks of his youth.

Over the years, we have met and become good friends with the whole family. It makes a memorable meal even more so. At Palozzo one orders by discussion, although there may well be printed menus. Before one even orders, the table is covered with antipasti: homemade sausages, local prosciutto, varieties of salami, briny olives, charred red peppers, and aromatic *passanella:* healthy slabs of that good country bread, first sprinkled sparingly with water, seasoned with salt and pepper, covered with pieces of fresh tomato and a dusting of fresh chopped basil, and finished off in a hot oven. The waiter pours generous goblets of the local red wine. It is nonsense to go any further. But Palozzo suggests some freshly made wide egg noodles, which, in this region of the hunter, are slathered with a thick meaty sauce of wild hare, *pappardelle alla lepre,* to be followed by little game birds—quail, figpeckers, ortolans, whatever is in season—grilled over charcoal, seasoned with laurel leaves and fennel seeds, basted with olive oil, then flamed with brandy. Buckshot is a likely, though unspecified, part of the dish. The best accompaniment is a dish of the wild mushrooms called *porcini*, sautéed with garlic and wild mint. There are alternatives: all sorts of game in velvet sauces redolent of wine and spices; *zingarella*, veal pounded thin and flat, floured lightly, browned in a mixture of olive oil and butter, then simmered in a splash of white wine, a dash of tomato-meat sauce, and a pesto of green olives, anchovy fillets, a clove of garlic, capers, gherkins, and parsley, mashed to a thick paste in olive oil. Spicy, like the little gypsy after whom the dish is named. Soft polenta is a good foil for this dish as well as for any of the game. A salad of mixed greens is the refreshment alongside, and there is always an offer of cheese, along with generous platters of fresh fruit and bowls full of water to wash them in. And then the sweet desserts, *dolci*, which end the meal. Except, of course, for a little *grappa* with the coffee.

The last time we were in Rome, we invited the Tortis and the Ronconis to dine with us in an old Trastevere restaurant on the Via Benedetta called Checco er Carrettiere. Since this was the Tortis' old stamping ground, Checco and its owner, Francesco Porcelli, were old friends. Porcelli's story was typical: The third generation of his family to peddle wine from a traveling cart, he grew tired of the nomadic existence, sold his cart, and converted a century-old tavern into a wine shop. Before long, he was serving food with the wine, and soon he was running a full-scale trattoria. Its name derived from "Checco," the nickname for Francesco, and cart driver, which in Roman dialect is *"er Carrettiere."*

Our guests included Rodolfo Torti, the Tortis' son, the youngster whom we had delighted with occasional gifts of Mickey Mouse watches or inflatable dinosaurs, and who in turn had delighted us with his intelligence and growing artistic ability. Now a married man himself, father of young Riccardo, he was a professional artist, painting large canvases with the boldness and vibrancy of Francis Bacon. In order to support his family, he used his skills at drawing to become one of the leading illustrators of the hardcover cartoon books, the *fumetti*, so popular in Europe. He works mostly for the French publishers of these one-story books, some of which run to more than fifty pages. Grazia, his wife, is of a sweet and gentle nature, sparked occasionally by a streak of independence. When we met that day in Rome, she told us that she had just begun belly-dancing lessons. Rodolfo and Grazia had spent a couple of weeks with us in the United States, then went on to see the Grand Canyon and the rest of the Wild West. We own several of his powerful paintings, and although his style has changed over the years, fortunately none of his fascination with cowboys and Indians has influenced his work.

Checco is that solid kind of restaurant that displays the ingredients for the night's cooking—fish caught that day and vegetables fresh from the Roman countryside—in luminous still life arrangements worthy of Chardin. The menu is full of favorite Roman dishes, such as beans simmered with pork rind and ham bones and covered with a grating of sharp pecorino cheese; oven-roasted suckling kid, *capretto*, light, moist, and tender, the meat perfumed by the garlic and rosemary that has been stuffed into slits, the skin golden and absolutely crackly; or tripe the way the Romans like it, with fresh-chopped mint and gobs of grated cheese.

That day we chose an assortment of appetizers: fried zucchini flowers stuffed with anchovied cheese that had become soft and oozy from the cooking, prosciutto and melon, various golf ball-sized fritters, and cold Roman artichokes—only in Rome can you eat the entire vegetable, including the undeveloped choke—braised in olive oil with spears of garlic and a sprinkle of oregano leaves. Our host suggested bringing two kinds of pasta so that we could have a taste of each. Two steaming bowls arrived. One contained ravioli, listed on the menu as *dischi volanti*, or flying saucers, stuffed with a finely ground mixture of chicken, turkey, veal, beef, minced garlic, two beaten eggs, some grated parmesan, white wine, and nutmeg, salt, and pepper. The other, the restaurant's variation of a traditional favorite, which they call *spaghetti alla carrettiera*, is sauced with tuna fish, tomatoes, and mushrooms. The scampi from the still life display looked so tempting that Renato and some of the others ordered them. They came from the grill garnished with lemon wedges and anointed with a glistening coat of oil and butter flecked with garlic. Enticing as they were, my husband and I could not resist one of our favorite Roman dishes, *coda alla vaccinara*, oxtails stewed with branches of celery. We had wild strawberries for dessert, intense from a syrupy blend of sugar, balsamic vinegar, and cracked black pepper, lots of it, but melded into the sauce in an undetectable way. The wine and conviviality flowed unabated, our host obligingly took pictures of the group, for everyone had brought cameras, and we lingered much longer than we should have. Finally, the drive back to Genzano became a stark reality and we parted with an endless series of warm embraces.

Early last fall, there was a letter from Rodolfo dated the seventh of September. Roughly translated, it said: This letter of mine unfortunately does not bring you good news. My father, Renato, died on the first of September. His illness was very brief. In July it was discovered that he had a tumor in his lung that left no hope. Papa's absence has left a great void and much sadness. But he understood his illness, had very great moral strength, and so passed away without too much suffering. Mamma wants to remain in Genzano. Grazia and I will be as close to her as possible. We send you hugs.

CHAPTER FOUR

The Villa on the Via Appia Antica

Another year when we planned to spend the summer months in Rome, we put an ad in the paper, something like "responsible professional family, two children, want small apartment south of Rome, in l'EUR or close to the beach." We accepted the very first reply because it was an offer we couldn't refuse. In a clipped British accent, the voice on the phone said, "It isn't small, it isn't an apartment, but I need somebody responsible."

Our prospective host, a man in the diplomatic corps working in the British embassy, had previously served in Greece, where he had bought part of a mini-island. In order to go there with his family for the summer, he needed someone to employ his maid, take care of his dogs, and keep silent about the sublease because it was a no-no. In exchange, we would be masters of a very large villa on the Via Appia Antica, across from St. Sebastian, surrounded by five or six acres of gardens, paying the diplomat what we would have paid for an apartment.

The sixteenth-century, six-bedroom, six-bath villa had been completely refurbished, including the addition of a modern, California-style living room, dining room, and kitchen. Floor-to-ceiling glass, doors opening to the terrace—that sort of thing. The land, screened from the street by a high wooden fence, had a road within, meandering among the fruit trees and wild arugula, that was big enough to permit our daughter, who was too young to apply for a legal permit, to learn to drive without breaking any laws. But the unbelievable, very best part, were the private catacombs under the property. With access through the locked kitchen door, there were miles and miles of them. Not smoothly excavated nor electrically lighted like the ones across the street at St. Sebastian, they retained their original form. Chiseled out of the tufa, they were eerily clammy and dripping and irregular underfoot, which made the going slippery and stumbly at best. Most of the skeletons were still entombed behind their stone closures, buried one over the other in ranks up the sides of the walls. On one side, there was a first century chapel decorated with frescoes that had faded and flaked somewhat over time. The Vatican, who owned the catacombs, forbade anyone to enter the sacred ground without an official guide. You could easily lose your way in the endless tunnels and wind up just another skeleton. Whenever we wanted to go down the very steep, long, narrow stairway, we would call St. Sebastian's. For a thousand *lire*, the equivalent of $1.60, one of their guides would come with his key and his lantern, and we would descend into ancient history.

When one of my husband's former professors, a devout Catholic, visited Rome, we arranged for a guide to take him and his wife through the catacombs, knowing that it would be a particularly meaningful experience for them. We went on to dinner at a nearby trattoria, where because of the warm weather, people were seated outside in the spacious flower-decked patio. As we were eating, a group of wandering musicians strolled from table to table singing *stornelli*, spontaneous songs in which the singer inserts details pertinent to the person he is singing to—the color of their eyes, the beauty of their golden tresses, sometimes humorous observations, that sort of thing. The songs are based on a formula of three-lined ditties, of which the first has five syllables and rhymes with the third, but it varies. We were not at all sure that our American guests, unfamiliar with the custom of wandering minstrels, didn't find it more intrusive than amusing.

Alas, with prosperity, the wandering musicians are no more; they have gone the way of the self-appointed parking custodians, the *commendatori*. That honorific title, if bestowed on them ironically, still gave them a certain dignity not equaled by the driver's usual fifty *lire* tip. Although they took up their unofficial stations at perfectly legitimate parking places, their function was not to park your car—most *commendatori* probably couldn't even drive—but to watch over it while you went securely about your business.

During our tenure on the Via Appia Antica, we had many visitors, including Manlio Rossi-Doria, his wife Ann, their teenaged son Marco, who was at that time a fervent Chinese Maoist, and Mateo, Marco's little brother. Grown men now, Mateo is an art restorer in the north of Rome, and Marco is a teacher, gathering together the hoodlums and street kids of Naples and conducting lessons in his peripatetic sidewalk classroom. Manlio, who came from a distinguished Roman family, had long since moved the family to upper Posillipo, a neighborhood in northern Naples. He was a professor of agricultural economics at the University of Naples in Portici, a neighboring community just south of, and contiguous to, Naples proper. At the time of our stay on the Appia Antica, he was in residence in Rome in a pied-à-terre he used when the legislature was in session. Previously, because of his vocal anti-Facist sentiments in the World War II era, he had spent five long years in Mussolini's jails. After his release, he had become a Socialist with strong anti-Togliatti feelings (Togliatti then being the head of the Communist party). Even when the Socialist party's reputation took a dive, he remained a member for the rest of his life. He was now in Rome for the legislative sessions because, as an articulate orator, he had been persuaded by his political friends to run for senator from Puglia—not a chance in hell that he would win, but he could be an eloquent spokesman for the south (in Italy called the *Mezzogiorno*) and the causes to improve the lot of its impoverished farmers and disadvantaged workers. To the shock of the practiced politicos and against all odds, he won handily.

When we visited him and his family in Naples, we drove to Torre del Greco, a beachside community south of the city, to have lunch in a restaurant perched spectacularly over the sea. Shortly after we were seated, eight men commandeered a table nearby. They radiated an authoritative presence, the kind that made you wither, even in the hospitable confines of the restaurant. As if in uniform, they all wore white linen suits set off by brilliantly colored silk ties, vests buttoned concealingly over their paunches, heavy gold chain bracelets, and rings set with marble-sized precious stones. *"Camorra,"* Manlio told us *sotto voce,* the name for the Neapolitan Mafia. It was hard not to stare, not to imagine a gun being whipped out, a groveling waiter, slow to brush up the crumbs, going down in a pool of blood.

But without any such incident, the waiters paraded, showing off various fish on oval platters for selection or rejection as the main course. There was white-suited arm-waving, the men discussing animatedly and at length which pasta to have, goblets of wine refilled, waiters scurrying to and fro like skaters on a rink, until the lunch was finally decided on. Meanwhile, Manlio, smoking his strong, nasty, omnipresent little black cigar, beckoned us to the kitchen where the chef, in his own proper white uniform, displayed the catch of the day, fish that had moments before given their last gasp, and now stared at us through sparkling clear eyes. The chef suggested some prosciutto and melon as the antipasto, followed by *spaghetti alla puttanesca*, whore's pasta, spicily sauced with capers, olives, garlic, anchovies, and a touch of tomato. Then a simple grilling for the chosen fish, to be ornamented only with a splash of olive oil and quartered lemons. We returned to our table with anticipation. As we glanced out over the sea crashing onto the beach below, a bikini-clad man emerged, glistening in the blazing sunlight with the droplets of water left from his swim. In his large powerful hands he held a thrashing octopus, tentacles encircling his arms, gyrating, waving to obtain release. He held it aloft for a moment for all to see, then in a sudden, victorious sweep, he had it in his mouth and bit deep until the arms, one by one, shuddered and stopped contorting.

Among our other visitors on the Via Appia Antica were two young men, Anesti Yorgiyadis, whom everyone called Taki, and his friend Vladimir Rayçanovski. We had first met Taki in Istanbul, when our Greek ship put in to port there for several days. After a week of motoring on the mainland of Greece, we had decided that the best way to see the islands was by boat, a kind of built-in hotel that eliminated packing and unpacking, checking in and checking out, yet offering frequent and long enough stops for exploration, including two stops in Turkey.

When we docked in Istanbul, our second Turkish port of call, we were given a magnified version of the stern warning we had received before disembarking at Ephesus, our first stop. And that was: NEVER, EVER talk to a stranger on the street, in a store, in a restaurant, anywhere. You are sitting prey for con artists, swindlers, thieves, and no-goods of every description, and if you don't heed the warnings, you will be lucky to come away with your head still attached to your body—or something like that.

With our daughter in tow, we explored the behemoth jewels of Topkapi, the mosaics in the Hagia Sofia, which I had studied as a college freshman at Bennington, the Blue Mosque (named, I mused facetiously, because when you took off your shoes, which of course was mandatory, the frigid temperatures of the floor made your toes turn blue). Animated by our look into Istanbul's great and gaudy bazaar, we decided that the spice market would be fascinating as well, but we didn't know where to find it. No one understood our English, and we in turn knew no Turkish, so we resorted to our rather large map. As we tried to make our way, map unfolded before us, a young unshaven man stopped us. In hesitant English, he offered to help. We were terrified. This was exactly what they had warned us about. We tried to shoo him off. He was gently persistent, convincing us that he would lead us to the spice market and leave us there to our own devices, and it being broad daylight, the streets filled with people, what harm could possibly come of that? Besides, he could practice his English, which he was studying, but had little chance to use. We would all benefit. We agreed to follow him, at a distance.

When we arrived at the market, the vendors all knew him and greeted him warmly. When he asked them to give us tastes of the various spices, we didn't even hesitate, by this time having given up any previous suspicions of being drugged or poisoned. Embarrassed by his day-old beard, he asked if we would accompany him home so that he could shave. Throwing all warnings aside, we did. The apartment was elaborately and expensively furnished, if a bit overblown for our California taste. There we met his mother, a statuesque woman in a long printed gown, wearing gold slippers that curled up at the toe, and enough kohl eye make-up to give her an uncanny resemblance to Maria Callas. She spoke French, Greek, and Turkish, so we tried to chat in the first while the young man shaved. They were Greeks, now living in Istanbul. The young man was a student, a very good photographer (she showed us various Nikons, lenses, tripods) and most hideously embarrassed to have us meet him in this unkempt, unshaven state. She offered coffee. The young man, now disbearded, reappeared. In his nervousness he had cut himself once or twice, but the transformation was impressive, for he had also changed his attire and now Anesti Yorgiyadis stood before us looking like a model for some gentleman's magazine.

Taki, as we soon learned to call him, was an excellent guide and took us all around Istanbul. He introduced us to the local jitneys—when they became overcrowded, the passengers near the far door who boarded first were shoved out to wait for the next vehicle—and to a delicious drink, a cross between kefir and cream of wheat, that we tried at a local café. One day, we went by taxi way up the Bosphorus to a tiny restaurant that Taki knew. There we had a simple but exquisite lunch of the freshest fish imaginable. We wanted to reciprocate, so we invited Taki to come as our guest to dinner aboard our ship.

Visibly shaken by our invitation, he was compelled by good manners to accept, meanwhile fearing for his life that the Greek ship would kidnap him and return him to Greece. In spite of our reassurances, he was nervous. Very nervous. But the crew welcomed him warmly, and by the end of the evening he was such good friends with several of them that he promised, on the ship's next trip to Istanbul, to supply them with the slingshots for bird hunting that were not available in Greece.

When we got back to Rome, we corresponded. One letter announced that Taki and his friend Vladimir were planning to come to Rome, hitchhiking most of the way. When they arrived, they checked in at the local Y, where they showered, shaved and changed clothes before turning up at our house. Their baggage consisted of one knapsack each, into which they had packed their food and changes of clothes for the trip, an elaborate Turkish silver and turquoise necklace with matching bracelet and dangling earrings for Lissa, and a complete brass Turkish coffee set—cups, saucers, tray and carafe—for me. Their packing was like the unbelievable number of clowns crammed into one car in the circus.

The first thing they did was to fix our television set, which was misbehaving badly. It enabled us to see the landing on the moon, which some of our Italian friends believed was actually staged in a studio. The second thing they did, and with the utmost seriousness, was to impress upon Lissa, now age fourteen, that she must beware of, never fall in love with, a man from Turkey. Men from their culture had an attitude towards women that an American could never accept. It would be a disaster. The third thing they did was to pay a call on the Turkish embassy. It turned out that they had been summoned by the draft back home and should have turned up at an assigned Turkish army outpost instead of in Rome. But that was not a problem, they shrugged; they would simply bribe the officials. At the embassy, they tried the bribe. No one took it. They wrote us that after they had returned home, they had to serve thirty days in jail, thanks to the unheard of noncooperation of the Turkish officials.

Several years later, we made a trip to Italy for the sole purpose of acting as tour guides for my husband's sister Alice and her husband Orville. It was their first time in Italy, and it was with considerable trepidation that we agreed to shepherd them from city to city, oversee hotel reservations, select some of the high points culturally, and not least, explain menus. Aware that we could come across as overbearing instead of helpful, we gingerly shared some of our discoveries, cautiously acquainted them with some of our favorite places, and little by little introduced them to many of our Italian friends. Much to our relief, they embraced everything and everybody with enthusiasm.

One day, the four of us decided to try a very off-beat restaurant because it was so unlike anything you would find in the United States. A Roman friend had taken us there, and it had quickly become one of our favorite places. It was very hard to find because it nestled in the wall of a church, Santa Maria in Pianta, that was not currently in use (repairs had yet to be made to damages that had occurred during an earthquake, the church services having been diverted to the undamaged chapel). It had no name nor sign, although the regulars called it Sora Margherita, after the woman who did the cooking (*"sora"* is Roman dialect for *"signora"*). The restaurant, in the ghetto, was on the Via di Santa Maria de' Calderari on the Piazza delle Cinque Scole, and it did have a number, 30, alongside the door, but nobody seemed to notice that.

The entry to Sora Margherita, through an unassuming doorway cut through the wall, was obscured by a curtain of dung-colored, vertical chenille cords, easy enough to pass through if you knew where you were going, but completely concealing the interior to passersby. The restaurant clearly didn't depend on walk-in traffic. The dining room on the other side of the chenille cords was stark, but the family who owned it was friendly. We joined others at communal wooden tables laid with long paper runners. The place was open only for lunch because the owner-in-chief, a policeman, had to work from afternoon through the dinner hour. His mother-in-law was the cook—the Sora Margherita of the title—and his wife helped him serve.

The meals were simple: a pasta or two, maybe a risotto, a choice of two or three main courses, fruit and cheese for dessert, red or white wine in tumblers, every single thing delicious, as only the best home cooking can be. At the end of the meal, the policeman would write what you had eaten—*spaghetti alla carbonara, pesce spada al pomodoro*, etc.—on the paper tablecloth, tear it off with a flourish, and present you your bill. It was a big hit with Alice and Orville, who were not only enjoying themselves but by now believed that we knew the city inside out, that we were the ultimate tour guides.

On January 23, 2000, there appeared an article in the *New York Times*, "Gastronomic Pilgrimage Through Rome," a review of a dozen or so traditional restaurants that not only included a paragraph on Sora Margherita, now "one of Rome's favorite holes-in-the-wall," but had a large photo of the aproned Margherita Tomassini holding a handful of homemade *tonnarelli* cascading into a wicker basket in her other hand. She was standing in the restaurant doorway, which now sported a miscellaneous collage of awards or reviews—it was hard to tell from the picture—and a poorly hand-lettered sign saying SORA MARGHERITA. Was this manufactured especially for the photograph? Had word-of-mouth publicity really changed to this? It should have been a warning. When we went there for lunch in the spring of 2002, the shabby green door in the wall was closed and padlocked and the phone had been disconnected. No one in the neighborhood seemed to know why they had given up, but clearly the trattoria was now only a fond memory.

Update: We learned the last time we were in Rome that the closure was because Sora Margherita had fallen ill. When she regained her health in 2002, there were no liquor licenses available for restaurants, so they could not reopen. However, they found a way out. They formed the *Sora Margherita Associazione Culturale*, and every member, without any fee, has a card for life, with name, date, and number officially filled out on the back. Mine is Number 0497 D. This allows me to dine anytime with full assurance that I can buy wine, beer, or alcoholic beverages such as *limoncello*, to drink with my meal. The more cheerful, reopened dining room has been spruced up a bit, and the chenille rope entrance curtain is now red. I must say that I miss the dung-colored one.

We drove one afternoon, at Alice and Orville's request, out to the Via Appia Antica to show them the old villa that we had lived in a few years before. Behind what had become a higher fence, you could no longer see any part of it from the street. What once had been a welcoming entrance had now become a forbidding, solid locked gate, halting all comers like an official stop sign. A highly polished brass plaque, mounted on the gate, was etched with the name of an English private school, the new occupant. Several times we rang the bell. We hoped they would permit us to view the grounds unobtrusively, to see at least the outside of the house. But there was no response. Reluctantly we realized that our brief residency was just a miniscule part in the history of the villa on the Appia Antica.

In Rome, the four of us had been staying at the Hassler hotel at the top of the Spanish Steps. On our last day, we checked out by midday, our car piled high with the baggage the hotel's crew so skillfully jigsawed into place. Tips given, farewells and *buon viaggios* said, we drove off with bravado, heading into the extensive park of the Villa Borghese as a shortcut to the highway. Charles, who was driving, discovered, much to his dismay, that since our last visit the once familiar road now led directly into a parking garage. It was too late for any alternative, so into the garage we went. In order to get out, we had no choice but to pay the parking fee—sort of like the involuntary voluntary contribution to the opera. Charles paid. We exited. We had goofed, royally, our reputation as tour guides instantly shredded. My brother-in-law delightedly kept that parking receipt in his wallet until the day he died.

CHAPTER FIVE

Positano and Capri

Since we had the good fortune to have a live-in housekeeper in Rome, it occurred to us that we also had the good fortune to have a live-in babysitter. That suggested the possibility of a trip without the kids. We asked our friend, Elena, who knew Italy well and was currently living in Rome, for suggestions. Born in Milan, she had moved to the United States many years before, along with her parents and sister. As a graduate of the University of California, she was currently in Italy for three years to attend graduate school. Her interest in Carlo Goldoni, the eighteenth-century dramatist and the subject of her intended thesis, had attracted her to the university in Rome, where the current professorial expert on Goldoni was on the faculty. But the professor, relying almost entirely on his assistant to conduct classes—a typical modus operandi in many foreign countries—never turned up, considerably cooling her ardor for graduate school. Fortunately for us, it didn't cool her ardor for Italy, and we therefore had the advantage of her invaluable knowledge and advice. And so it was that with her help we chose the destination of Positano, on the Amalfi peninsula, which we knew only by its glorious reputation. By this time, of course, Elena was included in the plans.

Our route included long stops at Pompeii, excavated from Vesuvius's molten lava and ashes, and Herculaneum, perhaps better preserved because of its burial in mud. Both places were humbling reminders of nature's power. Equally humbling, but more immediately terrorizing, was the man-made Amalfi Drive, dazzlingly cut into the rocks in the mid-nineteenth century without the aid of computers or heavy earth-moving equipment. Clinging to cliffs precipitously plummeting hundreds of feet into the sea below, with hairpin turns every five seconds, or so it seemed, the roadway was so narrow that two cars abreast could barely fit. Yet, tempting as it was to close your eyes tight when a vehicle approached from the opposite direction, to do so would have meant certain death on that serpentine road. Certainly, it was not a place for someone with a fear of heights—if you didn't have acrophobia to begin with, you had a full-blown case by the end of the drive—but that was the least of it. Not only did buses pass us on blind curves, but at the same instant a hurtling Ferrari would maniacally zing past the bus. They would tuck into single file, at full throttle, just as the same configuration would round the bend in the other direction. It was white knuckle time, with a little vertigo thrown in, a time for prayers, even if you were an atheist.

Once in Positano, we continued along the one road that was accessible to vehicles, searching for our hotel. Although we knew that the Albergo Miramare was on the Via Trara Genoino, there were neither street signs nor hotel marquee to suggest that we were anyplace near it. We stopped a passerby who happily gave us directions and pointed out that, since no actual roadway went there, we should park and walk to the hotel, far below us. The hotel was accustomed to sending someone to fetch the luggage. Apart from the street that we were on, all the others were actually steep pedestrian passageways, most of them an unending series of steps, helpful in ascending or descending, but not possible for vehicles. We followed the instructions, climbing endless stairs until we reached the hotel. We were overwhelmed.

Perched breathtakingly high on the side of the hill, it overlooked the Gulf of Salerno, part of the larger Tyrrhenian Sea. Glistening in the brilliant sunlight, the sapphire-blue water sparkling below, the hotel was straight out of paradise. When we were shown to our rooms, we were altogether speechless. The view out over the sea and of houses spilling down the hill to the beach far below was not confined just to our windows: The end of our black bath tub, set into the wall, was actually a see-through aquarium swimming with live tropical fish, who enjoyed the same stupendous scene of the hillside and turquoise sea as anyone who entered the bathroom. Taking a bath was like going to heaven.

Both our room and Elena's, although differently luxurious in their fabrics, colors, and furnishings, made the same ubiquitous use of ceramics as the hotel in general: All light switches, door knobs, switch plates, lamps, ashtrays, flower vases, and any other possible accessory used myriad patterns and figures in mixtures of bright colors to create an effect at once frolicsome and harmonizing. When we ate dinner that night on a vine-trellised balcony edged with flowers and overlooking the same incredible view, the food was served on a progression of ceramic plates, not one having the same color or painted characters as another. As the light began to fade, the waiter lit the candles anchored in a slightly off-center, three-pronged ceramic candelabra.

Intrigued, we asked the owner and the man responsible for this fantasy, Carlo Cinque, where the ceramics came from. He enthusiastically supplied the name of the small factory that he dealt with in the nearby village of Vietri sul Mare, a town famous for its colorful pottery. Besides the people he bought from, there were numerous other sources there. He encouraged us to pay a visit. We drove there early the next morning.

Vietri, which sits between Amalfi and Salerno, was a warren of shops and factories, some displaying samples of their wares on the stoops. The cheerful figures that decorated the tile facades on many of the buildings were similar to the images on the plates that we had been eating on at Miramare: peasants gathering fruit, herding goats or cows, fishing in boats, playing flutes, drawing water. An occasional mermaid swam through the waves, and a playful octopus wriggled its eight legs in every direction. Although the hand-painted designs appeared almost childlike in their simplicity, it took a certain sophistication to make them as naive as they seemed. In both their charm and exuberance, they reflected the spontaneity of life in the region, the closeness to and dependence on the sea, the primary colors that abounded in the sunny climate. Bordered by stylized curlicues and furbelows, simpler ceramics created signage for businesses and house numbers for residences. Even the dome of the church was covered in tiles.

The tradition of ceramics-making dates way back, by some accounts to the ancient Greeks who once settled in the area. Paestum, a colony that they founded around 600 B.C., is in the neighborhood, southeast along the Gulf a little way past Salerno. One day, we also drove there to see the three magnificent Doric temples that the Greek settlers left behind. In more recent times, the sprightly designs of German artists who took up residence in Vietri became a lasting influence on the local wares. At the time of our visit, the current number of shops and factories was proof that the ceramic industry was certainly thriving.

When we followed the directions to the factory whose address Carlo Cinque had given us, we were surprised to find it housed in a sizeable building. Endless stacks of plates, bowls and platters, rows of cups, jars, vases, and collections of accessories covered the floors. The proprietor, as sunny as his wares, welcomed us with effusive hospitality. After he showed us about, he left us to make our selections in a leisurely fashion. When we had settled on the dinnerware that we wanted—a difficult choice since each plate was more enticing than the next—Elena spotted candleholders like the ones at Miramare. We couldn't resist adding one to our pile of dishes and bowls.

More than forty years later, we are still using our Vietri plates, although there is now a chip here and there among the shrimp and the cowherds. On a foray to Positano a couple of years ago, we decided it was time to restock, and so we drove one day to Vietri. We had a vague feeling on entering the town that the lack of self-consciousness that had made it so appealing in the past now somehow had just an edge of commercialism about it. When we sought out the factory where we had bought our plates and bowls, the same warmth and hospitality greeted us, and as before we were free to range through the stacks of finished ceramics to pick out what we wanted. But the dishes had fewer figures, and the designs were more deliberately childlike versions of our dinnerware, somehow less colorful and lacking its subtlety. When we described our original dishes, in the hopes that we had possibly missed the stacks that contained them, our salesperson told us that those designs were now primarily made for export. She suggested that when we got back to the States we should look in Macy's, "one of our big accounts." When we did, we discovered that the newer dinnerware was jolly enough but less sophisticated than before, nice dishes, but certainly not the same. Suddenly our little chips and blemishes diminished visibly.

In 1964, in an effort to promote and identify regional Italian cooking, the *Unione Ristoranti del Buon Ricordo*, a group of a dozen restaurants in Italy, started giving away hand-painted ceramic dinner plates made in Vietri. To get one, all you had to do was eat the local specialty that the dish illustrated. Jaunty and humorous designs of the food, as well as the restaurant name, the town it was in, and the name of the dish depicted, made these the best kind of souvenirs. Now there are dozens and dozens of participating restaurants. When the specialties change, which they frequently do, it necessitates a new plate with a new design. Not for sale, and originally intended simply as a memento of a memorable meal, these dishes almost immediately became valuable collectors' items. Italian antique shops, when they can get them, sell the dishes for outrageous prices, and within the last few years restaurants in Switzerland, Australia, Hong Kong, Singapore, Japan, Austria, and the United States have joined the consortium.

We have, of course, become collectors of the plates commemorating the restaurants in Italy. (For now, the rest of the world seems too much to cope with.) They capture with even more humor the spirit of our original dishes from Vietri. We now have sixteen of them. Although on many occasions we prefer something else on the menu, it becomes harder and harder to resist ordering the special recipe that gets you the plate.

Our original stay in Positano occurred several years before the *Ristoranti del Buon Ricordo* plates were even invented. And it wasn't many years more before some of the shops in town began offering a modest selection of Vietri ceramics, thereby saving you the tortuous drive that we had made to the village where they were produced. Although it seemed, when we were staying at Miramare, that the delicious food tasted even better on the colorful pottery plates, occasionally we abandoned the flower-decked balcony, descending to one of the trattorias nestled on the dark pebbled beach below. That is where we swam on most afternoons, although for walking the pebbles were not as kind as sand to the bottoms of your feet. The beach restaurants we tried, brimming with flowers and overlooking a dozen gaily painted fishing boats, offered simple dishes: marinated anchovies, a risotto made with local shellfish, a pasta with wild mushrooms or clams, a fresh fish cooked plump and juicy. And then to end the meal, *limoncello*, a liqueur based on the lemons that grow in such abundance along the Amalfi coast. Every restaurant in the area has its own homemade version. Our favorite, served as a dessert rather than an after-dinner drink, was a combination of vodka and *limoncello* poured over lemon *granita*. It rivaled our other favorite, a discovery we made on an excursion to Ravello, an ancient town high above Amalfi. We dined in the Hotel Caruso Belvedere, from which there are breathtaking views of hillsides terraced with olive trees, vineyards, and lemon groves, and beyond them the sea. Although we ate sumptuously, the one thing that we all remember is the luxurious chocolate mousse with cherries.

Carlo Cinque had opened the Miramare with half a dozen rooms in 1934, eventually expanding it to three times that size. Its precarious perch, incredible view, and a décor executed with such extraordinary flair, made it unique among hotels at that time. But in 1970, Signor Cinque surpassed even his first creation with his new hotel, the San Pietro, hewn into a precipitous rock cliff on the outskirts on the other side of town. To get to the tennis courts or the bar and bathing area that repose 250 feet down near the bottom of the hotel, an elevator chiseled through the rock descends to the level of the sea. For those who do not want to swim in the ocean, which can be reached from a small pebbly beach or by steps from the bathing deck, there is a swimming pool in the hotel up above. As they did at Miramare, San Pietro uses the same colorful miscellany of dinnerware from Vietri—clearly all of it didn't go to Macy's—and in addition, enormous curved ceramic benches, hand painted in a more rococo style, border the terrace. If anyone ever feels the need to leave this self-contained village, there is a chauffeured car to take you to and fro.

When Carlo Cinque passed on from his heaven on earth to the one in the sky, his niece and nephew, Virginia and Salvatore Attanasio took over both the San Pietro and the Miramare. Their mother Carmela, who was Carlo's sister, owned yet another hotel, the Palazzo Murat, further down the hillside. Each place has a unique personality, yet they all have that Cinque style. Being a *hôtelier* must be in the family's genes.

Reluctantly we left Positano by ferry for our final destination, the fabled isle of Capri. Just off the point of the Amalfi peninsula, the tiny island is only four miles long and half as wide, but its legendary reputation belies its size. The Roman emperor Augustus started it all with his lengthy idylls there before Christ was born. Remnants of his stay and that of Tiberius, the next emperor in residence, dot the island. The craggy hillsides, abundant sunshine, cascades of flowers, and staggering views over the sea have made it a crowded mecca for everyone from the rich and famous to the legions of ordinary folk who want to investigate its fame. Hating crowds, we almost decided not to go, but because it was still off-season we guessed that the island, in spite of its magnetism, would lack its usual cheek-by-jowl tourist population. Little did we imagine that we would be among the few, if not the only, foreigners in town. It was absolutely tranquil.

Once checked into our hotel, we immediately set off on foot to explore. When we came upon the Piazza Umberto I, which the Capresi call La Piazzetta, we decided to stop for a coffee. Three men finishing up their Camparis sat around the only other table occupied. Of the three, the youngest, who was deeply tanned, dark-haired, and exceedingly handsome, looked like one of the current advertisements for tooth whiteners every time he smiled, which was frequently. The second, the most gregarious, was fairer of complexion, a bit older, pleasingly plump and jolly, with the blond hair so common to people in the Amalfi area. The third man was tall, trim, and quite good-looking, though no way near as dashing as the man with the sparkling smile. He seemed to preside over the table, chatting amiably with the waiters, ordering a second round of Camparis when the group had downed their first. Before our coffees had even arrived, the three of them had introduced themselves, welcomed us, moved their chairs over to join our table, and become our fast friends.

We exchanged information. It turned out that the young man with the fabulous tan was a cliff diver, one of those incredible, fearless athletes who dove with swanlike grace off the precipices into the sea far below. It was how he earned his living. In the off-season he lounged about with his friends. When we got to know him better, we learned that his ambition was to go to South America to make a pile of money. It was clear to us that once he was rich, he would of course find no better place to vacation than Capri, where he could watch the gorgeous young men dive off the cliffs.

The fair-haired man was an attorney who didn't let work interfere with his pleasurable lifestyle, which included sitting around the square with like-minded companions. The third man who had chatted so amiably with the waiters turned out to be a waiter himself, a job that freed up his afternoons and in this case also his evenings, since in the slow season he often had time off.

Our newfound friends squired us to ancient ruins, to high vistas where each new view was more breathtaking than the last, along meandering paths to the harbors, up to the town of Anacapri. One day, they decided that we should see the Blue Grotto, normally the biggest tourist attraction on the island, but not the usual rip-off if you are in the charge of locals. Small boats take you through the rocky opening, so low that you have to bend quite flat to keep from smashing your head. Thanks to our friends, we avoided the assault for outrageous tips as well as the guide's warbly bel canto along the way.

Perhaps the favorite pastime of our group was to go to dinner together at the trattoria Da Gemma, where the robust food was as welcoming as the staff and the guitarist knew not only all of the popular songs but every Neapolitan lyric ever written. The excellent pizza and seductive music would have been reason enough to return, but even more, Da Gemma had become "our place," by now a nightly ritual.

Finally, tearfully, we had to face the fact that it was our last day on Capri, time to resume our normal lives. Our last night at Da Gemma was bittersweet and we agreed to meet our friends for cappuccinos in the morning. A glum-looking trio appeared, bearing a small nosegay for Elena and beseeching us to stay just one more day. They were so sad and so convincing that we finally gave in, much to the relief of all of us, and began to plan our final day. The next morning when we met for our farewell cappuccinos, three morose men presented us with a poem they had stayed up half the night composing. Sometimes eloquent, sometimes humble, always sad, it begged us to reconsider for just another day. We were touched. Of course we agreed to stay. And so it went for four days. If Elena had not had to resume her studies and we to take up researches and parenting once again, we would be there still.

CHAPTER SIX

The Giants of Riace

I n 1972, during his annual stay in California, our friend Carlo told us about a marvelous archeological discovery that had been made that past August in southern Italy. Apparently a snorkler by the name of Stefano Mariottini, on vacation from Rome, while diving in the Ionian sea off Riace, had discovered the heavily encrusted arm of a statue poking through the sandy bottom that had buried it. Through a succession of dives, he had managed to brush away enough of the sand to determine that the hand was part of a complete metal statue buried some twenty-five feet below the surface of the sea. Before he was done, he had uncovered a second figure of similar size a few feet away.

He reported the find immediately to the Antiquities Department of Reggio. They in turn set up a guard over the spot and began arranging for official divers with the necessary equipment for retrieval. Some four or five days later, with the help of air-filled balloons to aid in the statues' flotation, three divers tortuously brought the first six-foot figure up, and overcoming the difficulty presented by its weight—each of the statues weighed in at more than five hundred pounds—and with the aid of a boat, finally managed to get it to shore. By the next day, crowds of the curious had come on foot, by car, and in the water, greatly hindering the official efforts at recovery. Besides the numerous boats, the human obstacles, and a turbulent sea, it was much harder to dig out the second figure, embedded more tenaciously in its sandy grave. The first attempt at raising the statue, finally free of the bottom, went awry and it plunged back into the sea. The second try, in spite of the difficulties, was ultimately successful. After more than 2,000 years of submersion, the two warriors, for that is what they turned out to be, were transported from the beach to the workshop of the museum in Reggio Calabria for cleaning.

Because they were covered with shrouds of barnacles and calcareous incrustations that not only concealed, but actually had been fundamental in preserving the splendidly refined work hidden beneath them, the statues were at first thought to be of cruder Roman origin, possibly copies of Greek works. It was only gradually, as the restoration revealed the fineness of the workmanship and the elegance of the details, that scholars and other experts realized that the sculptures they had before them were, in fact, original fifth-century Greek bronzes, among the few surviving rarities from that era. It also became clear that in spite of more than two years of meticulous cleaning in Reggio, it was now time to employ more advanced restoration techniques using equipment unavailable in the southern museum. The place to complete the work was the Archeological Museum in Florence with its advanced center for restoration. In 1975, the Reggio technicians turned the bronzes over to their colleagues in the north.

By the time of their transfer, the two nude warriors, previously referred to as "Statue A" and "Statue B," had revealed enough differences to earn dubbed names. Statue A, clearly the younger of the two men, long hair and beard falling in curlicued splendor, became known as "The Youth," or sometimes, no doubt because of his handsome features and fit body, as "The Beauty." He is missing his shield and possibly a weapon such as a lance. The other statue, distinctly an older, sterner man, though with equally fine physique, has a full wavy beard, but only the hair that would have stuck out below his missing helmet. He is called "The Old Man." He has also lost his shield, his lance, and his left eye. An examination by the Florence laboratory further revealed that his right arm was an inferior replacement of the original, apparently soldered on sometime later. Collectively the two became known as "*i bronzi,*" "the bronzes"; Carlo always referred to them as "*i giganti*" or "the giants."

The Florence team labored for five years, discovering through various tests and further cleaning that the lips and nipples of both statues were of copper, as well as the eyelashes of Statue A; he also had a perfect set of silver teeth. Statue B revealed no teeth since he was sculpted with his mouth shut. Although the pupils of the younger warrior and the entire left eye of the older are missing, the remaining pupil turned out to be opaque and glossy, a mixture of glasslike materials, the cleaned corneas a mixture of limestone and ivory. The restorers thought that the headband that circled the hair of the curly-headed youth, as well as both of the missing shields, were probably originally overlaid with gold leaf. One further step completed the restoration: the removal from the insides of what-ever remained of the original casting molds, now a mixture of claylike earth and infiltrated sand, as well as the lead pipes that had once anchored the figures to their bases. The empty interiors and the smooth bronze exteriors, now devoid of the subterranean incrustations that had protected them, then got a chemical treatment to prevent deterioration.

Once the work was finished, and before the statues were returned to their rightful home in Reggio, the southern archeological museum gave permission for their display in Florence. The exhibition, which lasted for six months, brought overwhelming and enthusiastic crowds, among them our friend Carlo. On their way back to Reggio, the bronzes had a stopover in Rome. Their brief display in the sixteenth-century Quirinale Palace, the official presidential residence, brought equally ecstatic responses. Nine years after their discovery, they finally went back to the National Museum of Reggio Calabria, where they would remain on permanent display in an exhibition hall, part of a new submarine archeology section that had been especially prepared for the purpose.

On our very next trip to Italy, enticed by what Carlo had told us about these magnificent bronzes, we determined to go to Calabria to see them for ourselves. Some months later, we and the kids, heading south from Rome in a rented car, were on our way to Reggio. It was already dark when we arrived. We checked into our hotel, the Ascioti, which seemed to sigh for a little refurbishing. It was one of only two recommended in the town, but it had no restaurant. When we hesitated, the desk clerk assured us that we could get breakfast in the morning. Since it was quite late, we were famished and asked for advice on where to go for dinner. Within minutes of taking our bags to our rooms and perfunctorily washing up, we were heading for "the best place in town," the Ristorante Bonaccorso, near the Piazza Garibaldi.

The Bonaccorso's interior was done up in a sort of faux Belle Epoque style: deep red brocade walls, drapes, and valences; numerous paintings in gilded frames; tables set with ochre cloths overlaid with matching red damask cloths and napkins. The chairs were bentwood,

the tables trimmed with bulbous glass lamps and vases of red pop-
pies. There were, optimistically, three bulky wine glasses at each
place. The crowning glory was a number of light fixtures mounted
from the ceiling: large, dome-shaped, ochre shades, possibly of
stretched fabric, set off by three inches of undulating fringe on the
bottom, for some reason reminding me of the cinch-waisted corsets
of ladies of the night who might have populated a high class bordello
of that era. But we were there to eat and the robust food and wine—
no match for the décor—was abundant enough to satisfy our hunger.

In the morning, looking out of our window, we observed first
hand some of the conditions reflecting the poverty of Calabria:
the cracked and hobbled sidewalks and the widespread disrepair of
buildings, evident in our own hotel. There seemed to be a gray
shadow everywhere, even when the sun was shining. We were certainly not tempted to stay in Reggio any longer than it might take to
see the bronzes. Northerners had told us, whether it was true or not,
that the local Mafia's control over regional politics and the resultant
subjugation of the populace assured their power and promoted the
financial extortion that went along with it. Money spent for repairing sidewalks and refurbishing buildings was obviously not high on
their list.

Breakfast was served in a sort of upstairs lobby that stretched long
and narrow across the hotel. Along with cappuccinos for us and milk
for the kids, not standard breakfast fare for Italian children, we also
asked them to bring whatever breadstuffs they might be serving.
Would we like toasts, the lady serving us inquired. Pleasantly surprised by this further accommodation to American tastes, we happily agreed. Shortly, the lady returned with two glasses of milk. A
bit later she brought the cappuccinos. But no toasts. We waited. We
sipped our drinks. Still no toasts. After some time had passed, we
sought her out and gently inquired. She had not forgotten, she

replied somewhat impatiently, it takes time to make toasts. Her testy reply made us feel as guilty as misbehaved children caught in the cookie jar. We silently sipped away at our coffees. And waited. We finished our drinks. And waited. Suddenly, triumphantly, our lady appeared bearing a heaping platter of grilled cheese sandwiches, more than the four of us could possibly consume. As we faced this mountain of melting cheese and toasted bread we remembered, too late, that in spite of our generous interpretation of them as an accommodation to American tastes, "toasts" in Italy means grilled cheese sandwiches.

After breakfast we waddled over to the museum only to discover a handwritten sign taped to the entrance that informed us that the museum would not open that morning but would be open late in the afternoon. Having no choice, we wandered aimlessly through the town. Unfortunately we were so full of breakfast that we could not even think of filling the time by stopping for a snack, or better, going to a restaurant for lunch. At two, we returned, only to find that the sign had been altered. Now they weren't going to open until 6 P.M. Although it was frustrating, we shouldn't have been that surprised. Even our green Michelin guide to Italy warns that there is a constant change in opening times, sometimes even unpredictable closures for restoration work or because of staff shortages. It strikingly reminded us of a similar experience in Anagni where, several years before, we had gone to see some newly restored thirteenth-century frescoes in a crypt under the town's Romanesque cathedral.

Anagni, a little-known medieval hill town some forty miles south and east of Rome, came to our attention only because we read of the vault's restoration in an article in the *New York Times*. The frescoes, which had remained unscathed for some hundreds of years, fell victim sometime in the late 1960s to a leak in the town's well. It changed the balance of water underground, resulting in a cataract of crystalline salt accumulating on the surface of the paintings. It took some three years to clean it off.

Since it was only a short drive to Anagni from Rome, we started out early one morning to see the frescoes. We found the cathedral already gloriously bathed in sunlight. Surprisingly for a nontourist town, there were also a large number of parked cars. We soon found out why. The church was closed to the public for a wedding but would reopen after the ceremonies were over. We were disappointed, of course, but Anagni had a thirteenth-century medieval quarter to occupy us until we could get into the church.

We came back from our sightseeing just in time to see the wedding party emerging: a radiant bride and groom being gently pelted with candy-coated almonds, an Italian custom supposed to insure fertility, much like our shower of rice. When everyone had driven off and we started to enter the church, the custodian stopped us. It was now noon—the afternoon closure time—and we would have to wait until the cathedral reopened at four.

When we returned from a leisurely lunch to enter the church at last, we found that it was still decorated with the flowers from the wedding. The most remarkable were long green garlands of leaves interwoven with fresh lemons, years before chic florists in this country incorporated fruit in their floral arrangements. Skirting the flower-decked aisles, we made our way to the nave where, according to the custodian, we would find the stairs descending to the crypt.

Although the well-worn stairway showed its age, once at the bottom there was such an explosion of color that it quite took the breath away. Every inch of the space was carpeted with paintings and mosaic tile flooring, itself quite a work of art, all of it vibrant from its recent restoration. The vaulted room, about sixty feet long and half as wide, was intersected by columns that divided it into aisles. The arches, supported by the columns, as well as the walls and the curved ceilings, were elaborately painted to glorious effect. The frescoes depicted scriptural tales from the Old Testament as well as themes from history and early science. Five small altars indicated where saints were buried. Some of the paintings illustrated the stories of their sainthoods.

Somehow, the rich overlay of pattern and color was not what we had expected, nor the intricacy of the architecture. We felt that we had happened upon a real treasure. We all agreed that in the end, all of the delays, so typically Italian, seemed insignificant: The brief frustration had faded into a memorably happy ending.

As we faced the delays in Reggio, we wondered whether the bronzes would be worth the long drive, the drab hotel, the aimless wandering through the impoverished town to kill time, whether the outcome could possibly be as fortunate as seeing the frescoes in Anagni had been. At least, when we returned to the museum at six o'clock, there was no amended note telling us of further changes of schedule: This time around, we were actually going to get into the museum and see the prized statues.

Contrary to our expectations, the bronzes' whereabouts were anything but obvious. Somehow we had thought that they would be spotlighted, the area of their display, if not in plain view, at least well indicated. But there was nary a sign of them. In answer to our inquiries, the guard gave us a route that seemed to take in most of the museum: first through exhibits dedicated to prehistoric archeological discoveries in Calabria, then to displays devoted to the Greek colonies in southern Italy (and more of the Greeks on the floor above, along with a numismatic section; and on the floor above that, a Byzantine collection, all of which we opted to skip). When we came to the end of these numerous halls, stairs led to the basement level below and to the newly created submarine archeology section. But yet again, before we could reach the Hall of the Bronzes proper, there was a room devoted to various materials and finds related to the statues. Finally, at last, through a glass door, we arrived at the very large Hall of the Bronzes dedicated to the Riace statues.

No one had mentioned that in this room, straight in front of us, was a magnificent sculpted male head, which had been completely overshadowed by the notoriety of his fellow bronzes. He was stunningly beautiful, in spite of a missing left eye, an elegant three-dimensional portrait in bronze, an older man with a long undulating beard and a serious face, seemingly deep in thought. The head alone, without any bust, made the figure that much more startling and intense. According to the *Guida al Museo Nazionale di Reggio Calabria*, the sculpture known as the "Portrait of a Philosopher" (or variously, the "Philosopher from Porticello," for that was where he was found) was thought "to be the only Greek facial portrait in existence and dated to the fifth century B.C."

After lingering on this splendid and unanticipated find, we suddenly realized that this was the hall in which the warriors, the real focus of our visit, were supposed to be. But there was not a sign of them. We were astonished. We made strenuous inquiries. The answers were very disappointing: It seems that the interior corrosion of the warriors had been more extensive than originally thought and the experts had ordered corrective measures to prevent further damage. We were aghast. Had we come all this way not to be able to see the bronzes?

Because we seemed so deflated, our guide threw in a little consolation. The workshop where this restoration was going on was right on the premises. We could, if we wanted, see the work in progress. We wanted. In the center of the designated room, a raised platform, accessible by ladderlike wooden stairs, was totally fenced in. To see the restoration, it was necessary to mount the stairs and look down into the laboratory from a kind of catwalk that encircled it. From this vantage point, at last, we saw the statues. They were lying on their backs, endless wires and probes entering and exiting their bodies, some of them connected to television screens. The whole operation distinctly resembled surgery of the gastrointestinal tract. Although we had only a frontal view, by circling the catwalk, we could avoid the interference of hovering workmen and see the statues from several different angles, including upside down.

Even in their prone position, they were extraordinary. One could only imagine how imposing they must have been upright. The quality of the workmanship, more familiar to us in the marble carvings we had seen, was equally detailed and refined. How astonishing that we could get such an aesthetic thrill from work done by artists twenty-five hundred years ago. In spite of the limitations of the surgical theatre in which we had finally found them, we still had a marvelous view, and we were glad that we had persisted.

As we looked down admiringly from the walkway above, we suddenly made a crowning discovery. By positioning yourself just right, you could actually see the televised views of the bronzes' innards and the painstaking removal of the corrosive polyps. Millions of people, first in Florence and Rome, and then in Reggio, may have seen the outsides, and indeed the backsides, of these magnificent warriors, but only a few of us are among the privileged who can also claim to have had an intimate view of their insides.

CHAPTER SEVEN

Bacchanal in Rovescala

Knowing our love for Italy, some academic friends were quick to introduce us in the 1950s to Carlo Cipolla, a newly arrived professor from Pavia. An eminent economist, he had just begun a decades-long arrangement whereby he taught for half of every academic year at the University of California in Berkeley, the other half in Italy. For us it was the beginning of a fortunate friendship, which lasted until his death in September 2000.

Carlo was not your usual teacher of economics. Among his other attributes, he was the youngest person in Italy ever to receive the rank of full professor. He had studied at the London School of Economics, where he had perfected his English, and at the Sorbonne, where he had polished his French. He spoke not only classical Italian but the Frenchified dialect of his native Pavia, as well as the regional patois of Catania, Venice, Turin, and Florence, all places, besides Pavia, at which he had taught during his long career in academia. His last affiliation was a prestigious appointment to Pisa's Scuola Normale Superiore, the Italian institute for advanced study.

His scholarship, informed by a prolific intellectual curiosity, was inventive and unusually insightful. He wrote highly acclaimed, brilliantly succinct volumes on subjects as wide-ranging as miasmas, humors, and the plague; the consequences of the first sailing ships to be armed with cannons; the influences of mechanical clocks on society; and monetary developments from ancient history to the modern *lire*. His historic works on health brought him a recognition that he perhaps treasured more than any of his other honors, especially since his brother was a medical doctor: The University of Pavia bestowed on him an honorary doctorate of medicine. He was admitted to membership, as had been Galileo before him, in the Accademia dei Lincei, he won the Balsan Prize (which is like getting a Nobel), and he was on the roster of both the Academy of Arts and Sciences in this country, and Great Britain's Royal Historical Society.

In 1976, he wrote for fun a short essay in English, *The Basic Laws of Human Stupidity* characterizing human behavior in seven basic laws, complete with graphs and charts, lightly satirizing the traditional and rigid mathematical economist—the kind he was not. The first basic law, for example, asserts that "Always and inevitably everyone underestimates the number of stupid individuals in circulation." As part of the spoof, the text is heavily footnoted in the best scholarly tradition. As a gift to him, his Italian publisher, Il Mulino, printed a limited number of copies for his acquaintances and friends. And for this occasion, keeping to the spirit of the satire, they changed their name to The Mad Millers (*mulino* is a mill).

The thirty-page book became an instant underground success. The president of a Milan investment trust was so taken with it that he had an Italian translation made and gave leather-bound copies to his board of directors for Christmas. Il Mulino, realizing the overwhelming demand, decided to publish it as a book for the general market. Recognizing the limitations of its size, not quite sufficient for a small commercial book, they combined it with another of Carlo's short essays ascribing the economic development of the middle ages and the subsequent dawning of the Italian Renaissance to the wine trade, the wool trade, and the aphrodisiac effects of pepper. The combined essays were called *Allegro ma non troppo*.

The book immediately became a bestseller, and remained at the top of the list for seventeen months. The president of Italy awarded Carlo a gold medal designed by Arnaldo Pomodoro, the famous sculptor. (I once had the pleasure, when they were both on the Berkeley campus, to introduce Signor Cipolla to Signor Pomodoro—"Mr. Onion, meet Mr. Tomato.") The book was first translated into French, then German and Japanese. A theatrical troupe in the French provinces turned it into a play that was such a success they brought it to Paris. We and our mutual friends, Hillary and Danny Goldstine, flew over for the opening. Barbara came up from Rome and Ora, Carlo's wife, and their daughter Tanya, flew in from Florence.

Carlo was the subject of innumerable newspaper and magazine interviews. My favorite was in the Italian magazine, *Panorama*, which ironically had on its cover four sun-bronzed young women, naked except for thongs, standing ankle-deep in the sea and bearing aloft an equally nude, except-for-thong, male. In complete contrast, the interview on page 90, prefaced by a description of Carlo as having an "old-fashioned elegance," being "very aristocratic," "looking a little like Henry Fonda," asks serious questions about the hygiene of the seventeenth century and is illustrated with such classic paintings as Veronese's "Visit of the Doctor," and a somber photograph of Carlo. It appeared because the famous author of *Allegro ma non troppo* was about to publish a new scholarly book, *Miasmi e umori*. Carlo always lamented that, over the course of his academic career, he had published some twenty scholarly books, but it was *Allegro ma non troppo* that captured all of the attention.

Reflecting his wide-ranging writing and research, he collected ancient and medieval coins; clocks (including one which we also own—Carlo directed us to the store in Bern where he had found his —a copy of a sixteenth-century, pendulated timepiece that not only ticks and tocks but tells the time with only one hand); and a vast assortment of old maps and medical instruments. He also had a stunning collection of wine, which he shared with abundant generosity. Besides all of which, he was tall, thin, and suavely good looking. More Fred Astaire than Henry Fonda.

When they were in Italy, he and his wife, Ora, lived in a large, modern apartment in Pavia, overlooking the Ticino River— Scandinavian furniture, significantly chosen antiques, beautiful old paintings, examples of Carlo's vast collections, and the view of the shimmering river were part of the décor. As is the custom in Pavia, where floors are made of marble, shoes were shed at the door in favor of large felt slides which polished instead of scratching. Although they were high up in the building, the Cipollas used their ample storage room in the basement as a *cave;* it had the perfect temperature for keeping wine, and it was easily accessible by the elevator just outside their door.

In later years, when Carlo had to spend much time in Tuscany, they bought a small *villetta* that had been built, along with several others, on the grounds of a grand estate in the hills above Florence. We once had the good fortune to stay in one of the other houses, whose owners rented to us during their absence. There was an extensive view of the Tuscan countryside out over the silver green foliage provided by myriad olive trees.

One December, Ora and Carlo invited our whole family, as well as our mutual friends, Barbara and Piero Pozzi, to Pavia for the Christmas holidays. It was Carlo who had introduced us to Barbara in the first place; Piero, comparatively speaking, was a "newcomer" to our circle: Most of us had been guests at the Pozzi wedding in Rome many years before. Across the street from the Cipollas' apartment was a hotel where we could all stay, with a wonderful restaurant run by Carlo's friend Bolfo.

Throughout the area there had just been a huge snowstorm, creating a perfect winter landscape, as well as an ideal playground for California-born children, who didn't have many opportunities at home to toss snowballs, create icy forts, or build snowmen. We all felt as if we were living in a Christmas card. The silence and the snow made the Certosa, the exquisite Carthusian monastery to which Carlo took us one day, magically descend into time, although it was as cold as I ever remember it being. Years later, Bolfo moved his restaurant to a site across from the Certosa, affording diners a view over the monastery, especially appealing when it was lit up at night. It was startling to see peacocks parading around the restaurant grounds and sometimes perched high in the trees.

One evening during our Christmas visit, Carlo suggested that once the children were fed and bedded down, we go to dinner in a very simple place on the outskirts of town: They prepared only one pasta, one main course, one dessert, but all of it was excellent, and he was sure we would like it. He added that there was no need to get dressed up since the place was extremely casual. After a long drive, we pulled into the parking area in front of an undistinguished, nondescript building housing a tavern. On entering, we found only one table occupied: Four men, even less casually dressed than we were, cigarettes ablaze, wine glasses half empty, were in the midst of a raucous game of cards. It was then that I learned the word *poltrone*, idler, often applied to those who lounged around endlessly playing cards.

Both the friendly ambience and indoor temperature were warming, especially to those of us who never grew accustomed to the chill of Italian winter temperatures. The convivial woman who took our coats and seated us made us feel instantly welcome. She poured some of the good local wine, dark, rich, and purple, into large tumblers all around. With only one menu offering, there was no need to order. The encouraging smells coming from the kitchen suggested that Carlo knew of what he spoke. We sipped our wine and after a time the woman arrived bearing steamy dishes of spaghetti blanketed in a meaty wine sauce. She grated cheese over each one. It was delicious.

After a suitable interval, she brought the next course. It was a pot roast that had been braised until the wine and aromatics that it cooked in had thickened and reduced, resembling the sauce on the pasta that had preceded it. Carlo explained that it was, in fact, the very same. They braised the meat, along with the vegetables and herbs, in the local wine until it was so tender that it didn't need a knife. At that point, the slowly intensified sauce was almost sludgy, as delicious with the pasta as it was ladled over the meat. Zucchini sautéed in garlic and olive oil came along with the beef. There were slabs of country bread to mop up with as well as to go with the *taleggio*, the cheese that followed. The basket of fruit came Italian-style, with a bowl of water to wash it in. We didn't know whether our incandescent glow was the result of the good food, the abundant wine, or the warmth of the cozy room. Perhaps a little of each. As we parted with profuse compliments all around, we noticed that the card players were still at their game, faces a bit redder, voices more animated, more boisterous than ever.

The next night Carlo informed us that he had made reservations at an elegant place for dinner, to be followed by a performance at the local opera house. He had already arranged for tickets and had secured a box for us. Dressed in our best, the six of us crowded into the car and drove off. The drive was long and—we suddenly realized —strangely familiar. When we neared the scene of our previous dinner, the car slowed and Carlo pulled into the parking area in front of the same building that housed the *taverna*. We were all puzzled and certainly overdressed; our only explanation from Carlo was that we were not overdressed and in a minute all would be clear. Dutifully we followed him to the back of the building, ascended a staircase, and entered a charming private dining room one floor above the tavern.

It was furnished with a long single table set with starched white linens, glowing silver candelabra, stemmed wine glasses, elegant china and flatware, and a profusion of well-arranged flowers. The waitress, the same welcoming woman of the night before, was now done up in a black uniform with a white organdy apron tied properly around her waist. We had the exact same dinner, the exact same wine; but what the night before had been an excellent country repast now transformed itself into a three-star meal: an elegant pasta, a delicious *daube* of beef, first-rate *taleggio*, deep purple wine, choice fruits, with a meticulous waitress to serve it all.

The opera turned out to be another of Carlo's surprises: We saw Puccini's *La Fanciulla del West (The Girl of the Golden West)*, a subtle tribute to the westerners among us.

Ora and Carlo had been going for some time to Rovescala, a small village less than an hour's drive from Pavia. It was a typical Italian country town, perched at the promontory of a conical hill, with cascading vineyards unfurling downward on all sides. On occasion, we would accompany them on their excursions. They introduced us to all of the local characters, and the excellent food and rich purple wine provided by the local trattoria. They had such an endearing relationship to the town that once, on the occasion of the annual polenta festival (a ritual in which huge pots of polenta are cooked and stirred with a six-foot-long pole, then served and eaten by the assembled community), the townspeople, carried away with their enthusiasm for the couple, had honored the beautiful blonde Ora by presenting her with the inescapably phallic polenta stick. She told me later that, not knowing exactly what to do with it, she had left it in the car. One day, when she became mired in the mud, it proved to be just the thing to get the car out.

When a hillside property, one that could be planted to grapes, came up for sale in Rovescala, they bought it. The house they constructed was a simple country retreat, with vineyards planted immediately to the front of it, forming a lacy pattern all the way down a gently sloping hill. One sparkling fall day, the four of us decided to take a rather elaborate "picnic" there to eat on the patio of the house overlooking the vineyard. As we drove into town, people spotted the car and came waving onto the sidewalks with great animation. Charles and I were impressed that the local citizens expressed their friendship so exuberantly. As we drove down the street, the number of wavers grew, and we realized that they were trying to flag us down. Carlo rolled down the window and an excited crowd, all burbling at once, told him that thieves had broken into the vineyard house. They didn't know what was stolen or damaged but urged an immediate inspection.

We drove straight there and found that the robbers, who had obviously come when it was dark, hadn't managed to find the light switches and consequently had left a trail of burned matches in their attempt to see what was worth stealing. Since the light of a match gives little illumination, they finally gave up, taking only the wonderful old metal matchbox that had been a gift from Carlo's brother. It was the one thing of sentimental, irreplaceable value.

By this time some of the villagers had arrived by foot, vociferously urging Carlo to report the incident to the police. Since there were no police in Rovescala, Carlo had to drive down to the trattoria, where they had a phone, and place a call to Santa Maria della Versa, the nearest village that had a force. By the time Carlo returned, Ora and I had set out the lunch that she had prepared: pasta, slices of juicy rare roast beef, salad, cheese, bread, and a bottle of local purple wine. Much relieved that there had been little damage and little taken, we sat down to enjoy our meal in this bucolic setting.

We were midway through when there was a loud rapping at the door. Ora answered and found before her the chief of *carabinieri* from Santa Maria along with two uniformed subordinates. They had come to investigate, the chief said most solemnly. He was a character straight out of Gilbert and Sullivan: black trousers with a strip down the side, his jacket buttoned in brass, the shoulders made broader by protruding fringed epaulets. His hat was tall and plumed. He clicked his heels together, military-style, by way of a greeting, and as often as possible thereafter.

With a wave of the hand, he dispatched the subordinates to investigate, meanwhile accepting the glass of wine that Carlo had offered. He dutifully jotted down in a small notebook such few details as Carlo could give him. Meanwhile the two underlings were picking up the burned matchsticks one by one, using thumb and forefinger as if they were holding some fetid offal, then grasping each gingerly by the stem end, in order to give a thorough perusal. They were employing, even without a magnifying glass, the old Sherlock Holmes technique. When they had finished, they consulted, heads together, demeanor most serious, and reported their conclusions: The thieves had used matches to light their way. Since they had found no other clues and the chief had taken his report and finished his wine, their investigation was complete. With a click of the heels and a salutary flourish, they bid us _arrivederci_ and were off. The culprits, not surprisingly, were never found.

During the summer, we were all invited to a grand dinner at the trattoria. The evening was clear and balmy. Enzo, nicknamed Stan by the Cipollas because of his resemblance to Ora's brother-in-law of that name, was the owner of the trattoria. His wife did the cooking. Her name was Dina, but she was always called Dina la Cuoca, making her vocation a part of her name. Also in attendance was the mayor, inconsequential next to his wife, a woman with a voluptuous figure, obviously dyed blonde hair, and an overabundance of makeup that gave her a startlingly alarming resemblance to a street walker. Nobody called the village priest by his name, so I never learned it, but the padre was a hearty eater and even more of a wine lover, and his presence was incumbent at such a gathering. There was one local couple whom we hadn't met before. And then there was Piero Valli, _Il Professore_, dubbed that, and never called anything else, because he had once taught in a local art school. He was accompanied by his steady girlfriend.

Besides his regular residence, _Il Professore_ owned, and sometimes lived in, a medieval castle set high on the hill overlooking the town. Once, when they were doing some repairs there, workers had discovered the skeletons of two youths between the thick stone walls. Murder? Unwanted princely inheritors? Without either an oral or a written historical record, and there was none, no one would ever know, but the speculation was rife with gruesome intrigue.

As we assembled around the table, we noted that everybody had brought at least one bottle of the wine that they had made (this was a village of winemakers), and there was much uncorking and pouring around even before the first of many courses arrived. When we were seated we found large platters, abundantly filled with salami, prosciutto, *culatello*, mortadella, and assorted olives, centered on the table. Along with them came *bruschette*, thick slices of country bread, grilled and oozing olive oil, redolent of the garlic with which they had been rubbed. Those platters were replaced with plates of wild mushroom ravioli, followed by bowls of fettuccine dressed with a cheesy sauce studded with ham and fresh peas. On the table was a big hunk of parmesan with its own grater.

By the time the little birds came, stuffed with fennel, roasted mahogany brown, and placed alongside a wedge of grilled raddichio, Stan had descended to the cellar to fetch an even older, more wonderful wine than he had at first provided. Then the unknown couple insisted that the man dash home to get one of their wines that they thought was even better. It was first-rate. Stan, challenged, went to the cellar once more and brought up an even dustier, older example. We were all immensely pleased by the ever-escalating caliber of the wines we were drinking, pretty grand to start with, and with the savory food that Dina la Cuoca was producing in such abundance.

When we had polished off the last of the gorgonzola and nibbled our last Muscat grape, the Rabelaisian priest rose to thank our hosts, which he did profusely, ending his speech with an invitation to all of us to come with him to the church to taste his wine, "perhaps even better than what we had been drinking." Enthusiastically following his billowing robes, we all marched merrily down the street, Stan and Dina la Cuoca right behind him. Once arrived at the village church, he pushed open the creaking door and threw on the lights. The procession followed him through the nave straight to the altar. Next to it, concealed in the floor, was a trap door. When he pulled it open it revealed a set of narrow steps, which we descended one by one.

The room in which we found ourselves was a revelation. Ripening salamis and curing prosciuttos hung from the rafters. The Professor, giving unto temptation without the slightest hesitation, sacred or otherwise, pulled out his pocket knife, slashed a cord overhead, and secreted one of the pendant salamis under his jacket. The priest drew two bottles from among the many that lined the walls and uncorked them. The wine tasting took place directly beneath the altar at a round table already provided with several glasses. We sipped. The priest stood back expectantly. He was right: The wine was excellent, clearly the equal of any we had drunk during the evening.

Then the Professor spoke. Why didn't we all come up to the castle? He had several bottles that we should taste. Everyone thought that was a splendid idea, the priest closed up shop, and we were off to the hill. On the way to our cars, we lost Stan and Dina la Cuoca, who pleaded the lateness of the hour. At the castle, the Professor whipped off the dust covers that draped the furniture when he wasn't in residence, and the tired, closed-in smell was replaced, when we threw open the doors and windows, by the perfume of jasmine and roses. In the background was the lilting song of resident nightingales. It was suddenly a full-fledged, medieval castle.

The Professor uncorked his wine, sliced his stolen salami, put a record on the Victrola, and some of us danced to the slow, romantic music. The night was still balmy, and the garden outside enticed us. Soon we were all gathered around the wooden table, trying a few sips of the Professor's fine purple wine and breathing in the calm night air. Suddenly someone, I don't remember who, had the idea— it then seemed quite rational—of getting Stan to make us some Italian-style *panini*, because we must surely all be as starving as he was. Thinking of those sandwiches, we felt instant pangs of hunger. One of us was dispatched to drive down to find Stan. We waited only a short while before he turned up, still in pajamas and bathrobe, cheerfully bearing an assortment of *panini* garnished with toasted red peppers and olives. To go with them we finished the few drops that remained of the Professor's wine. We suddenly realized that it was two-thirty in the morning. A customary evening in Rovescala.

CHAPTER EIGHT

The Nuns of Populonia

Nestled among a string of beach resorts on the west coast of Italy, the small hamlet of Populonia was unique among the coastal towns because of its lack of facilities and its downtrodden ambience. We once visited the village on a driving trip along the Tyrrhenian Sea with our friends Ora and Carlo. Since Carlo knew the mother superior of the convent there, and that it took in guests, he offered to call to make reservations for an overnight stay.

When we arrived, even though we had been forewarned by Carlo, we were surprised to see a place that was so clearly neglected, especially since the numerous adjacent towns seemed to be thriving, filled with tourists, hotels, and bustling restaurants. Carlo explained the situation. Years ago, while engaged in routine excavations, workers had uncovered an area of Etruscan ruins. Immediately the digging stopped, the *Sovrintendenza delle Belle Arti*, always referred to simply as the *Belle Arti*, took over, and no one was able to come to a conclusion as to who had jurisdiction over what part of the ruins, who should dig, who should pay for any work done, what disposition should be made of the site or the artifacts—in short, who could or should make any decision whatsoever. Meanwhile the town, in spite of its ideal location but now governed by the rules of the *Belle Arti* (similar to our restrictions for landmark preservation), was unable to build or change anything at all and thus lost out to its now prosperous neighbors.

The lack of traffic, of course, made parking easy. We carried our bags up the steps to the covered front porch of the convent. Next to the door, in place of a doorbell and in keeping with the ecclesiastical tone, we found a large brass bell hanging to one side with a rope to activate the clapper. Carlo signaled our presence, and shortly we heard the patter of feet scuttering closer. Suddenly, the door swung wide to reveal a tiny woman dressed head to hem in a long brown habit. Her wrinkled face, besides its huge smile, sported very long hairs sprouting from her chin and making a semimoustache above her lips. She was overjoyed to see us—not many people, she confided, came to Populonia those days. In fact, before the Etruscan discovery, the convent had served dinner to its guests, but alas, for the nuns, that was now but a fond memory. The Church could no longer provide them with more than trifling sums for support. Attrition had reduced the resident population of sisters to four elderly survivors, the other three of whom had by now scurried forth to greet us.

After effusive welcomes from all, they took us to our rooms, absolutely insistent that they carry our bags. Up the darkened stairs we marched, the nuns chattering vigorously all the long way. We were to have two separate bedrooms and a shared bathroom. The Cipollas' room was one that the bishop used on his rare visits. It was grand, with a baldachin flowing from an ornamental knob, no doubt a church symbol, over the bed. I recall that it, as well as the bedspread and window draperies, were of somewhat faded maroon velvet. Our room, in contrast, was bare bones; obviously from the number of narrow cots, formerly some kind of dormitory. The mattresses were straw, a first for us, and the simple well-worn bedspreads were patched, where they needed mending, with Scotch tape. There was one dim lamp, not giving nearly enough light for the two of us to read by.

The large bathroom contained an aged tub; a sink with a rim so small that no article of toilette could possibly fit on it, but a stool on which several of them thankfully did; and a small toilet with a brown wooden seat and a tank suspended above, far up on the wall. To flush, one pulled on a long metal chain with a wooden handle that connected to the tank overhead.

The nuns fluttered around, jabbering among themselves, making sure that everything was perfect so that our stay with them would be as comfortable as possible. Was there anything, anything at all that we might need, they inquired repeatedly. Finally, keeping in mind the early curfew after dinner, and the prospect of wanting to read before retiring, we got up the courage to ask if there was perhaps another lamp that we might use. They were absolutely delighted and assured us that a lamp would be installed by the time we returned. Clearly, they were pleased to offer assistance so we asked for advice about restaurants in the neighborhood. Where a minute before there had been smiles, now there were four chagrined faces. They were obviously crestfallen. Since they never dined out, and were therefore innocent of the simplest information, they could not guide us, even with a name. After profuse apologies, including assurances that we would no doubt find a fine place in one of the nearby towns, they excused themselves so that we could wash up for dinner.

As we took our turns in the bathroom, it was immediately obvious to us all that the toilet was not functioning properly. It wouldn't flush. So on our way out, we had to confess our problem. Immediately happiness was restored. Not to worry, they assured us, it would be in working order by the time we returned. They wished us good appetite and we were on our way.

We drove the serpentine road down the hill to Piombino, the town below, where you take the ferry to Elba. There we found the Ristorante Canessa and had a fine dinner overlooking the sea. On our return, Carlo sounded the bell, three cheerful, grinning sisters answered and asked, almost simultaneously, whether we had found a restaurant, whether we had had a good dinner, how we liked the coastal villages, and on and on. When we ascended to our rooms, the lights were on. There, on the top of a tall ladder leaning against the tank above the toilet, her sleeves rolled up revealing long white underwear, was the tiny fourth nun. She was fixing the flushing mechanism. It turned out that she was an excellent plumber, and we had no further difficulties during our stay. In each of our rooms, the sisters had laid out glasses and bottled water. In our room, next to the bed, attached to serpentine twists of wires and extension cords, there stood a huge lamp, its bulb burning dimly away.

The next morning, after a simple breakfast, we headed toward the Etruscan ruins. The site was surrounded by a fence but accessible, as we recall, after you paid an admission fee. It turned out there was little to see. Not until 1980, during the tenure of Antonella Romualdi as superintendent of archeology for Populonia, did actual excavation begin. For nineteen years, ending in the fall of 1999, a consortium of archeologists from the universities of Florence, Siena, and Pisa explored the site under her supervision. They dated the Etruscan city from the fifth to the third century B.C. When they discovered the area of its ancient acropolis, it was beneath a Roman house, which led to other Roman finds. By the time they ceased their excavations because funds had been cut off, they were convinced that there might be an extensive Etruscan city yet to be uncovered, very important archeological finds still to be made, much work ahead before the final completion of the project.

When the funding stopped, the government gave the archeologists only 100 million *lire* (about $5,000) to use during the next year for the restoration of monuments already excavated. Antonella Romualdi tried to get some explanation, some elucidation, as to the prospects for future funding, without which new excavations were doomed. Perhaps private funds will come from outside officialdom, but it is not likely.

Recently, we went back to Populonia to see what the archeologists had uncovered. We parked outside the convent where we had stayed, just inside the stone gateway to the town, and discovered that in the huge municipal parking lot outside the walls and below the crenelated turrets of the castle, there were numerous large buses ferrying groups of schoolchildren to the Archeological Park of Baratti and Populonia. They could walk to the Etruscan acropolis of Populonia and drive some distance to the extensive necropoli of Baratti. Next to the excavations there are huge parking lots and the area itself is well developed. They obviously draw many tourists besides the school kids on fieldtrips.

The whole vast area, as well as many other regions in Italy, had been peopled by Etruscans for some thousand years, their cities built over first by the Romans, then by the medieval inhabitants, and last giving way to the layer of modern civilization that now exists. That means that the Etruscan remnants are the least well preserved and the most difficult to dig out. The best archeological finds have been from the necropoli. Most recently, Giovannangelo Camporeale, a professor of Etruscan civilization from the University of Florence, has been in charge of a dig in Massa Marittima, where they have unearthed evidence of an extensive Etruscan city at least three thousand years old. It is an extraordinary find, consisting of clusters, whole neighborhoods, of as many as a dozen dwellings each, many of them having several rooms, plus artifacts that describe daily life in that ancient place.

There is now in Populonia, under the auspices of the state, a very handsome small Etruscan museum that houses a private collection consisting of amphorae, plowshares, pedestals, monoliths (partly preserved), sarcofagi, plaques from the tombs, partial sculptures, marble burial epigraphs, and many bowls, vases and cooking utensils. On the back of the entrance ticket it lists a Web site for the city, "castellodipopulonia.it," which supplies information as well as a listing of apartment rentals.

The town itself has been spruced up. On the one principal street, there are no weeds poking through the cobbles. Bright flower boxes and hanging planters lend color. A notice announces that the Friends of Populonia (actually an association from Piombino) conduct free guided visits to the acropoli every week or so in March, April, and May. Now, besides the residents' houses, the street is lined with ground-floor boutiques: a clothing shop, a jewelry store, a leather shop, a glass store with handsome modern offerings, an antique shop, a fabric store, an outlet for local ceramics, and a souvenir shop. It looks like a small-scale art village. All the shops, according to the decals in their windows, take credit cards.

There is a two-fork restaurant, Il Lucumone, now listed in the Michelin guide and, next to the convent, the Taverna di Populonia. Outside the town gate a sign advertises the Cantina Buia, which specializes in homemade bread cooked over wood and typical organic products from the Val di Cornia. Just off the street, in a very small square, is a ticket office and entrance to the tower of the castle. Across from it is the tiny church of Santa Croce.

The convent is closed, its locked gate and a sign proclaiming it "private property, entrance forbidden," standing as mute evidence. We made inquiries of the man running the tavern next door. Some ten years ago it moved, he told us, to Piombino where the order of nuns now runs a school. But since they moved, the convent has remained vacant. Perhaps, now that there are tourists, they should reopen it and take in guests once again.

CHAPTER NINE

The Vinegar of Spilamberto

O nce on a visit to Bologna, Carlo took us to the office of Il Mulino, his publishers, whom we had not previously met. Before the visit was over, these generous and hospitable people insisted on taking us all to dinner. The restaurant they chose was Silverio, new to Charles and me, a fine place on the Via Nosadella. The evening turned out to be memorable.

We ate figs stuffed with a mixture of soft cheese and prosciutto, and *bresaola*, thinly sliced dried beef, atop cucumbers dressed with oil and lemon juice. Next came large envelopes of pasta filled with a mixture of ricotta, egg, parmesan, and enough béchamel to bind them, the whole topped with spears of asparagus and a dusting of cheese grated at the table. The main course was a medallion of veal, lightly dusted in flour and sautéed nutty brown in butter with onion greens, then scattered over with mixed wood berries and spoonfuls of sauce made by deglazing the pan with white wine, then simmering until the juices were thick and syrupy. Along with this we were drinking a straw yellow Collio sauvignon and then, with the veal, a grand, intensely ruby Vignarey Barbera from Angelo Gaja.

The cheese course featured regional products: a finely grained *parmigiano reggiano*, an almost spreadable *robiola*, and from the Colli Bolognesi, the hills of the province of Bologna, a *pecorino dolce* made from ewe's milk. They were, of course, in peak condition, and perfect following the veal. Then, because he knew the publishers and Carlo so well, Silverio Cineri, the proprietor, placed on the table a very special treat, several small bottles of differing shapes, with enough demitasse-sized spoons for each of us. They were for tasting and comparing the very old balsamic vinegar, the *aceto balsamico tradizionale*, that the bottles contained. It was a revelation. This was vinegar so smooth and syrupy that one could taste it without puckering, almost as if it were a full-flavored *digestivo*. There were also very subtle differences among the bottles, between their viscosity and their sweetness. Fortunately, because they are extremely expensive, only a few drops of these intensely flavored traditional balsamics add an indescribable richness to meats, a savory touch to cheeses, and become a nectar on ice cream and on strawberries.

Which is what we had next. Wild strawberries, their perfume intense, tossed with sugar and balsamic vinegar. If you want to try them, these are the proportions: Add up to two tablespoons of good balsamic vinegar to one basket of wild berries (my market at home in Berkeley, California, carries them, but if yours doesn't, substitute regular, fully ripe strawberries, and slice them into sections). Mix gently and let stand about ten minutes. Add sugar to taste—a tablespoon or two or more—and stir in until a thick syrup coats the berries. When you add coarsely ground black pepper, lots of it, as some restaurants do, it intensifies the perfume of the berries and does not convey pepper at all. Highly recommended.

After our evening was over, we couldn't stop talking about the dinner, the kindness of Il Mulino, the publishers, and above all, the flavors of the really old balsamic vinegars that we had tasted. And that is when Carlo suggested that our very next excursion must be to Spilamberto, where for as long as anyone can remember, almost the entire town has engaged in making balsamic vinegar in the traditional way. He told us that, thanks to the local extremes of climate— hot summers and cold winters, a primary factor in the production of traditional balsamic vinegar—it has been made in this region for centuries. During the *Festa di San Giovanni*, on the nearest Sunday that falls between the 24th and the 27th of June, there is an annual competition, or *palio*, to choose the twelve best vinegars. The rivalry is fierce.

We had many questions about the history of balsamic vinegar, but documented facts, it turns out, are few, although legends and suppositions abound. In preparation for our visit, we looked up as much information as we could find. There were abundant references to the long history of ordinary vinegar, widely and variously used in many parts of the world as a medicant, disinfectant, preservative, food stuff, and even in the practice of alchemy. In the 1630s it was sometimes prescribed to counter the effects of the plague. In the eighteenth century the great Modenese scholar and priest, Ludovico Antonio Muratori, in a treatise entitled *Del governo della peste e delle maniere di guardasene (On the governing of the pestilence and some manners of guarding against it)* attributed the same powers to balsamic vinegar, supplying several remedies based on it

There is a mention, in the official *Gazette* of the Italian government, of documents and manuscripts from the sixteenth century and also from the year 1796, that refer to the well-matured grape must that is used in the production of vinegar made in the style of Modena. In the same section of the *Gazette* is a notation of thirty-six barrels,

presumably used for vinegar, supported on a rack kept in the third
tower of the ducal palace. Most historians agree that the first
recorded use of the term "balsamic vinegar" was in 1747, in a secret
inventory of wine from the private cellars of the Duke of Este, who
ruled over Modena at that time.

There are some early accounts about "special" vinegars from the
Modena area being used as gifts to VIPs, most often royal ones.
However, according to the various reports, none of them seems to
have been made in the complex formula that yields balsamic. But
they may have been precursors. At least, in one written account
from the sixteenth century that describes the process of making
such a vinegar, there were rudimentary similarities: Grape juice, first
warmed by the immersion of a hot brick, then aged in wooden barrels, resulted in a "special" vinegar.

By way of actual documentation, there are two letters, written in
1862 (although some documents say 1860) and in 1863, by a Modenese attorney, Francesco Aggazzotti del Colombaro, setting forth
the precise formula for making *aceto balsamico.* The first of the two
recipients was Pio Fabriani, a resident of Spilamberto, which attests
to the fact that people in that area were passing around the recipe at
least by the early 1860s. Aggazzotti's directions included two pages
of precise handwritten instructions down to such details as covering
the barrel opening with a piece of cloth to repel flies and wasps, a
custom still in use today. Among the instructions, there were directions for simmering the pressed grape juice before fermenting it
until it had been slowly reduced to half, thereby intensifying the
sweetness in the syrupy liquid. Called *saba,* the cooked must of
grapes had long been an important ingredient in the culinary preparations of the region. In fact, there are references to the Counts of
Salimbeni of Nonantola, a town seven miles to the north of Modena,
having used it in the early 1700s (but whether for vinegar making or

cooking, is not clear). The history of the area shows that there was, indeed, good vinegar there long before that. The site of a Bene-dictine monastery in the eighth century, Nonantola was ruled by the beginning of the eleventh by Bonifacio of Tuscany, then succeeded by his daughter Mathilde. One of the resident monks named Doni-zone, writing a chronicle of Mathilde's life, mentioned an excellent vinegar made by Bonifacio in the Castle of Canossa in 1046, a bar-rel of which was given to Enrico II, the king of Franconia. Clearly that area had an early penchant for acetification.

Part of the lore suggests that it might have been a batch of *saba* intended for cooking, somehow put aside and forgotten, that had fermented and become the original base of balsamic vinegar. The tale persists, but so also do its debunkers. Only recently I read in *Slow Food*, a book by Giorgio Triani, a convincing argument that cooked grape juice, which must often have fermented inadvertently in various areas of Italy, never elsewhere resulted in the complex Modena formula of making balsamic vinegar. Why, for example, would a batch of fermented grape juice lead to such steps as simmer-ing the must for a couple of days outdoors and aging it for years in a progression of barrels? It seems that fermented *saba* could not have been the culprit behind its beginnings. Another questionable theory on the origins of balsamic is the climate in the zone of Modena, hot summers and cold winters that prove ideal for the production of bal-samic vinegar. But since this phenomenon occurs in a much wider geographical area, weather, likewise, could not have been the causal factor behind the regional invention.

I have seen a reproduction of a medieval picture of vinegar-making in a book by Renato Bergonzini, an authority on balsamic vinegar, that clearly depicts the first step in the special process pecu-liar to Modena. In full color, it illustrates an herbarium of the middle ages. Two figures, clad in garments appropriate to the times, attend to the cooking of a caldron of must, or so the caption identifies it, which is suspended over an open fire. The turreted fireplace is distinctly of stone or brick and clearly in the out of doors. One man is fiddling with the fire with a long splayed tool, perhaps putting another log on it. The other, just behind him, is emptying liquid from a small barrel. Although he is using a large pitcher to collect it, another vessel sits on the ground to receive it, a ceramic container strangely resembling, both in its shape and its size, the earthenware storage jugs currently in use in the vinegaries, or *acetaie*, of Modena. Perhaps the scene shows the making of *saba*, and the vessels now used for vinegar were first used in the middle ages to store the cooking condiment. No one will ever know.

One thing is certain: The true balsamic vinegar, *aceto balsamico tradizionale*, whatever its origins, has always been confined to the geographic area of Modena and was until recently more or less an artisanal product, made in relatively small batches, used for family consumption, and—for the most precious and aged vinegars—given as gifts to important people. The lack of any mention of it by prestigious Italian chefs or in prominent Italian cookbooks until the 1970s bolsters this idea. In the early 1960s, I had strawberries doused with balsamic and sugar in Al Moro, a restaurant in Rome. The recipe that they gave me specified only "vinegar," not balsamic. Since the eighties, when the traditionally made vinegar became recognized as a very special thing, so-called balsamic vinegar has been increasingly used by cooks the world over, but most of it is not the painstakingly-made product. In the mid-sixties, the minister of agriculture set official guidelines for a lesser product known as Balsamic Vinegar of Modena, lacking the word "*tradizionale*." This resulted in an enormous increase of production and the creation of a huge market for export. These days, even a few entrepreneurs in California are making the vinegar, mostly using the traditional method, but they can't label it "from Modena."

With a somewhat better, if still limited, idea of the history of balsamic vinegar, one Sunday in June, a week or so before the actual competition, Carlo, his wife Ora, and Charles and I set off by car for Spilamberto. We figured we would be able to learn more, to ask more questions about the history, before everyone was caught up in the throes of the contest. The town, not far from Modena and about twice that distance from Bologna, has a population of about 11,000 and, among other things, is the source of the original recipe for a liqueur made from the green skins of walnuts, nowadays also produced elsewhere, but in those parts still called by its original name, *nocino Modenese*. Traditionally, the women pick the still-green walnuts right before the *palio*, where, in between the vinegars, bottles made in previous years are for sale.

The four of us entered Spilamberto through a medieval archway below a fourteenth-century brick clock tower crowned with majestic crenellations. They knew how to build turrets in the middle ages. It was early afternoon, just after most people had finished their major meal of the day and the piazza was filled with leisurely strollers engaged in the customary *passeggiata*.

We followed Carlo up the steps to the vinegar depository. The door was locked, and no one responded to our knocks. Obviously it was closed on Sunday afternoons. But to Carlo that was only a temporary obstacle. We quickly descended behind him and went into the piazza full of walkers where he spotted his friend the mayor. After Carlo's brief introductions and explanations, the mayor went into action. It seems that the tailor had the key. If we hopped in our car and followed him on his bicycle, he would lead us to the tailor's house, where all would be set right instantly. So off we went to the outskirts of the village, and following the mayor's lead, parked in front of a modest one-story house.

The tailor and his family, just finishing their Sunday repast, graciously welcomed us all. After a few explanatory words from the mayor, the tailor sought out his keys, got out his bicycle, and became our official guide. Back to the center of town we went, two bicycles and one car in procession, back up the stairs, key turned in lock, and suddenly before us, set out on tables, were a thousand small glass containers, mini flasks with bulbous bottoms, half full of dark brown, velvet balsamic vinegar, all of them contestants in the annual competition.

The tailor explained the process. Normal vinegar is sour wine (the French word for vinegar, *vin aigre*, means just that). Anyone who has kept an unfinished open bottle of wine knows that, after a short period of time, some of the bacteria, the *acetobacters*, once exposed to oxygen, convert ethanol alcohol into acetic acid, i.e. vinegar, from which the Italians derive their name for it, *aceto*. Balsamic vinegar, *aceto balsamico*, is another thing entirely.

It starts with the must of gently pressed grapes and skins, most usually made from overripe white Trebbiano grapes, although several other varietals grown in the region are allowed. First boiled slowly until it becomes concentrated into *saba*, the same syrupy liquid that has been used in cooking for a long time, it lends the finished vinegar its sweetness. Then an infusion of regular vinegar starts a fermentation process in the boiled-down must, after which it is mellowed and aged a minimum of twelve years (but sometimes more than a hundred; legend has it that in the case of the ducal family of Este, who had ruled over the Modena area since the 1500s, for as much as 360 years). The process takes place in a *batteria*, usually five to seven barrels—sometimes as many as ten—of different woods and sizes. Some barrels have been in the same family for generations.

Fermentation takes place in the largest cask, many times started first in a wooden container, aging goes on in the small ones, and mellowing in the sizes in between. No barrel is ever completely filled. Each winter, a small quantity of finished vinegar, possibly no more than half the barrel or enough for one family's yearly supply, about a gallon and a half, is drawn from the smallest keg, which is then replenished by an amount from the next keg, and so on down the line, somewhat like the *solera* process in making sherry. The last cask gets its deficit replenished with the new must. The different woods—mulberry, chestnut, English oak, juniper, cherry, and in more recent times, ash, acacia or locust—each impart a different characteristic to the flavor. Evaporation concentrates the vinegar, adding to its viscosity and density. Traditionally, the opening, many times rectangular, is covered by a square of cloth often held down by a metal grid or wooden block. This keeps the bugs out while allowing the contents to breathe and intensify. The barrels are traditionally kept in the attic where, during the summer, the temperatures are high and the atmosphere dry, both of which are needed for the fermentation to proceed. The colder temperatures of winter slow the process and allow the vinegars to clarify.

The *Consorzio Produttori di Aceto Balsamico Tradizionale*, founded by the late Rolando Simonini in 1967, is the official body that authenticates traditional balsamic vinegar (according to the government's edict), enforces the strict rules for making it, runs the training program for the tasters, and conducts the annual *palio*. The grapes used must only be of specified varietals. The reduction, cooked over a fire outdoors and slowly simmering for almost two days, must reduce the original pressing to half. The aging must take place in different wooden barrels of decreasing capacity. The minimum aging must be for at least twelve years. Those that are aged for twenty-five years or more can be labeled *extra vecchio*. Preservatives or sugars are a no-no. And the vinegar must be made within a geographically defined area of Emilia-Romagna, specifically in Modena or Reggio, the limited regions that were once the Este Duchy of Modena.

The labeling of balsamic vinegars is confusing. The real thing has a D.O.C. *(Denominazione di Origine Controllata)* certification, must come from the designated area of Modena, and must be made in the traditional style. The labels usually say *Aceto Balsamico Tradizionale*, and the vinegars cost a good deal—the really old ones well over $100 a bottle. Vinegars that say *Aceto Balsamico di Modena* are made in the traditional way from boiled-down must, but may have caramel added to enhance the flavor, as well as a small amount of aged vinegar, which allows the label to proclaim six or eight or ten years of age, although the bulk of it may have aged for less than a year. These can be comparatively inexpensive to moderately expensive and are made in large part for commercial sale. Vinegars labeled simply "Balsamic Vinegar" can be made from any grape, have added sugar, have no barrel age, be made by a process that is not traditional, and indeed come from any region at all. They are usually bargains but do not resemble the real thing.

When the tailor had done with his explanations, interrupted by our frequent questions, it was time to sample the vinegars. He picked out several for us to taste that would best show the differences in flavor, viscosity, and the balance of sweetness to acidity. Although they varied, each was an excellent example of a true balsamic. We wanted to know what would happen to all these samples after the judging took place. He explained that the best were mixed together and then poured into small bottles—I would guess they held no more than two or three ounces—corked, sealed with red wax, and labeled with various identifications: *Aceto Balsamico Tradizionale di Modena, Consorteria di Spilamberto Produttori, Festa S. Giovanni Spilamberto.* Then they were packaged in small cardboard boxes and offered for sale. How wonderful! But where could we buy them? From him, of course. It turned out that the repository of bottles was in the back of his tailor shop which was in his home, and since he was a member of the producers, the *Consorteria di Spilamberto*, he could sell them to us directly.

Back to the shop we went, first he on his bicycle and we following in the Fiat. Between the Cipollas and ourselves, we bought several bottles. Pleased with our purchases and the delightful afternoon, we realized that it was late, in fact evening was setting in, and we were getting hungry. It was time to make our reluctant departure. As we drove out of town, we shortly passed Vignola, a village known for the quality of its cherries and plums. The first cherries of the season, bursting with purple juices, were already for sale at stands bordering the road. We couldn't resist, especially Carlo, who was a cherry lover supreme. Although he shared with us liberally, we realized that, in a flick, Carlo had inadvertently consumed the greater part of the kilo we had bought—two pounds plus.

Somewhat later, in the piazza of one of the villages down the road, we stopped for what we expected to be a modest dinner— those cherries hadn't made a dent—in a humble trattoria. The cooking was indeed home-style but had sophisticated nuances that took it one step beyond. It was utterly delicious: a little ham from Modena with some olives and country bread to accompany it; agnolotti stuffed with *pancetta*, ricotta, and parmesan, splashed with a thick garlickly tomato reduction, and served up in a deep bowl to capture the sauce; and then some local duck that had been roasted simply with aromatics and herbs until it was succulent, brown, and tender. Of course, there were cherries from Vignola afterwards and ethereal little cookies that had come from Spilamberto, different from the usual *amaretti* found elsewhere in Italy. These had a predominant mixture of almond-honey combined with the usual anise flavor, and used beaten egg whites to give lightness and lift.

Several years later, we returned to Spilamberto, without Ora and Carlo this time. As we approached the clock tower, we noticed what we had not been aware of before: colorful planting, a mixture of roses, begonias, gazania and juniper bushes, and a statue dedicated to the Spilamberto members of the military who had served against the Nazi oppression between 1943 and 1945. Once inside the archway, we were at the beginning of the long street that leads to the Rangoni castle. The noble family has been connected to the town at least from the mid-fourteenth century. One of the women, Bianca Rangoni, is particularly remembered because of a silk mill that she had built early in the 1600s and which remained a source of employment for the townspeople until after the Second World War.

Now the town has all the usual shops, including Armani and Missoni boutiques, a bakery, a pastry shop, a store that sells fruit and vegetables, one that sells perfume, a place that sells beer, two or three cafés. It was to one of these that we went for lunch while we waited for the reopening of the Villa Comunale Fabriani, the municipal building that is now also the headquarters of the *Consorteria dell'Aceto Balsamico di Spilamberto*. We sat on the terrace at a table, one of four or five, covered with a red crocheted tablecloth anchored by a red elastic band, which kept it from blowing off. The terrace, surrounded by vines in planter boxes, was mercifully shaded by a red awning, and we enjoyed our simple lunch.

When we went back to the Villa, we were welcomed by Signor Vecchi of the *Consorteria*, who gave us a detailed and lengthy tour of the premises. In this new location there was room for tasting tables, and in the attic there was an actual *acetaia*, for making vinegar. Two groups had their barrels there: one representing the township, the other the cooperative belonging to the *Consorteria*. The latter group also conducts training courses in tasting balsamic vinegars, using sixteen different samples in a series of twelve lessons. To run things there are various ranks of directors and community representatives, and even *gli alfieri*, or appointed officers, assigned each year to collect the samples of balsamic vinegar for judging at the *palio*. The wide membership of the consortium is divided, according to their experience, into apprentice tasters who are just learning, *allievi assaggiatori*; accomplished tasters, *assaggiatori*; and the true master tasters, *maestri assaggiatori*, who are only certified after passing the nine-year course.

The tasting, except during the yearly contest, is done in small groups seated at tables centered by a candle in a tall brass holder, a help in judging the density, color and clarity. During the *palio*, there are seven tasters per table. The small bulbous flasks that we saw on our first visit are still the choice of vessel for the specimens of vinegar, and small spoons are still the way to taste them. On each table there is also a wicker basket of *crostini* to aid in clearing the palate. Over the years, the *Consorteria* has developed and refined an official tasting form. Besides the identity and signature of the taster, the table number, and the date, it includes the specific categories to be judged, as well as the maximum number of points that each can score. These are divided into visual values; olfactory qualities, such as finesse, acidity, and intensity; and taste factors, such as flavor, harmony, and fullness. These broad categories are further divided into such components as syrupy, mature, well-balanced, robust, and exquisite (for flavor) on the positive side, and four lesser rankings, each with successively fewer points, going all the way down to such disagreeable faults as inconsistent, turbid, lacking, unpleasant, weak, pungent, or absent altogether. There is also room for a line or two of written observations. This is serious business.

The attic where the vinegar is made is a large painted room

whose pitched roof is lined with massive wooden beams. Ranks of barrels on wooden platforms extend from the sides and line some of the walls. The floor is handsomely cobbled, there are several chairs and a tasting table or two, and on the wall, besides shelves containing various implements and ceramic vinegar crocks, there is a cabinet containing bottles of vinegars combined after the tasting.

The glass containers for sale had changed somewhat since our last visit, now holding more like four ounces in a bottle of a slightly more modern shape, pasted with amplified labels showing that this is documented, extra-old, traditional balsamic vinegar of Modena. In fact, the official government decree now specifies exactly what the container should look like, insuring the preservation of the quality —and incidentally the prestige—of the product inside. The uniform bottle must be used for the traditional vinegars put up by the official consorterie of the area, the major one in Spilamberto, and two lesser, and later, groups from Modena and Reggio Emilia. It must be spherical in shape, of white clear glass, with a rectangular solid glass base. The labels show which town the vinegar came from and differ slightly in other details, such as logos and colors. The red wax is no longer a part of the packaging, but now you don't need to go all the way to the tailor's shop to buy a stash. You can get it directly from the *Consorteria di Spilamberto*, attested to in three different places on two separate labels, which is what we did. It is so good that our only problem is to make it last until the next visit.

CHAPTER TEN

Sicilian Idyll

From the moment we attempted to drive onto the car ferry in Reggio, we knew that Sicily was going to be different from any place we had been before. Just in the area of the dock, there were vast crowds of people, not unusual in Italy, who seemed friendly, completely unsophisticated, welcoming us more warmly than any Italians we had yet encountered. Many of them were carting squawking chickens and squealing baby animals, the women almost uniformly in dark clothes with babushkas tied behind their ears but otherwise covering their heads—everyone shoving and jostling to get aboard. Once the boat was on its way and we out of the car, the sense of overcrowding did not diminish; we rode out the voyage cheek by jowl with poultry, vocal livestock, and lively, chattering people, many of whom were missing teeth, which didn't seem to deter their gregarious ways in the least.

Our intent was to circle the island, hitting the major and not so major towns, and to drive inland to Gangi, a remote village high on the massif, where we had introductions to an attorney, the uncle of a friend in Berkeley. As far as our friend knew from his relatives and other townspeople, he had been the first American to visit that remote town and we would be the second. When we saw how difficult it was to get there, that seemed entirely possible. These days, almost fifty years later, there are three or four hotels. They may well have been there when we first visited; we probably just didn't notice. But there is good reason why local tourists might come: The town observes many religious celebrations and festivities based on old traditions derived from a mixture of folklore, religious beliefs, mythology, and pagan practices. The participants, always clad in colorful period costumes, sometimes embroidered in gold and silver, or wearing the uniforms and carrying the flags and emblems of the various fraternal organizations, march in procession from church to church, many times accompanied by timpani or bands, often with statues in celebration of the various saint's days. The goddess Ceres, prominent throughout Sicily, is particularly acknowledged in Gangi in August in a fete dedicated to fertility, abundance, and the harvest, all of which are associated with the deity. On Palm Sunday, at the start of elaborate festivities celebrating Holy Week, the palms are carried in procession to be blessed in every church in town, starting and ending with the Mother Church. It seems that no matter the theme, everyone loves the parade.

One of the traditions that is most familiar to us, and which the Sicilians inherited from the time of the Spanish occupation, is the breaking of the *pignati*, better known to us as piñatas. In the Gangi version, the clay pots are filled with sausages and sweets, then hoisted on stout cords that are manipulated to keep the vessels from being broken. An army of assembled stick wielders tries, and eventually manages, to bash the pots and obtain the hidden treasures. But one pot, filled with either soot or water, rains a black ash or a watery shower on the unlucky person who breaks it.

Once we had visited Gangi, we planned to continue on toward Palermo. Our friend had given us a second introduction, this one to another uncle, the brother of the attorney, who lived in that bustling city. This brother happened to be the chief veterinarian of the island. It occurred to us little by little, although we certainly can't verify it, that to get to be chief veterinarian of Sicily, one must surely be a member of the Mafia. Because of that possibility, the two shall remain nameless and, although he died several years ago, their nephew, too.

Our ferry landed in Messina, which we found to be a lively town. We had once read in a guidebook that the area had been subjected over its history to numerous earthquakes, one of them so severe that it destroyed almost the entire city. You'd never know. The recovery was complete. Once we got the car clear of the crowds of people and animals at the dock, we headed toward the coastal highway and drove briefly north until the road turned west. Following along, with the sea to our north, we were struck by the clarity and true blue color of the water, by the simplicity of the many fishing villages and beaches snuggled along the route, and by the thriving stands of prickly pear and espaliered citrus.

We were planning to spend the night in Cefalù, a small beach town, which would give us an early morning start to Gangi, necessary because the drive to that remote village involved following an ascending road that was extremely coiled and winding. It was dusk when we finally arrived in Cefalù, our children by now restless from their too long confinement in the car; obviously they would enjoy a frolic on the beach. We drove directly onto the sand, parked there, and released our shoeless hostages. The sand was still warm enough to feel good between the toes, and the kids cavorted and rollicked until we reluctantly corralled them, feeling it was time to check out a place to stay and get some dinner. We wandered back to the car, past a few boats painted a bright primary blue, and a miscellaneous band of ragamuffins, who acknowledged our presence by a friendly wave. They were also without shoes and were playing a game of sand soccer using a somewhat battered orange for a ball.

After a rudimentary attempt to clean off the sand and to put on the children's shoes, we piled into the car and tried to drive off the beach. The tires spun, digging further into the sand. Instead of going forward we were going deeper. The young brigade of soccer players, having seen our futile attempts to free ourselves, abandoned their game and came to our rescue. Out we got. They positioned themselves along the car and managed, half nudging, half lifting, to get the thing to the roadway once more. They were all smiles at their success, and we were eternally grateful for their friendly intervention. We gave them all of our coins, much to their evident delight, and they waved and yahooed to us as we drove off.

In the morning, we found that after a time the tortuous road was indeed as serpentine as the map had suggested. As we motored along, we came to a railroad crossing with the gates down; there was no gatekeeper in sight. We seemed to be the only travelers on this road, a line of one waiting for the train to pass. We waited. No train came. We surmised that this was one of those situations, not infrequent in rural Italy, where the keeper had put the gates down on the chance that the train might arrive before he or she got back from marketing or some similar chore. The gatekeeper's responsibility, to insure that no driver would be in peril, was therefore fulfilled.

We waited. Still no train came, and no gatekeeper appeared. An hour passed. Suddenly a motorcyclist barreled up, gunned his motor, looked both ways, then lifted the gates high enough for him to pass under safely. He roared away into the distance. If he could lift the gates, why couldn't we? Who knew when the gatekeeper would return? Who knew how many hours before the train was scheduled to pass? Charles got out, looked down the track in both directions, then lifted the gates just enough for our car to clear them. I drove through. We switched places and Charles, once again in the driver's seat, put us on our way to Gangi.

A few miles further along we came upon the *polizia*, who had pulled a motorcyclist to the side of the roadway. He was, of course, the man who had lifted the gates before us, now in deep trouble, judging by the facial expressions, voluminous gestures, and serious paper work being filled out. We were sure that this poor man would spend at least several years in jail for his misdeed. We were as guilty as he was, but no one had paid us an iota of attention. We construed this to be the courtesy that the police might show to people from other places, a fact evidenced by our Roman license plates. Only later did we learn that raising the crossing gates automatically stopped the train, a rather grave offense, so we considered ourselves blessedly lucky.

Feeling a bit guilty, we nonetheless drove on. Finally, many hair-pin turns later, we caught sight of the distant village of Gangi, which crowned Mount Marone like a miniature tiara, the distant shining houses stepping up the slope. As we went higher, the temperature went lower. On the road that snaked up the side, we began to pass villagers in increasing numbers. They had obviously been gathering wood. The men, all of them astride donkeys, were huddled against the cold in their heavy capes of deepest blue, the brilliant kelly green linings flashing when one end was tossed over a shoulder. The women, dressed all in black, with head coverings and shawls to match, bore on their backs the heavy loads of kindling they had collected. They walked ahead, leading the donkeys by stout ropes. This was clearly a place that had not given a thought to the equality, much less the warmth, of its women.

When we drove into town and parked in the square, we were immediately surrounded by curious townsfolk. There were males of all ages, but no women in sight. The men and boys unabashedly examined our license plates, then us. We consulted the paper that had the address that we sought. We asked where it was, and everybody eagerly answered at once. They pointed, directed, accompanied us, until we reached the destination. The crowd did not go away, jostling and staring until the attorney appeared. He shooed everyone off, graciously accepted the gifts of chocolates for the invisible women (we had carefully been instructed by our Berkeley friend to bring lots of goodies), and then proudly took on the duties of official guide to the village of Gangi.

He had handsomely Italianate features and a trim figure that showed off his well-tailored suit to advantage. His hospitality to us and the obvious pleasure with which he engaged our children did not deter from his firmness in addressing other townspeople or in making immediate decisions regarding our destinations. No hanky panky whatsoever. We felt very lucky to be toured about by such a commanding figure, a more cosmopolitan and citified man than we had ever imagined would come from this remote interior village.

We walked on grey cobbled streets through the town, past shops of golden stone that dated to the sixteenth century, many of them with typical arched doorways. As we passed numerous churches, we remarked to ourselves on the evident religiosity of the people. The attorney then suggested that he show us a particularly famous religious painting, at least well known in those parts, and led the way to another church. It was dark inside, and we crept behind our guide to the wall where the painting hung. It was so dark that we couldn't see it well, nor completely make out the subject, even though our friend discoursed at length about it. We spent some time studying the various figures that we could decipher, and concluded silently that even in full glaring light, it would not have turned out to be a tremendous work of art.

After we had considered the painting for a suitable time, the attorney took us down one floor to view the catacombs. For centuries, every priest had been interred in the crypt below the church until there was no more room. More recently bodies were buried in a graveyard neighboring the church. The catacombs we were viewing were an endless series of arched recesses, each bearing an erect skeleton, clothed in the official vestments of office, and held in an upright position, arms dangling, head inclined forward, scary even to us adult Americans. As we walked past, some of the disintegrating garments, stirred by the breeze of our passing, fluttered dustlike to the floor. To make matters even more eerie, at some point long ago the people in charge had decided to replace the flesh that had clearly rotted away, with applications of wax. Over the years, the wax had begun to peel and ooze and now hung in grotesque shreds where hands and faces once had been. Several skeletons wore fairly new garments, the colors still discernible and the fabrics whole. These were the remains of priests, the attorney explained, whose American relatives had sent money to buy new vestments for their kin. Our kids, fascinated by these bony figures, asked many questions, ending with one from Lissa asking Charles if one day he would be dead, too, like these priests.

At no time during our tour did we see any women, except for those wood-gatherers on the road leading to town. Although personally he could not have been more gracious, the attorney never introduced us to his family or invited us into his house. Nor were we offered such comforts as a bathroom. By the end of the day, I was in serious need of same. The café had facilities for men, much to the relief of Charles and Jeff, but not for women, much to the chagrin of Lissa and me. Judging from their absence, women, I guessed, were not welcome in such public places and therefore did not frequent them, which would explain the men-only facilities. Uncomfortable as we girls were, we somehow managed to get through the thank-yous and goodbyes, but by the time we were on the road descending from Gangi, we were desperate. In full view of any passersby and anyone who happened to be looking down from the town—there was no possibility of privacy anywhere—I led the way into a field next to the road, hoisted my coat, squatted down, and being careful to avoid my boots, relieved myself. With some help with her garments, Lissa did the same. Charles said I looked very funny, like some oblivious animal—I believe he mentioned cow—doing what came naturally. I, who had never before even bared my backside in public, wished that I were as unconcerned about privacy as my four-year-old daughter.

Palermo turned out to be as cosmopolitan as Gangi was unsophisticated. Whereas Gangi remained a remote village cherishing its old ways, Palermo, a thriving port and capital of the island, seemed instead to expand within and beyond its layers of history. Its architecture, splendid mosaics, and lush gardens, even its food, reflected the many civilizations that had dwelt there: Phoenician, Roman, Byzantine, Norman, Moor, Greek, Saracen, French, German. In fact, Palermo was a microcosmic reflection, an inheritance, of the various peoples that had left their marks on all of Sicily. That island, the largest in the Mediterranean, because of its prominent physical position and dominance over the sea, had managed to seduce one conqueror after another.

When we found the chief veterinarian, a hospitable and cordial man who was equally delighted with our children, he had already mapped out strenuous plans for sightseeing. A man clearly proud of his city, he perceptibly enjoyed his role as tour guide. Like his younger sibling, he was a handsome man, sported a haircut that men could get only in Italy, and a sartorial finesse that is usually associated with bankers.

As we followed him around the center, we marveled at the vitality that the blend of civilizations had imparted. Pink-domed churches fit right in with Gothic facades, oriental roofs, Byzantine mosaics, and baroque fountains. The three historic main squares, the abundance of sculpture and painting, the museums, the huge Norman palace, the *Orto Botanico* with its palm-studded tropical gardens on the other side of town, all of these divergences should have produced a distracting jigsaw of a city, not the harmonious place that it was.

We also marveled at the fact that as we walked along, vociferous postcard sellers and aggressive souvenir vendors who approached us immediately became silent and quickly faded away like a receding tide, at an almost imperceptible hand gesture from the veterinarian. Well protected—by the Mafia?—we plodded along and after a long but fascinating period of sightseeing, our prescient host thought that it was time to stop for a refreshment.

In a nearby bar (really more of what we would call a café), we ordered *spremute di arance* for the kids, pressed orange juice with water and sugar that you add to taste, and espressos for the grownups. The good doctor then commanded a tray of sweets, or *dolci*, originally brought to the islands, along with citrus and pistachios, by the Arabian invaders. Whatever the source, Sicilians have a sweet tooth that is insatiable; the vast array before us only hinted at the variety available. Our friend insisted that we must try a typical selection, which he then chose for us, directing the waiter to serve us "these"—pointing—"marzipan fruits, those babas, these *cannoli*, those assorted candied fruits, these *cassate*." *Cannoli* are crisp fried pastry tubes filled with ricotta mixed with various candied fruits, chocolate bits, and pistachios; *cassate* are refrigerated cakes layered with ricotta melded with rose water (or a sweet wine or a liqueur like maraschino), chopped candied lemon, citron, and orange peel, along with glacéed cherries, and sometimes chocolate bits or chocolate icing. An even richer version incorporates a layer of bitter almond paste. In Sicily, *cannoli* and *cassate* taste even better than elsewhere, including the mainland of Italy, because of the unique flavor of the Sicilian ricotta with which they are made. Still, for me, a little goes a long way.

On top of everything, the veterinarian also ordered a *brioscia* filled with pistachio ice cream. Although the ice cream flavor may vary and the brioche usually looks more like a hamburger bun than its French counterpart, it is a standard Sicilian combination, eaten even for breakfast. Just to make sure that we wouldn't go hungry, our friend also ordered one *granita di limone*, lemon ice—"just to taste"—little realizing that we had before us enough to kill our appetites for weeks to come. The Arabs also get credit for bringing the idea of ices and ice creams to the island, purportedly at first mixing the syrups of roses, citrus fruits, and jasmine with snow. That eventually led to *granita*, ices flavored with citrus, berries, or coffee, then to sherbets and ice creams. As we sampled all of these goodies, the sweetness and abundance of the selection made our teeth, already aching, unbearably sensitive. I felt that I could never eat another dessert as long as I lived, but this was an offer that we couldn't refuse: Slowly, dutifully, we consumed enough confections to turn us into instant diabetics.

The next morning the veterinarian took us to the great street market, the Vucciria, the oldest and no doubt the biggest on the island. Overflowing stands, tables, stalls, stacked wooden crates, and open-sided shops, many shielded from the sun by colorful canvas awnings, lined a vast neighborhood of narrow, winding cobbled streets. Vendors offered every conceivable foodstuff: prickly pears, all colors and kinds of grapes, varieties of citrus including the unfamiliar citron, much resembling a small grapefruit or very large lemon but more convex in shape. One of the favorite Sicilian salads consists entirely of sliced oranges, one of the citrus fruits readily available in the market, with a simple dressing of oil, vinegar, and a bit of coarse black pepper. Sometimes, as a garnish, chopped nuts are sprinkled over the top.

Among the vegetables there were wild asparagus; all kinds of peppers and tomatoes, including trays of them sun-dried, and others concentrated into a paste shaped into a bright red pyramid and sold in bulk; mushrooms, including *porcini* in season; artichokes and cardoons; eggplant and zucchini; and squashes, many of which we had never seen before, of all sizes and shapes. Some were narrow and three feet long; others were crook-necked or curling, like the *cucuzze*.

In the spice and herb section of the Vucceria market, we saw the famously aromatic capers from the Sicilian island of Pantelleria, wild fennel, wild parsley, and wild mint, side by side with saffron, bay leaves, myrtle, lemon verbena, oregano, thyme, and basil, and such perfumed spices as cinnamon and cloves. Salt, which came from still extant salt flats that one could see on the road along the bay of Mozia just north of Marsala, was parceled out in bulk. Garlic was abundant, olives ubiquitous. Bitter almonds, pine nuts, and pistachios, all grown in Sicily, had their displays. There were fava beans and chick peas, alternately called garbanzos. Chick pea flour, used on the island to make pasta, was more commonly fried into flat, rectangular fritters called *panelle*. We ate both. In Sicilian dialect, the *panillaru*, the fritter maker, offered his wares in street and market stands. They made a nice snack when sudden hunger pangs assaulted you.

The market display of cheeses was overwhelming. The most well-known was the *ragusano*, made from sheep's milk, or the cow's milk *ragusano*, similar to a *caciocavallo*. Alongside them were *pecorinos* made from ewe's milk and sometimes studded with black peppercorns, a *canestrato* made from cow's and goat's milk, and a couple of *provolas*, one of them from the mountains of the Madonie massif, although it was not one we saw in Gangi. And, of course, the ricotta, made usually of sheep's milk, but sometimes using cow or goat milk. One, which I have never seen elsewhere, is called a ricotta infornata: Covered with a dusting of black pepper, baked in a stone oven at a very low temperature, it is ready when it is soft-solid and has formed a delicate crust.

When we saw the meat stores, which seemed to sell everything, it made us sad that we had no kitchen in which to cook. They did an especially good business in Italian bacon known as *pancetta*, pork, prosciutto, and lard, all essential parts of the Sicilian culinary pantry. Game was available. Stands carried offal, such things as spleen, or *milza*, a favorite topping for bruschetta but also used as a filling for savory pastries. For consumption on the spot, some stands sold buns drippy with cooked spleen, first sliced, then fried, and seasoned with cheese and lard. We didn't try any. Other stands offered snacks of *arancine*, breaded and fried rice balls, popular not only in Sicily but throughout southern Italy. They are variously stuffed with some mixture of cheese or béchamel, prosciutto, ground veal, or vegetables such as peas.

Fish stands displayed a glorious variety, often arranged in silvery compositions. Surrounded by the sea, the island has always relied on its abundant supply of water creatures, much more widely consumed than meat. Swordfish and tuna were, and still are, extremely popular, but sardines, anchovies, calamari, ling cod, red mullet, lobster, whitebait, and various shellfish, among others, turned up frequently in many succulent dishes. Stands offered sea urchins, or *ricci* which, once cracked open, revealed golden gonads, which the eater scooped up, as if they were soft boiled eggs, with hunks of bread. Boiled *neonati*, newborn fish no bigger than a needle, once cooked, were a favorite topping for pasta. Men sometimes ate them still alive and wriggling in an act of extreme machismo. Squid and octopus, boiled on the spot, were chopped into suitable portions and served up on plates for a market breakfast or snack with quartered lemons for squeezing over them.

Despite this amazing array of foodstuffs, and the mixture of culinary traditions, the cooking of Sicily usually seemed quite simple. However, often relying on marinades or sauces, both aromatic and piquant, the flavors that resulted could be complex. We tasted combinations of savory, sweet, and sour, a reflection, in particular, that showed a gastronomic inheritance from the island's historic Arabian and North African inhabitants. We found in the eastern part of Sicily, however, a decidedly more Spanish and Greek influence.

Anchovies, usually marinated as part of every antipasto, were also commonly used to add spark to other dishes They were minced into sauces or added to vegetable mixtures. Chopped fine with fresh garlic, they were frequently stuffed between the leaves of artichokes and baked under a christening of olive oil. Fish were often served whole, roasted or grilled on a spit, a particularly toothsome way to prepare such fresh catches as calamari or sardines.

The national pasta dish, *pasta con sarde*, relied on sardines. We had tasted it before our visit to the island when a Sicilian friend, visiting in California, had made a typical dish of spaghetti with sardines and grapes. *Bottarga*, pressed and salted fish eggs (from a variety of fish including cod and tuna—they all taste a bit different), was weighted down to form solid blocks. Thin slices were then shaved to top pasta. Strongly flavored, they were used sparingly. Sicilians were also fond of the pressed eggs sliced over raw tomatoes. *Bottarga*, available as well in crumbled form, was used primarily as an addition to pasta.

Sicilians are bread eaters and especially pride themselves on their home-baked breads and homemade pastas. But dried pasta, always cooked extremely firm, or *al dente*, was eaten copiously throughout the island. Outside of the Orient, Sicily claims the oldest history both of making and consuming dried pasta. From the earliest days, it was the Mediterranean center of wheat cultivation and flour making. In the form of semolina, the grain was also the source of couscous, another food that the Arabs introduced. It is widely made and a specialty in the region of Trapani, where they often combine it with seafood.

One of the most famous and widely available dishes in Sicily, *caponata*, makes use of the abundant produce grown on the island. It resembles, in a more complicated sweet and sour form, the French *ratatouille*. On our travels around the perimeter and inland, we found it everywhere, with frequent additions to the basic dish. We never tired of it. I often make it at home, but as good as it is, it lacks the Sicilian olives and the capers from Pantelleria that give it such piquancy in its place of origin. *Caponatina*, which you often find on Sicilian menus, is the same thing sliced into smaller pieces. Giuliano Bugialli, the famous food authority from Bologna, tells us that the dish originated with sailors. Whenever they hit port, they bought cooked vegetables from inns called *caupone*, then ate them back on the ship. They piled them on sea biscuits softened by the sugar and vinegar used to season the veggies. Here is the modern recipe that evolved:

ℛ ℛ

Dice an unskinned eggplant weighing about 1 pound into two-inch squares. Sauté the cubes in abundant olive oil, salting lightly, until golden. Set aside. Coarsely chop 1 large onion, two stalks of celery, and slice two or three bell peppers. Sauté them in the same pot, adding oil if necessary, until the celery is translucent and the onions have begun to take on color. Add two cups of chopped red tomatoes. When the vegetables are just soft but not mushy, return the eggplant to the pot. Add a tablespoon or two of capers, a dozen or more pitted and chopped olives, a small whiskey glass of red wine vinegar (about 1 ounce), 1 table-spoon of sugar, and salt and pepper to taste. Cover and simmer until the flavors have mingled and the vegetables are soft all the way through. When cool, refrigerate for at least a day to marry the flavors. Serve as part of an antipasto.

ℛ ℛ

Frequently in Sicily, *caponata* is made into a main course by the addition of such ingredients as tuna fish, anchovies, boiled lobster meat, shrimp, fried baby octopus, hard boiled eggs, artichokes, asparagus, tuna eggs, pine nuts, or any other compatible commodity. In Syracuse, on the diagonally opposite corner of the island, the basic dish is often prepared without tomatoes, and sometimes with the addition of a small amount of grated chocolate.

Chocolate is used in foods that are not desserts more commonly than one would think. A few years ago, R. W. Apple, known to many of his friends as Johnny, traveling for the *New York Times*, found that in Modica, a town not too far distant from Syracuse in southeastern Sicily, one sweet shop still used an old artisanal process to make chocolate. Both in Oaxaca, Mexico, he wrote, and in certain towns in Catalonia, do they still employ this ancient process. Going on to describe dishes that he and his wife Betsey had tasted, he listed ravioli stuffed with mincemeat and chocolate, pastry filled with eggplant and chocolate, a dish of rabbit simmered in a sauce including chocolate, and a chocolate candy heated up by the addition of red chili pepper. It came as no surprise to him that the use of chocolate as a food rather than a sweet reminded him of the great mole sauces of Mexico. According to Johnny, the Spanish, who brought chocolate to Sicily in the fifteenth century, had gotten it from the Aztecs. In Tuscany, we have eaten wild boar, *cinghiale*, with chocolate in the sauce. Perhaps it was a culinary trick that was long ago passed on from Sicily. In any case, the chocolate was as imperceptible and enriching in the dish of wild boar as the Apples found it to be in the foods that they sampled in Modica.

In subsequent days, after our visit to the market, we went back to a few of the sights that our preliminary overall view had necessarily slighted. In particular, we returned to the enormous Palace of the Normans, which is now the seat of the Sicilian Legislature. The veterinarian had recommended that we see there its splendid twelfth-century Palatine Chapel, open to the public, and its treasure of sparkling mosaics. It turned out to be astonishing. The upper walls and apse of the chapel glittered with Byzantine tiles of a quality that our guidebook compared to that of Ravenna. We would sorely have regretted missing them. However, there was one piece of advice that we didn't follow. The veterinarian had told us that we must visit the Catacombs of the Capuchins where, beginning in the seventeenth century, about eight thousand cadavers, mostly mummified, were entombed in long subterranean corridors. Apparently it was an awesome sight, but one which, after Gangi, we happily passed over.

On the next morning, we headed for Monreale, a town about four or five miles to the southwest of Palermo. The cathedral there is famous, particularly for its mosaics, although the quality and beauty of its patterned marble floors, bronze doors, and adjacent cloisters make a tour of the whole ensemble more than worthwhile. The remarkable mosaics, resplendent with gold and covering all of the upper walls and arches, re-create the stories of the Old and New Testaments. In one of the apses there is a striking mosaic, an enormous Christ figure depicted from the waist up, giving his blessing. A recounting of some of the Bible scenes depicted in the mosaics kept the children happy.

From Monreale, with its panoramic views over the lemon and orange groves of the vast valley called the Conca d'Oro, we headed to the Greek ruins of Segesta. The whole island is studded with archeological treasures, particularly the ruins of ancient Greek and Roman structures, and our aim was to see the most important of them. Which is what we found in Segesta: one of the finest and best preserved Doric Greek temples anywhere. Dating to 430 B.C., the golden stone temple, with a colonnade delineated by three dozen columns, perches majestically on its promontory. As an added bonus, about a mile up the road, chiseled out of the rock, is a semicircular Greek theater.

We went on to Selinunte, where there are ruins of several Greek temples, the oldest of which, Temple E, was being restored. Temple G, in disrepair, had once been huge, but was now mostly remnants on the ground. Agrigento, much further along the same road, turned out to be a modern hillside town with an ocean view and an older medieval section above it. Mysteriously, the archeological zone, called the Valley of the Temples, was on a plateau, not in a valley, but easily accessible on foot from the designated parking area. Named the Sacred Way, the pedestrian route passed right by the major temples. Originally ten, nine were still distinguishable although in various stages of destruction or repair. The Doric Temple of Concord was in the best condition. Most of its columns, the entablature

and triangular tympanum above them, and the stone steps surrounding the temple, were preserved more or less intact. It gave a
sense of the majesty that this edifice had once projected. In the same
archeological zone were traces of ancient houses, streets, a theater,
and burial sites, the remains of the Greek city that had dominated
the site in 582 B.C.

Agrigento owes its existence to Greek colonizers from Gela,
many miles east along the sea. That town, which is where we headed
next, had itself been inhabited by settlers from Rhodes and Crete,
one hundred years before some of them moved on to found Agrigento. Our interest, however, was not in the remains of the Greek
fortifications nor the archeological museum for which the town was
known, but in its beaches where American troops had waded ashore
during the invasion of World War II. My husband Charles, as navigator of a large landing ship, had vivid memories of constantly going
back and forth from Africa, discharging tanks and troops along those
shores, and of being bombed and strafed by German planes. His
recollections, once we were on the spot, were more overwhelming
than he had expected. He was even seized for a moment by a sobering, involuntary chill.

He remembered that later in the campaign, after the Germans
had been expelled from Sicily and the German embassy in Palermo
had been turned into the naval officers' club, he had eaten hamburg-
ers there accompanied by a wonderful red wine from the cellar—all
for fifty cents. It was only some years afterwards that he realized that
the wine that he had been served, with the funny little tower on its
label, had been a pre-war Château Latour.

We left the beach in a somewhat somber mood, which soon dis-
sipated with the discovery that our car was nearly out of gas. At the
nearest gas station the attendant chatted amiably while he pumped,
asking where we were from—our American accents clearly revealed

that it was not from Rome, in spite of our license plates—how we liked Sicily, where we had been, what we had seen, and so on. It turned out, according to him, that the most important sight was still ahead of us. Some kilometers to the northeast, he advised us, was a singular imperial Roman villa, the floors of which were covered with world-class mosaics, only recently excavated, really the best any-where, not to be missed. Before he waved us off, he enthusiastically gave us detailed information on how to get to the marvels in Piazza Armerina. Isn't it wonderful, we thought, how everybody thinks that the monument or relic in his part of the world is the best there is. We sailed right on past the road to Piazza Armerina.

Much to our chagrin, we later found out that the attendant had been absolutely correct. We had missed one of the most monumen-tal Sicilian discoveries that had ever been made. Years later, on another trip to the island, Piazza Armerina was first on our list of things to see. But by then there was no more walking on the pave-ments. The site had been immaculately organized: restrictive cat-walks for viewing, protective glass covering some of the mosaics, transparent new louvers, roofs, walls, glass doors here and there— enclosing, to be sure, but in such a light and airy way, one had to applaud the measures taken to preserve this treasure. Even in its manicured state it was a stunning site, its scope and beauty breath-taking.

The town of Piazza Armerina, inland on an ancient consular road midway between Agrigento and Catania, is a harmonious cluster of light-colored houses on a hillside slope dominated by a huge domed cathedral. The Roman Villa of Casale, the scene of the excavation and long covered over by many feet of earth, is a few miles away. Constructed at the end of the third and beginning of the fourth cen-turies A.D., it served as an imperial country retreat, which explains the many murals devoted to hunting, fishing, exercising and other leisure activities. From the scale of things, it is immediately clear that this was a luxurious undertaking. There were hot, warm, and cold baths, with swimming pools and dressing rooms. An aqueduct had branches to the private apartments in the residence and to the elaborate furnaces that heated water for the bathing rooms. By maneuvering the windows above the furnaces, servants could control the temperature in the hot bathing room, or calidarium. Steam for the sauna in the warm bathing room, or tepidarium, was generated by the hot water that ran under its floor. In the adjacent room for massages and oiling, the mosaic floors depicted servants performing those functions for their masters.

The semicircular Great Latrine—one among many, including a private toilet in the family apartments—got its water from the overflow of the fountain in the large courtyard. Marble seats, which have never been found, purportedly lined the curved wall. A sort of canal carried a stream of water which served for public urination. It pays to be imperial: One of the higher class latrines came equipped with a bidet. In the master's private latrine, there was a mosaic. It portrayed a three-eyed Cyclops, Polyphemus, receiving a cup of drugged wine from Ulysses.

Besides the quarters for the royals, there were numerous guest rooms, long connecting corridors, an immense dining room, kitchens, a ball room, a gymnasium, various entrance halls, and ornamental pools, fountains, and gardens, all of which have been uncovered. Appropriate mosaics covered every inch of flooring. In the entrance hall were welcoming figures bearing lit candles and branches of laurel; in the ball room there were twirling dancers; in the gymnasium chariot racers portrayed the games in Rome's Circus Maximus.

Fishing, by cupid fishermen, and small game hunting each had their room, the latter with a scene depicting a sacrifice to Diana, the goddess of hunting. One long corridor depicted big game hunting, from baiting, chasing, and catching the animals, to carrying them wrapped in nets, jammed in boxes, or transported by oxcarts to a mosaic sea full of fish, where they were loaded onto waiting tile ships. Bloody depictions abounded: spearing a wild boar, hunting down tigers and lions, dragging a roped bison to its doom, capturing a rhinoceros. One bare breasted female figure personified Africa, surrounded by a tiger, an elephant, and a phoenix raising from its fiery nest.

Besides panels depicting the labors of Hercules, and Ambrosia metamorphosing into a vine, there were three mosaics that we found particularly amusing. In the room of the children was a satire on the Circus Maximus in miniature. Fantastic giant birds, one web-footed pair resembling oversized ducks, pulled wheeled chariots driven by whip-wielding youths. The victor received a palm from another boy. Other scenes in the childrens' room, a commentary on the full-scale escapades that elsewhere portrayed adults, showed young boys engaged in a hunt, the prey also being on a befittingly smaller scale: a hare, a cock, and a rabbit.

The second panel that particularly caught our attention was designed in a series of geometric patterns alternating with women's heads and portraits of the four seasons. These busy distractions, perhaps intentionally, delayed our attention from the central erotic scene: an embrace of two young lovers, the woman suggestively removing her clothes.

Lastly, there was the room that has come to be known as "The Girls in Bikinis." In the upper panel, four girls scantily clad in strapless red bras and well-below-the-naval matching red bottoms, were lifting weights, competing in a race, and preparing to throw a discus. One sported an ankle bracelet, two arm bracelets, a necklace, and earrings. A precursor to the modern day tennis player? In the lower scene, two girls batted a ball in what looked like a game of handball, while the other three figures, one in a gold drape that exposed one of her breasts, represented victory, rendered pictorially by bestowing or wearing a crown, a palm, and a symbolic wheel.

These amazing mosaics, most of them in a remarkable state of preservation, achieve vitality and humor through the brightness of their colors, the naiveté of their style, and the fluidity of their subjects' depicted movements. The sheer number of mosaics is in itself overwhelming, and the glimpse of history, however brief, is profound.

On our first trip to Sicily, although we regretfully missed Piazza Armerina, we did go on to stop at Syracuse, a city founded by the Greeks in the eighth century B.C. One of the attractions for us was the baroque cathedral built on the site of the doric temple of Diana, in which some of the original fifth-century B.C. columns are incorporated along the north aisles of the interior. Another highpoint was seeing the remains of the ancient quarry, the *Latonia del Paradiso*, in which an ear-shaped artificial grotto called the Ear of Dionysius displayed extraordinary acoustical properties which echoed and amplified voices to the delight of our children. They also liked the large Greek theater and the Roman amphitheater built several centuries later, both chiseled out of the rock, perhaps because the vast outdoor spaces were less confining than the walled in churches.

We went on to Catania, a city many times leveled by eruptions from Mount Etna, in spite of the fact that St. Agatha, the city's patron saint, was supposed to offer it her protection. We discovered her beatified remains residing in a reliquary in the church bearing her name. They rest there permanently except for one ceremonious day a year, her feast day, when they are paraded through the streets.

The black lava, incorporated in the rebuilding of the city after a tumultuous earthquake in 1693, gives it a somber cast in some places. Not, however, in the Piazza del Duomo, where an amusing elephant fountain has presided since the seventeenth century. Rising out of the water on a central pedestal, the black lava elephant sports ivory-colored tusks and an Egyptian obelisk, which seems to grow out of his back.

About eleven miles north, on a road skirting the sea, is the town of Acireale, whose attraction, at least for us, was the folklore theater devoted to puppet shows. A long tradition on the island, Sicilian puppets, which are actually marionettes, stand at least three feet tall and are elaborately costumed in sumptuous silks, real furs, bejeweled headgear, gaudy shields, flashing swords, and golden armor. Their repertoire includes many of the five hundred tales that make up the *Orlando Furioso* epic. Numerous museums are devoted entirely to puppets, their history, and accessories. Theaters throughout the island give live performances. There are shops that sell puppets—a rather expensive and cumbersome souvenir. Professionals who work the strings will tell you that to produce a thrilling mock swordfight takes great talent and training. Unfortunately, skilled puppet masters, called *pupari*, are becoming infinitely rarer.

Such also is the case with donkey-cart carvers. Although when we first visited Sicily, donkey carts and horse carts were everywhere, their numbers on the road have sadly diminished. Even on our first visit, there were few old masters left who could create the traditional painted side panels, metal work, and carved back panels. The best ones from the past now highlight the collections of ethnographical museums. A century or so ago, the side panels bore carved borders, and the elaborate metal work on the axle connecting the wheels depicted human figures, animals, and entwined flowers. Gaudily decorated carts do still participate in festivals and celebrations, the animals who draw them colorfully garlanded in floral wreaths, fancy harnesses, and feathered plumage.

Because on our Sicilian travels we shared the road with many a donkey cart, our interest in them piqued, particularly our interest in the side panels, paintings mostly of St. George slaying the dragon, scenes from the *Orlando Furioso* stories, the medieval uprising against the French, or the invasions of various conquerors. But we soon realized that the back panels, called *chiave*, three dimensional depictions of actual or legendary historical events, were more sophisticated examples of local folk art. Toward the end of our journey, when we were heading up the eastern coast, we had started inquiring of drivers whose carts bore particularly well carved *chiave*, if they knew the names and locations of the artists. We hadn't made many inquiries because good carvings came along infrequently, but one day, struck by the artistic caliber of a St. George, we hailed the driver and asked our questions. He knew exactly where the panel had come from and gave us directions to the village of Randazzo on the side of Mount Etna. He didn't give us the name or address of the carver, the only one in the village, because anyone, he explained, would know who and where he was.

The village was the most depressing place we had ever seen, being built entirely of blocks of black lava. Crumbles of dark rubble from various past eruptions lay scattered here and there. It was unrelentingly dreary and monochromatic. We stopped to inquire of a shabbily dressed man whether he knew of a carver in the village. Yes, he certainly did, but why didn't he just show us the way, he asked, hopping on the running board of the car. With the aid of his gestures supplemented by a few verbal instructions in a dialect that we could barely make out, we arrived at a very small house, partly converted into a wood worker's shop. Smiling broadly, he hopped off and started down the hill.

We rapped on the double door of the workshop. Shortly it opened to reveal a thin middle-aged man wearing a dark visored cap and a dirty blue apron covered with wood shavings. We told him we were admirers of his work and had learned his whereabouts from a driver whose cart bore one of his carvings. He hospitably invited us into his shop, all the while protesting that he didn't have anything worth showing us. His carvings were rather primitive and displayed a good deal of whimsy, but they were mainly works in progress.

Stacked behind one of the uncompleted panels we discovered a small carving, maybe a foot and a half long by half a foot high and a couple of inches thick. Although it was from a solid piece of wood, it was made to look like a three dimensional carving atop a decorative base. The paint had faded enough so that the figures below had all but disappeared, except for some lightly carved curlicues and delicate fawns' heads. On each end above the base were two green fish, or maybe sea serpents, whose tails curved skyward. Abutting them, two growling Venetian-looking lions with stylized manes swiveled their heads backwards. They had looped tails that circled back through their rear legs. What looked to be eagles with their wings fully extended perched on their rear haunches. These were painted a faded red. Under each lion's belly a mysterious fifth foot extended, pinning down what appeared to be a snake with a head raised on each end. One of the lions' front paws rested on a four petaled flower; the other supported the corrugated sides of a green medallion. Several brown sticks stood in a bundle in the absolute center. Next to the sticks, an ax that may once have been black completed the center grouping.

We liked its funky, shopworn quality and offered to buy it—to no avail. The carver was emphatic. It was old, it had never been good in the first place, and it was absolutely not for sale. We poked through the other work, but found nothing that was complete. Disappointed, we thanked him and bid our farewells. He walked out to the car with us and as the engine started up he thrust the carving we had liked through the open window. Charles drew out some money, thinking there had been a change of heart. The artist waved it off. "It's a gift," he explained. "I'm not proud of it but you like it and so you shall have it." Then, grinning generously, and waving us off, he added, "And besides friends never exchange money."

It was almost time for our Sicilian idyll to end. In a few days, we would be taking the Messina ferry back to Calabria and from there returning to our ordinary life in Rome. But we had those few days left. Our final destination of Taormina, a lovely flower-filled city set high on a hillside by its original Greek founders, would be the perfect ending. Its elevated perch afforded panoramic views out over the sea. The fearsome Mount Etna formed a backdrop, its usually snow-capped peak and peaceful wisps of smoke belying the fact that it was still an active and mighty troublesome volcano.

Our chosen hotel, the San Domenico Palace, was surely one of the world's great destinations. A former fifteenth-century convent, it was converted to secular use as a hotel in 1896. In modern times, it has become a place to stay that is at once elegant, luxurious, and soothingly pampering. Just what we needed before returning to everyday life. San Domenico, during the occupation of Sicily in World War II, had served as the German headquarters. When the Allies had tried to bomb it, they had done much more damage to the ancient church next door. The repairs to the hotel were minor, and had restored it once again to its former glory.

San Domenico's halls and lobbies were furnished with stately antiques and paintings, as were the bedrooms, but such amenities as accessories, beds, electricity, lamps, and bathrooms were completely up-to-date. Every morning we enjoyed a leisurely breakfast on our balcony overlooking the sea, every afternoon we headed through the gravel paths of the gardens, themselves a spectacular horticultural fairyland, to the pool for a swim. Some nights we ate in the splendidly elegant dining room, where the food was exceptional. While the kids always chose pasta and grilled chicken, we indulged in seafood salads, eggplant and wild mushrooms, pasta with bottarga or sardines, veal cooked in marsala, or fish cooked with capers, black olives, and plum tomatoes. There was always an assortment of Sicilian cheese with which to finish off the wine. For dessert we adults once tried sliced citron sprinkled with sugar, because we had never had it (it turned out to be good—citrusy but not sour), but usually we all had one of those smooth ice creams like pistachio that the Sicilians make so well, or one of the sorbets that are the essence of lemon or blood orange or jasmine.

Sometimes, we would have an after dinner glass of *nocino*, a Sicilian specialty made from green walnuts that much resembles the nutty liqueur made in Modena. More often, we would have a *limoncello*, variously called *lemoncello*, which like its counterparts throughout the south of Italy, appeared ubiquitously in street stands, cafés, and restaurant dining rooms all over the island. Although the purists insist on a more complicated and lengthy process—whole lemons wrapped in cheese cloth, suspended over alcohol, sealed in a mason jar, and stored for months in a dark place before final filtering and sweetening with sugar syrup—the nonpurist recipe is really quite simple:

ℛ ℛ

To 4 cups of vodka add the rind of 4 to 6 lemons, depending on size. Cover the container and place out of the light for at least two weeks, better a month or two. When ready to proceed, simmer 1 cup of sugar, 1½ cups of water, and 1 teaspoon of fresh lemon juice until it is thick and syrupy. Remove the lemon rind from the vodka, add the cooled syrup, and strain into a glass bottle with a tight top or cork. After a week, store in the cooler. Serve it over crushed ice, ice cream, or sorbet, or drink it straight in small liqueur glasses. The newest trend in Italy is to use it in place of rum for soaking babas. *Baba au limoncello?*

℘ ℘

Having explored the Greek Theater, with its breathtaking view of the sea and Etna, and the terraced public gardens, which provide a similarly striking view, we decided one morning after breakfast that it was time to navigate the town itself. The Corso Umberto, the main street, was clustered with shops and galleries. The downtown area encompassed many squares, including the Piazza IX Aprile, from the terrace of which one had the usual splendid view over the water. We casually window shopped as we strolled along, stopping once in one of the piazzas at a café with outdoor tables. There we could enjoy a refreshment while resting our feet and doing some people watching before resuming our meanderings.

A half hour later, while browsing in the window of an antique shop, we spotted inside the store what appeared to be a *chiave* from a cart. Through the window it looked to be the finest example of carving that we had yet seen, and we hurried inside to take a better look. It was indeed superb. The subject was the martyrdom of the virgin St. Agatha, MARTIRIO DI S. AGATA VERGINE, clearly carved out on a titular band of red curving along the bottom. Painted flowers in various colors filled out the rest of the strip. The two ends, one of which had obviously been damaged and mended halfway up, depicted creatures who seemed to be half angel (judging from the huge wings coming from their backs) and half mermaid (based on their fishlike green and black bottoms that suddenly entwined and undulated like serpents before they split into tails). They were nude from the hips up and held fluttering birds, perhaps doves, painted blue. It was obvious that the carving and painting of the undamaged maid was much more accomplished than the cruder repair on the other side. The amazing thing was that this panel, unlike any other that we had seen, displayed sophisticated perspective, more agile carving, more detailed painting, and a whole palette of colors whose hues had only slightly faded. Clearly, this was a real find.

The central part of the carving delineated the actual act of martyrdom, the removal by pincers of Agatha's breasts. Before this, all of the depictions that we had ever seen, except the painting hanging in the Pitti in Florence, were of the saint displaying her severed breasts on a silver platter. In the panel before us, a serene and already haloed St. Agatha, her long red robe pulled down to bare her breasts, was restrained by one man while another applied the pincers. Five onlookers were in a viewing box in the foreground, four of them in different poses, all wearing various headgear, drapes, hairstyles, and differently colored costumes. The fifth seemed to be in charge, judging both by his authoritarian attitude, the halberd he was carrying, and the silver armor and red plumed helmet he was wearing.

In perspective, the three other civilian spectators appeared much smaller, because they were on a balcony in the background. There were also armor-wearing guards bearing lances, and a cupid, or maybe it was an angel, in a swirling blue cloud, who was holding a golden crown above St. Agatha's head. The carving also portrayed houses, city gates, balconies, stone columns, and cobbled courtyards, all brightly painted in an array of colors. Most importantly, they were rendered in perspective.

The actual legend of Santa Agata varies; historic records only verify her martyrdom. The various stories, which disagree as to her birthplace, as well as to most of the basic facts, are summarized best by recounting what the various proponents (mostly) agree to: the fact that she was born in Sicily—but in Palermo or Catania?—of noble and well-to-do parents, and that she was martyred (one faction) by the removal of her breasts—the scene depicted on the donkey cart carving—or (other faction) by being rolled naked over either potsherds (one version) or hot coals (another version). The story behind the double mastectomy is that, as a devout virgin, she repulsed the advances of the tyrant, Senator Quintanius (in some versions, Quintianius), who governed Sicily under the Emperor Decius, and who had summoned her because of her fame as a wealthy and reverent beauty. When she remained passionately undefiled, Quintanius put her under the charge of an evil woman, learned in transmitting the arts of seduction. Resolutely chaste, Agatha still resisted and remained a virgin. The spurned Quintanius had her breasts cut off, but St. Peter, or a vision of him (alternate version), healed her wounds. The persecutions continued. It was only when she asked the Lord to spare her from further tortures (on the occasion of the hot coals or potsherds) that her life ended, and according to some versions, martyrdom followed.

Whatever the story of the martyrdom might have been, it was clear that we had one fantastic *chiave* before us. We approached the lone salesman and asked the price. It turned out that he was substituting for his brother-in-law, the owner of the shop, who had suddenly been called away on an emergency. He, just minding the store, gave us a price of such-and-such. We, by now experienced in the art of bargaining, knew that one never accepted the offered price but suggested one that was much lower, the eventual price being some compromise that pleased both buyer and seller. We offered half. His response was to consult his brother-in-law. Since it might take some time to reach him, he suggested that we go for an espresso and come back.

We couldn't believe our good fortune in finding this extraordinary carving. We lingered as long as possible, impatiently, but confident in our bargaining skills, and above all propelled by our desire to have this masterpiece, we went back. The temporary clerk looked chagrined. He was most apologetic. He had made a terrible error in suggesting a price. This panel had been carved by a master named Russo—surely we had heard of him?—now in his late nineties and no longer working on *chiave*. It was worth more than double the amount he had quoted, no bargaining possible. Had we agreed to his original guessed-at price, he would have been forever in disgrace with his brother-in-law. He didn't care whether we bought it or not. He was just happy that we hadn't taken him up on his original estimate.

The wonderful carving of the martyrdom of the virgin St. Agatha now hangs in our living room. We are probably the only people who, after legitimate Italian bargaining, ended up paying double.

CHAPTER ELEVEN

The Medieval Tower of Barbarino Val d'Elsa

Our frequent visits to Tuscany had always centered around Florence. Although we had also made extensive explorations of the countryside, we had never settled down anyplace for more than a few days. Our city habitats had included various *pensioni,* among them an extraordinary one directly looking down on the Ponte Vecchio, and several agreeable hotels. The Berchielli fronted on the river Arno (noisy unless you had a room in the back, but a great location); the David, across the river, was gracious, comfortable, and quieter. Our favorite—it has been our preference for the last several years—is the Villa Azalee, once the family home of our friend Ornella Bracone. She has refurbished it handsomely, and thanks to frequent trips from her residence in Switzerland, runs it diligently. What we like particularly about it is that it has more the character of a home—a rather large one, to be sure—than a hotel.

When she is in residence, the *signora* is famous for riding around town on her bicycle. For guests similarly inclined, the hotel provides several cycles. For those who prefer walking, the villa is ten or fifteen minutes from the city's center. It also has the advantage of an azalea-filled garden, hence the name, and well decorated, unusually large rooms, modern bathrooms, and furnishings, *objets*, and paintings that were once family possessions. Sometimes, we stayed in the hills with the Cipollas; otherwise we were happy guests at the Villa Azalee.

For a long time, the Cipollas lived high on the slopes above Florence in one of the small homes that had been built to augment the original Villa Selva, a grand property with expansive views and rolling hills dotted with olive trees. It was the closest we had come in Italy to actually living in the countryside. Besides the olives and the undulating landscape, there was a persuasive calm that convinced us that some time we should try staying in some place more bucolic than a major Italian city.

When we learned that my husband's brother Len and his wife Draselle were going to Monaco for his month-long job as a consulting marine biologist, it was an obvious opportunity. In the past, when we had traveled together in Italy, they had shared our fervor for all things Italian. In fact, after returning home, Len had enthusiastically taken up Italian cooking and proved to be particularly gifted at making pizza from scratch, *panna cotta* in increasingly refined variations, and many delectable dishes in between. We suggested that they combine their trip to Monaco with a rented house in Italy first. They didn't need to be persuaded.

And that is how we came to rent a medieval tower in the village of Barbarino Val d'Elsa, halfway between Siena and Florence. Originally built high on a hilltop, a location that better protected it from its enemies, the handsome walled town followed the usual custom of the Etruscans and those civilizations that came after it. Only two or three blocks long and half as wide, it is entirely constructed of stone. There are narrow cobbled streets, anachronistic for the modern automobile, with a tall arched gate at each end of the main passageway. Except for the addition of electricity and drain pipes here and there, outwardly it probably has not changed much since its beginnings. The more recent and less picturesque modern town, with its cafés, supermarket, dry cleaners, and restaurants, spreads out below, from the foot of the hill into the valley.

The tower, rising from an attached villa, had belonged to a successful Italian diplomat, now deceased, whose last post was in North Africa. His daughter, a professor at a university some miles south, had decided after his death to try renting it out. We were her first tenants. Fluent in English, and no doubt many other languages, she did her best to insure that our stay was as comfortable as possible. One way was to provide maid service whenever we required it. Franca, the maid, came immediately after our arrival to greet us and was there to bid us farewell when we left. In between, we arranged cleaning times as we needed them. The *professoressa* had also thoughtfully left information about restaurants in the area on the large desk in the living room. After we had departed, she even sent us a photograph of the house as a fond reminder of our stay. Whenever we went across the street to the little grocery for olive oil or to the baker downstairs for our morning rolls, the villagers always remarked on what a fine man the diplomat had been and how sad it was that he was no longer with us. Although we had never met him, we always dutifully commiserated, but our secret vote was for the daughter.

Through the large wooden entrance door on the street, a flight of stairs led to the main rooms one level up, which the Italians refer to as the first floor. The diplomat's collection of helmets, arms, and other military paraphernalia, displayed in glass cases in the entry hall, were the first things to greet you. The tower itself contained the dining room with its arched ceiling, and above it a study tucked away under wooden beams. In the villa proper, the enormous living room, about sixty feet long, completely lined with fascinating books in all languages, had a similar timber construction overhead: gigantic wooden beams that looked as big as tree trunks running one way, narrow square beams connecting them in the opposite direction, the whole thing supporting a plank ceiling. The intricately filigreed black iron chandeliers, hanging from a triangular rope of chains, looked as though they had been converted from candle power to electricity.

Carved elephants and figurines on the mantel above the huge fireplace and on the shelves of display cabinets mounted on the walls, were no doubt trophies of the African days. The commodious couch, a large fur throw across its back, and the ample matching chairs, all suggested lounging in comfort. Obviously recently installed, a large modern window on one side of the room opened to a vast view over the entire valley.

Between the multitude of books and the various *objets* and works of art, we never ceased to find something to entertain us. The not very accessible garden down below in the back, clearly unused for some time, was the only thing in the entire property that was not appealing. Better, if you needed fresh air, to go out on any of the narrow balconies, one of which ran a good forty feet on the valley side of the villa.

A *salotto*, or small living room, also on the first floor, contained a charming tapestry running the length of the wall. A curlicued glass chandelier, obviously Venetian, provided light. Next to the pale blue silk couch stacked with multiple toss cushions sprouted the flailing arms of an incongruous coat rack that would have been more at ease in an office. The top of a wooden cabinet served as a showcase for various precious objects, such things as a silver urn, a wonderful glass bottle, and a baroque antique silver samovar, the latter of which turned out to have an importance revealed only at the end of our stay.

Our bedroom, off the living room, had its own tiny dressing room, a small balcony, a carved wooden headboard, and a crown-shaped metal *"baldachino"* on the ceiling over the bed. Nestled among the oversized pillows in their linen cases, one couldn't help but feel regal. Len and Draselle's room, on the floor above, was equally comfortable if not so royally decorated, and had the full run of the unoccupied second floor, including a whole complex—large living room, bedroom, bathroom, kitchen—that was still under construction. We each had quite modern bathrooms with all the facilities, although ours contained a rather old-fashioned hot water heater mounted from the ceiling.

The light and airy kitchen had two complete stoves, a wood-burning one with various ovens, warming compartments, and moveable metal plates that constituted the cooking top, all set into brick masonry. Overhead a fan imbedded in a substantial hood drew the smoke upward, the wide ledge of the hood doing double duty for storage of such culinary equipment as a giant mortar and pestle—an irresistible invitation to make a big batch of *pesto*. In contrast, the adjoining cook-top and oven were quite modern. A contemporary dishwasher and modern refrigerator made life quite comfortable. We ate every morning around the table in the center of the room, warmed by the heat of the stove's wood fire, which simultaneously cooked our breakfast.

On our first day, we unpacked, put in supplies, walked through the town, and had dinner at La Bustecca, a simple restaurant and pizzeria right in Barbarino. It was so satisfying that we returned many times during our stay. Beyond the pizza, which was excellent, they made a fine spaghetti with seafood, *spaghetti con frutti di mare*, and a pasta called *stracciate*, which means ragged or torn, named for its irregular, somewhat shredded appearance. It was at La Bustecca that we first ate a soup of *farro*, an old grain, a sort of wild buckwheat that is a Tuscan specialty. Since *porcini* mushrooms were in season, the chef often grilled the larger ones—each made a single main course portion—with olive oil and garlic. *Filetto alpino*, for heartier eaters, turned out to be a steak topped with a fat grilled *porcino*. Another good dish, more common but no less satisfying, was thin slices of veal cooked with lemon.

Equally good and equally easygoing, the Osteria la Gramola, just down the road in the nearby town of Tavarnelle, served tasteful cooking based on the flavors of old Tuscany. Wherever we ate in the region, we found that the simplicity and true flavors of the cuisine were the predominant characteristics. Even in the upscale Paese dei Campanelli in Barbarino, a charming, old, beautifully appointed stone farm house, we found that though the very good, sophisticated cooking was a bit on the fancy side, it still showcased the genuine flavors and freshness of the ingredients.

Almost at the beginning of our stay in Barbarino, we discovered among the books in the tower library one on the nearby village and church of Sant'Appiano. Written by Monsignore Ferradino Fiorini, who happened to be the parish priest, it described the tenth-century church so appealingly that it immediately seemed to us that it was a place well worth a visit.

On the day that we decided to go there, we were lucky enough to find the *monsignore* himself. He graciously took us about, explaining the history, showing us the burial slabs, carved to depict the early knights clad in their armor, who were interred under the paving squares in the simple brick interior. He led us out the back door to a grassy plot behind the church where rose the chunky stone remnants of four Roman columns. The altar of the tiny church was festooned with arrangements of white lilies, left over, he told us, from a wedding that had recently taken place.

When our leisurely and informative tour had ended, our intention had been to follow it by going to an Etruscan tomb in the countryside near Barbarino. But as we left the church we were distracted by two men who were crushing grapes in front of a three-story field-stone house in the cobbled street nearby. From under the machine they were using, a long green hose snaked its way into an adjacent barred window, the sill of which supported two clay flower pots ablaze with geraniums. Drying clothes hung from an upstairs window. Profusely blooming flowers filled several larger planters. A number of intermixed plastic buckets of various sizes and colors were clearly part of a winemaking operation. They surrounded a narrow wooden door on the ground level, which turned out to be the unmarked and completely unobtrusive entrance to the winery of Sant'Appiano. Up a few steps in the center of the house, to the left of the smaller entry, was the main door to the residence, handsome double wooden panels set into an archway. A tall modern street light, a thin metal pole with a single bulb encased in a glass bubble, stood at the corner of the house. Were it not for the wires strung here and there on the façade, the simple lines and pristine condition of the building suggested a contemporary structure meant entirely for housing. The only indication of vinous intentions was the two men crushing grapes and their rudimentary equipment. In California, there are some nine hundred wineries, but none of them is so close a neighbor to a house of worship.

Of course, we had many questions to ask the two men who were crushing. The stocky older man, perhaps the father of the other one and a head shorter, was dressed in work-a-day grey pants and a tan and black v-necked striped sweater, his sleeves pushed up to his elbows. His jaunty cap topped off a jolly face. The capless younger man, taller, thinner, and equally jovial, displayed a shock of black hair above his grinning face. He wore blue jeans and a tan sweater, the collar of which opened to reveal a slightly dark blue shirt. When we approached them, they were delighted in our interest and immediately invited us to follow them inside the narrow doorway into what turned out to be their miniscule winery.

We found ourselves in a very small, somewhat ramshackle room with wooden beams covering the ceiling. Dozens of bunches of purple and white grapes hung from the beams, which were also festooned with precariously strung electric wires culminating in a blazing bare bulb or two. On a tile table along one wall stood a clutter of empty and half-full bottles as well as a miscellany of funnels and corkscrews. A narrow, crooked stairway, its walls, ceiling, and the cave it led to below, were crudely chiseled out of rock fortified with occasional bricks and stone. Before we got to the *cantina* we had to sneak past large glass demijohns with handled coats of woven cane that lined the stairs. Stoppered against the air, they stored wine, but made the passage difficult, even in single file. But led by our hosts, down we went to the dark, humid rock cave. Under the arched ceiling various barrels held wine for aging, some of it identified by names like Mugnani, obviously people whose grapes they had vinified.

Upstairs, they opened a bottle of three-year-old Sangiovese and poured it into a communal glass. We all took turns tasting, and found it remarkably good. They poured another shared glass, and then another, meanwhile answering our questions, such as why they didn't have a winery sign. They didn't need one since the whole village knew where they were and what they were doing, including the approving neighbors from the church. It was all very jolly and hospitable, ending with their insisting that before we departed we had to try their Vin Santo, a dessert wine with a high alcohol content. It was splendid—and potent.

Each adventure in Tuscany turned out to be enjoyable and reve-latory in its own way. Given our interest in wine and the fact that we were in the middle of Chianti, one of our choices was to visit other vineyards and wineries during the harvest. Immediately, it became clear that the differences between the Italian and Californian approach to wine went beyond drinking habits. Ever since the Romans planted grapes wherever they extended their empire, it has been taken for granted by Italians that wine is part of the meal; in the United States such a concept has been an uphill battle. Grape growing, winemaking, and wine consumption are all part of Italian culture, whereas in our country only a small percentage of the pop-ulation regularly indulges. In our best known wine region, Napa Valley, wine and the tourism attached to it have become big business for many: there are winery tours and connected gift shops, tasting rooms and overhead tramways to take you to them, burdensome traffic, even a fancy wine train that serves elaborate lunches and din-ners and takes several hours to thread its way the sixteen miles or so from Napa to St. Helena and back. In Italy, by contrast, it is unusual to welcome tourists, let alone have elaborate tasting rooms, not to mention the rest of the hullabaloo. Ordinarily the only winery guests are those of the owners.

On the day that we decided to pay serious attention to the Chianti area, it was extraordinarily clear and sunny, the rolling hills lush and verdant, the vineyards heavy with fruit. As we drove along the wine road, well-marked with black roadside signs, the white lettering and rooster logo told us that we were in the official world of the Gallo Nero Chianti Classico. From the road, we observed several pickers harvesting the grapes into gondolas, in many cases a field mix of different varietals that had been planted side by side, sometimes including both reds and whites. This was not surprising. The classic D.O.C. formula for Chianti had contained as much as 30 percent white grapes from 1967 until 1984, when it changed to 2 percent. Since the late 1990s, there has been no minimum requirement at all.

Some of the scarecrows in the fields, unlike the stationary ones to which we are accustomed, wore brightly colored dresses, others pants and shirts, a politically correct statement, however inadvertent. Strung on ropes suspended from long bamboo poles leaning diagonally at the edge of the vineyards, they danced and fluttered in the breeze like some headless conga line, meanwhile frightening the birds and protecting the fruit.

Our first destination was the town of Greve, where we had a pleasant lunch in the old square. Afterwards, we headed toward the *enoteca*, or wine library, for which the town is famous. We couldn't leave without buying something. Our choice was a bottle of Antinori Marchese Tenuta '93. Thirty years ago, Antinori was one of the first revolutionists in Tuscan winemaking, ignoring the classic formulas, introducing foreign grapes into the blends, and aging in small oak barrels. Although he couldn't use the D.O.C. certification and had to call his wine "red table wine," he was one of the first to make what became known as "super Tuscans."

We had driven many times past wineries with familiar names, such as Tignanello, Santa Christina, and Gabbiano, but true to Italian custom, there were not the least signs of visitors being welcome at any of them. Since we were all used to Californian beguilements to entice tourists, it was frustrating, particularly during the harvest season. Our interest in grape-growing operations was quite serious. Charles and I had owned a Napa Valley vineyard for seventeen years, and Len and Draselle were at that point close to becoming vineyardists themselves. It only waited his retirement from UCLA, at which point they moved to Napa, planted vines, built a laboratory, dug a cave, and now make a very good red wine.

We couldn't help but feel as if we were full-fledged members of the grape-growing community. Perhaps that is why, beyond all logic, we followed a gondola full of just-picked red grapes slowly down the road in the hills of Barbarino Val d'Elsa, smack into the Isola e Olena winery. As we came to a stop, we expected a probable rebuff—no visitors allowed, that kind of thing—but instead we found a welcoming committee who responded to our interest with equal enthusiasm. Among the greeters was Paolo De Marchi, the son of the owner, wearing well-worn blue jeans, an open-collared knit shirt, and a sweatshirt draped over his shoulders in that casual way for which Italians have an instinctive flair. He looked uncannily familiar, and then I realized that I had seen his face in a thousand renaissance paintings. And by the greatest of coincidences, it turned out that he just happened to have studied winemaking at the University of California at Davis, famous for its courses in viticulture and oenology, before he became winemaker at the family facility in Tuscany. In the United States, we had long been admirers and drinkers of Isola e Olena wines, so it turned out that our welcome was doubly fortuitous.

We watched as workers unloaded numerous gondolas of black grapes into smaller containers, easier to feed into the modern stemmer-crusher which stood in an open concrete pit some five feet below ground level. After seeing several loads stemmed and crushed, the ever-increasing pile of stems discarded on the gravel above, we followed our host into a small tasting room. To our utter amazement Paolo poured a '93 Chianti into expensive, long-stemmed Riedel crystal, the glasses normally used for elegant dinner parties, but in this case the winery's choice for sampling the Isola e Olena wines.

He followed the Chianti with glasses of '93 Cepparello, one of our favorites, made entirely of Sangiovese. Because it is a big wine, it is considered one of the "super Tuscans."

While we were sipping, Paolo described the research into experimental grape clones in which the winery, with the collaboration of the University of Florence, was currently engaged. The aim was to find Sangiovese clones that would overcome such problems as uneven ripening, which often meant that the wines made from them had an unpleasant acid character.

Isole e Olena also makes an exceptional Vin Santo, one of the best in the region. When Paolo learned that we had never seen the process, he called on one of the workers to explain how it was made. Tracy, a handsome, very young woman from New Zealand, wore her red hair braided loosely to the nape of her neck, before it cascaded to her shoulders in a gentle pony tail. She wore no makeup, which made her look even younger, but her explanations were the assured and clear words of someone who knew what she was talking about.

It turns out that Vin Santo has its own set of rules, which differ greatly from ordinary winemaking. Usually based on such white grapes as Trebbiano and Malvasia, the initial step is drying the clusters for several months to concentrate the sugars. She took us to the part of the winery dedicated to the drying process where bunches of grapes on bamboo racks were stacked tier upon tier. Some producers, she explained, prefer to hang the clusters rather than place them on trays. When deemed sufficiently dried, which sometimes takes as long as six months, pressing takes place, the juice going into small oak or chestnut barrels. She showed us row upon row of double-stacked casks, where the wine first ferments. Then it rests and concentrates for a minimum of three but sometimes several more years, all the while growing more intense, particularly since some evaporation takes place and nothing is added to top off the barrels. The finished wines are usually between 16 percent and 18 percent alcohol and somewhat gold in color. Served at the end of a meal, they are the perfect foil for dipping biscotti.

That evening we ate dinner in a restaurant in the outskirts of Barbarino named La Sosta del Papa, so-called because long ago a pope had stopped there as a respite from his travels (*"sosta"* means "halt" or "rest" or "stay"). The proprietress, a charming and efficient woman of middle age, discussed the meal with us, took our orders, and delivered each dish. She also acted as sommelier, and recommended a Montóli Sicelle Riserva 1991 from the Pasolini Onda winery, which she said would be perfect with the things we had ordered. When she had uncorked it and we had tasted it, we all agreed that it was without a doubt the best restaurant wine we had had on our trip.

We started our meal with two types of *bruschetta*, that wonderful grilled country bread. One was the traditional *aglio/olio*, the toast first rubbed with garlic, then anointed with olive oil. The other came topped with *cavolo nero*, which in this country we call dinosaur kale. After the appetizers, we tried two egg pastas, *garganelli*, rough-cut shapes that resembled *penne*, and *tagliatelle*, a more familiar noodle to us, but not always so ethereal. Delicious wild *porcini* mushrooms made the sauce for both. Two of us followed with *pollo alla diavola*, chicken flattened and weighted so that when it is cooked the outside gets brown and crisp and the interior remains juicy and moist. Roasted potatoes and a mixed green salad accompanied it. The other two chose *tagliata fiorentina*, slices of an extremely well-seasoned Florentine steak, served in this instance with arugula and slices of raw *porcini* mushrooms. It was extremely good cooking, perhaps the best meal that we had had so far.

When we ordered another bottle of the same wine to go with our main courses, our hostess proposed bringing us a different one from the Pasolini Onda winery that, she assured us, we would like even better. When we agreed, she brought and decanted a 1991 Montóli Chianti Riserva. She was right. It was exceptional. Where did it come from, we wondered, for in all our travels we had neither seen nor heard of it. We asked and her reply astonished us: The winery was on the Via Francesco Barbarino, the main street just inside the arched gate in the village of Barbarino Val d'Elsa.

The next morning we hastened to the end of the street to see for ourselves. Sure enough, just inside the archway and at right angles to it, was a handsome metal entry gate, closed tight, of course, set between two slim brick columns. On one of them small metal letters spelled out FATTORIA PASOLINI DALL ONDA. We must have passed it a million times and not noticed the unobtrusive sign nor realized that the very tall stone wall adjoining the brick columns concealed not a garden but a winery. The owners, the Pasolini family, live just across the street at #1 Via Francesco Barbarino, in the very first house inside the entrance gate to town. How ironic that the best wine we had come across was produced just doors away from us and we didn't even know it.

On the hopes of buying some, we knocked loudly at the entrance. A man responded and grudgingly let us in. It was immediately clear why he was less than cordial. Among other things, their bottling machine had broken down, which meant bottling by hand, which a couple of men were busily doing. Other workers, packing the finished product into six-container cartons, joined them in hurrying to make space for this year's harvest, the picking of which was imminent. It was clear that we were disrupting their work, and so we timidly asked if it we could possibly disturb them enough to buy some wine before we left. They sold us six bottles of the Montóli Chianti Riserva. Happy with our purchase, we thanked them profusely, apologetically bid them farewell, and got out of their way.

Since it wasn't far to get to any place from Barbarino, and there were such varied choices, our hardest problem each day was deciding, sort of triage-like, which destination had the highest priority. We drove through striking landscapes to such places as Certaldo, where we saw the house of Boccaccio and were pleased to find in the library a copy of Charles's book *Chaucer and the French Tradition*. For pure scenery, the most wondrous of all our drives was the serpentine climb to Lamole with incredible views along the way and a breathtaking vista from the top. Another day, we drove to Siena to see once again the stunning Pinturicchio frescoes, brilliantly restored, in the library in the cathedral. We showed Len and Draselle the fine hotel in Vescine, where we had once stayed, located in a charming restored village, all stone, in Radda in Chianti. One day we drove to Lucca, choosing the freeway because it was faster, but opting for beauty over speed, taking the state roads, the *Quatro Corsie*, on the way home. In the old part of Lucca, you can walk on top of the city walls, which we did, and visit the ancient Roman amphitheater, now ringed by houses. It is the colorful scene of a big market on Wednesdays and Saturdays.

Since Len and Draselle had never been to Pisa, we spent a brilliantly sunlit day there. It was a stunning sight, the camposanto, baptistery, cathedral, and leaning tower all gleaming white in the sunshine and accentuated by the vast green lawns into which they were set. This manicured expanse of greenery was new since our earlier visit, but in older days the tower was open to the public and we had dutifully climbed to the top. Under *restauro* for many years, the structure was no longer climbable, therefore sparing Len and Draselle the vertigo that inevitably occurred in conquering the endless skewed and sloping staircases. Along one edge of the complex, in front of the very attractive row houses bordering the long side of the area, we found another new thing: a continuous conglomeration of schlocky souvenir stands—it seemed like a thousand of them—which displayed the worst kind of souvenir garbage imaginable.

One day we drove to Castellina and picnicked on the rock wall surrounding the Convento di Santa Maria near Radda. Another day, we poked around the hill town of Volpaia, a well-restored, fortified twelfth-century village. In Imprunetta, where we lunched on *ribollita*, a thick, twice-cooked Tuscan soup that is a meal in itself, the colorful ceramic plates on which we were served caught our fancy. Fortunately we couldn't track them down because packing and shipping would have been quite a project. On several occasions, we drove to the nearby Badia a Passignano, a practicing abbey, but never got inside because we always turned up when private prayers were beginning. We strolled down the long alley of cypress trees, very old ones judging by their great height and girth, and spent time taking pictures among the profusely blooming bougainvillea in the interior courtyard. The abbey, with its crenellated walls and towers constructed of squares of variegated yellow stone, although many times restored and even partly modified, still conveyed its very early medieval origins. We have a small triangular watercolor of it in our dining room in Berkeley, thanks to the owner of the Galleria Civetta in the piazza in Greve. He gave it to us on one of our many visits because a mutual friend had introduced us to his gallery. Only in Italy.

Whatever our daytime destination, in the evening we always ate dinner in one of a series of unusual restaurants. One night we dined in La Cantinetta di Rignano, a beautiful spot near Greve, with a marvelous view and an outdoor terrace from which to enjoy it. Their menu included homemade *tagliatelle* with fresh truffles, which none of us could resist, and it was one of the best pastas that we had ever had. Although the kitchen specialized in wild game, little was yet available, so we settled for a delicious grilled *galletto*, or young chicken, and roasted pheasant, accompanied by an '88 Chianti Classico. On another night we drove to l'Osteria della Piazza, in the village of Piazza, where we feasted on *pappardelle al cinghiale*, egg pasta with a sauce of wild boar, followed by duck slices that had been stuffed with a mixture of ground meats and finely chopped chestnuts sautéed in the roasting juices. With it, we drank a young Castello della Rampolla and a recently bottled Mona Lisa, both good sturdy red wines.

One of the most flavorful dinners we had was at La Fattoria in Romita close by Tavernelle. The dining room featured a great wood-fueled oven, not only cheerful and warming, but also used for roasting such dishes as crispy baby pork loin and addictively browned young kid, both of which we happily consumed. The only meal that was not up to standards was at La Toppa in San Donato-in-Poggio. Although the trattoria was pleasant enough and obviously popular with the locals, at least judging from the crowds, we found the food extremely salty and very oily. The town, on the other hand, was quite wonderful with its narrow passageways and handsome stone construction, so all was not lost.

Although sometimes we had lunches in the tower—such things as toothsome fresh white beans cooked by the local market, various cold cuts, ripe tomatoes, radicchio, country bread, fruit bursting with flavor, and that remarkable cheese, gorgonzola dolcelatte—we also wanted to try cooking local products for a dinner at home, especially since we had a couple of old wines from Carlo that we wanted to try with a meal. Since we had heard so much about the marvelous butcher in Panzano, one day we set off for that small village to buy a roast of veal. And that is how we came to make the acquaintance of Dario Cecchini, master butcher, and his shop, the Antica Maccelleria Cecchini on the Via XX Luglio.

Panzano, perched high on a hill, is presided over by a tenth-century stone castle. The old part of town, where the butcher shop is, once was the locale of a Roman settlement, like so many places in Italy. The shop itself, over two hundred years old, has been in the Cecchini family since its origins, passed on from father to son, with Dario the last in line to take over. The family has always respected the artisanal quality of their work, and Dario has even followed the old peasant practice of raising a few of his own sheep, pigs, and cattle. Together with the University of Florence, he has also been successfully engaged in ferreting out and growing regional spices, all of them long out of use, that might be used to flavor meat. I currently have a bottle of his special seasoning salt in my kitchen.

When we entered the butcher shop, strains of opera filled the air, and shelves of cookbooks, including volumes by Julia Child in English, shared wall space with garlands of peppers, braids of garlic, bunches of spices, various salamis and cured meats, and old instruments such as scales, meat hooks, and yokes for oxen, some suspended from long metal brackets. What remaining space there was contained oil paintings, a cabinet full of glass jars full of everything from "tuna" (really pork or rabbit put up to resemble tuna, a product for which the shop is famous) to a peppery conserve *(mostarda)*, various dried spice mixtures, and things like brined meats. There was also the door to a walk-in cold box: Through the glass portion you could see whole carcasses of meat waiting to be butchered or hanging to age. The speakers that broadcast the music emerged high among the peppers and herbs.

Tubs of garlic heads and dried spices stood on the floor alongside marble-topped tables crammed with mixing bowls, straw baskets full of apples and peppers, wire baskets filled with eggs, ceramic containers arranged casually with spikes of rosemary and branches of bay leaves, and an assortment of good-sized gourds and, propped against the wall, a huge pumpkin. Strings of small red peppers garlanded the ceiling in gently swooping arches. The meat case itself, on the top of which resided everything from bottles of oil to spicy greenery, showed off a variety of whole, two-foot long salamis and other cured meats, prosciuttos, raw chickens, and such prepared delectables as loaves of country patés, as well as the liver mixture that the Tuscans spoon warm on *crostini*. Little meat balls, *polpettini*, were stuffed with cheese and nuts, and there were slices of roast pork stuffed with spices. There were also many preparations ready to cook, such as pheasant prepared with grapes, a lamb roast that had been rolled around rosemary, or a leg stuffed with cheese and spices. Surprisingly, this warm and friendly conglomeration was not in the least bit chaotic but instead seemed remarkably orderly, like a well-painted still life. Everything in the case looked so appealing that we chose enough to provide several lunches. And then there was our veal roast, cut to size, artfully tied, and milk white. It looked too good to cook.

But cook it we did, stopping for accompaniments on the way home. At the Barbarino supermarket, small in spite of its name, we got the onions, carrots, and garlic to flavor the roast, and a dozen very small potatoes to cook with it. We found some flat romano beans and hearts of artichokes for vegetables, which we planned to cook in a mixture of olive oil, garlic, and minced anchovies. We bought the makings of a mixed green salad, and for dessert, a hunk of parmesan and two kinds of *pecorino*, fresh and aged, to go with Muscat grapes and fresh figs. But no place in the market could we find any herbs, and we needed both sage and rosemary to season the roast. I finally asked the proprietress. There weren't any, but if I waited a minute, she replied, she would go cut them from her garden, which was right next door. She asked how much we needed and, of course, cut more than we could use. And she refused to charge us, smilingly shrugging it off, as if every supermarket did this kind of thing.

With our splendid dinner—for the succulent veal, juicy fresh fruits, and pristine vegetables were really flavorful—we had the two bottles of wine that came from Carlo's cellar: a fine old Ratti Barolo '68, which said on the label, "bottled for Carlo Cipolla by Renato Ratti," and a remarkable '75 Fontanafredda.

Just last summer, we went to Panzano again to visit the butcher shop and found a few changes. First of all, just off the Piazza Gastone Bucciarelli, on a raised triangle where the Via XX Luglio converges with other streets, there is now a thriving bed of flowers and a startling, lifelike sculpture, in true color, of a cow — surely four times the size of the real animal. Next to the doorway itself there is a full-scale reproduction of a T-bone steak, glistening red, and under it the legend, "*Ridotta Invalida Preferí la Morte*," followed by, "*In Memoria della Bistecca alla Fiorentina—Scomparsa Prematuramente il 31 Marzo 2001*" ("Reduced to Invalidity, it Preferred Death"; "In Memory of the Florentine Beefsteak—Disappeared Prematurely the 31 March 2001"). It turns out that when Mad Cow Disease struck in Europe, the Italians passed a law prohibiting the sale of any meat off the bone, which included the T-bone steak from the Chianina cattle, one of the great specialties of Tuscany. Dario, of course, championed the cause of the *bistecca* everywhere, his campaign including menacing photographs of him holding the forbidden cut, sometimes cartoons showing him with horns and cloven feet. Various postcards, one with a "stamp" where the real one would go, show him holding forth the outlawed meat in blazing color.

We also found that the adjacent store, of which we had been unaware on our previous visit, was annexed to the butcher shop. Besides a small table and chairs, it contained an assortment of products under

Dario's label, such as spices and jars of "tuna" and *mostarda*, flasks of olive oil, and a good variety of other tempting edibles. The music now included popular jazz. Several shelves of the ever-growing cookbook collection had expanded into the annex as well.

Annie, Dario's slim red-headed girlfriend, chatted in perfect vernacular Italian into her cell phone. She lives and works in Italy, but hails from Texas. She showed us on one wall a framed article by Johnny Apple, written in his role as a renowned gastronome. Published in the *International Herald-Tribune*, it described the thirtieth birthday celebration of the famous Berkeley restaurant, Chez Panisse, complete with pictures of Alice Waters, the proprietress, and the program of events. It was particularly apropos because now we were visiting the butcher shop in the company of Christopher Lee, at that time the chef at Chez Panisse, his wife Janet, who was in charge of the dining room, and their young son Tom, who had already enjoyed the privilege of butchering lessons from Dario. The framed commemorative poster was on the wall for a reason beyond admiration: when the anniversary party for Chez Panisse had taken place, with the tables set outdoors under the campanile on the campus of the University of California, it had had among its many celebrity guests the butcher from Panzano, Dario Cecchini. Resplendent in purple cowboy boots, no doubt a tribute to Annie, he had regaled the crowd at length by reciting, in Italian, verses and verses of Dante's *Inferno*. Described in the framed article, his recitation was, along with the spectacular food, the high point of the event.

In Tuscany, there was always something new to see, and so many things, like the butcher in Panzano, changed each visit, yet stayed the same. Although the tower in Barbarino had obviously been updated, the feel of the place betrayed its age, and the old stone town, with its narrow cobbled passageways and arched town gates, felt more medieval than modern. Although we knew that we would be back in that area many times in the future, we reluctantly realized that our stay in Barbarino was soon coming to an end. It was necessary to face the practical preparations for our departure. One of which was paying the rent.

When we had originally been in correspondence with the owner of the tower about what the fee would be, she had asked, and we had agreed to, two million *lire* in cash, to be paid at the end of our visit. With that in mind, we had gone to our local branch of the Bank of America and obtained a cashier's check before leaving for Italy. It would cause no problem to exchange it in the branch of the same bank in Florence. A few days before the end of our sojourn, when we had called the *signora* to ask about how we were to deliver the money, she gave us instructions to stuff it into the samovar in the *salotto*.

And so, the day before our departure, we headed for Florence to get the money. We had made reservations for lunch at one of our favorites, the Cantinetta Antinori, a very small and enormously popular wine bar associated with the Antinori vineyards and winery. They serve wines by the glass as well as by the bottle and offer typical Tuscan dishes to go with them. We chose two different soups, a thick *ribollita* and a rustic *pappa al pomodoro*, a dish made with bread and tomatoes. Afterwards, we enjoyed some classic chicken liver *crostini* and *bruschette* topped with *cavolo nero*, and a shared bowl of stewed tripe, just to taste it. Since this was our next to last day, we indulged in a bottle of Antinori Tignanello, expensive even in Italy, but worth it.

After lunch, we stopped at the elegant Ferragamo store nearby. Even if you don't buy anything, it cheers you just to look at all those beautiful things. It had been a perfect afternoon—good lunch, then a leisurely stroll in sparkling sunshine in that most beautiful of cities

—but we finally, reluctantly, had to face reality. This was our last day in Florence, and we had to attend to tomorrow's departure. We headed for the Bank of America.

It wasn't there. We went into the Banca Commerciale d'Italia to inquire, only to find out that the Banca d'America e d'Italia, as it was called in Italy, had closed its doors. A cashier's check, no matter how secure and safeguarded, was not something that the Banca Commerciale would even consider cashing, particularly since it was a Bank of America issue. We made the rounds of the local banks with always the same response. Since we couldn't get two *milione* out of an ATM machine, and personal checks for that amount were not acceptable, we didn't know what to do. Until I suddenly thought of our old friend Sandro. For many years he had lived in Switzerland with his wife Ornella, the owner of the Villa Azalee in Florence where we had often stayed. As a banker he had once worked in the Florentine office of the Banco di Roma. We put in a call to Lausanne. Sandro was fortunately at home. Of course he knew all the bankers in Florence and would immediately call the manager of the Banco di Roma and ask him to honor our check. He phoned and the manager cashed. Suddenly we were coping with two million *lire* worth of paper bills that would not conceivably fit into that samovar.

Back home in the tower, we stuffed and stuffed, packed and crushed, pushed and shoved, crammed and cajoled, until the last crumpled bill finally made it into the silver urn. If we had had one more *lira*, we wouldn't have succeeded. It was a very Italian ending to our stay in the medieval tower of Barbarino Val d'Elsa.

CHAPTER TWELVE

Slow Food

The international organization known as Slow Food came about as a reaction to fast food and other symptoms of the frenzy in our society. The movement celebrates the conviviality of eating together, promotes biodiversity, protects foods on the verge of extinction, and encourages artisans involved in producing and preparing heirloom, local, and handcrafted edibles. Through its publications, it emphasizes the dependent connection of gastronomy to ecology. Its message seems to be that if we all slowed down we could achieve a happier, more harmonious society. Although they are all admirable goals, and ones with which we agree wholeheartedly, until our trip to Garfagnana Charles and I had never heard of the group called Slow Food. It was purely by accident that we learned of it and, although we didn't know it at the time, in a way absolutely true to Slow Food principles. It came about through our pursuit of a foodstuff called *farro*.

An ancient form of wheat, *farro* is the basis of several of the rustic peasant dishes that are a specialty of Tuscany. The grain certainly has been around a long time, at least since Roman times and perhaps a good deal longer. In English it's called "emmer" and comes from a family, *triticum turgidum dicoccum*, that includes the hard wheats used in pasta and bread making. It is often confused with, and sometimes labeled, "spelt," *triticum aestivum*, but the two grains differ, true *farro* being, among other things, much more costly. About fifty years ago, at a time when European food supplies were diminished, most postwar farmers began to replant the difficult-to-harvest grain with strains of wheat that considerably increased their yield. The exception was in the region of Garfagnana, which is still the area where the best *farro* comes from. Because many of their traditional dishes were based on it, the farmers just kept growing it.

Today, you can buy *farro* in specialty markets in the United States and many restaurants offer recipes incorporating it. For several years I have been able to purchase imported nutty brown pasta made with *farro* flour, and have even seen packaged spelt lasagna (but judging by the elevated price, probably it was *farro* mislabeled). In her book *The Essential Mediterranean*, Nancy Harmon Jenkins suggests that the word *farro* has Latin ancestry and gives this example. Before Roman couples married, they offered a white cake made of refined *farro* flour, a *confarratium*, in the Temple of the Vestal Virgins. Their offering evolved into the modern wedding cake.

When we, Len, and Draselle first tasted the grain in a soup in Italy, we all became true fans. We were staying in Barbarino at the time, which was within driving distance of the Garfagnana region, a fact that easily persuaded the four of us to make an investigative excursion. Having heard that there was a fine restaurant several miles above Lucca in the small village of Camporgiano, and that it featured dishes made of *farro*, we had a specific destination.

The drive, one of the most beautiful we had made, took us over mountainous country roads and through innumerable small villages. At last, we reached Camporgiano, where we should have found our restaurant, but in spite of our best Holmesian efforts, it was elusive, nowhere in sight. Armed with directions from people we passed on the road, we eventually found the well-hidden dirt road leading to it. Il Mulino del Rancone, as its name implied, turned out to be an ancient mill on the banks of the Serchio River, with a farm and restaurant attached. Ironically, the train from Lucca stops in Camporgiano not far from the spot. Although the mill has stopped grinding, there is still a working farm that supplies the restaurant. In addition, Il Mulino, as a member of the *agriturismo* group, has simple accommodations for people who want to stay.

Having left our car in the small dirt parking area, we approached the building that housed the restaurant. It being a fine day, those who were taking lunch were at tables outside in the back. The veranda where they were eating is perched high on the hill, partially surrounded by handsome stone walls that are low enough to allow a luxurious view of the verdant terracing across the way and the hillside cascading down below. The fields, planted with vegetables and grains such as corn, rye and *farro*, were the source of much of what was on the menu. For the rest, the farm animals supplied the meat, the rivers produced the fish. In addition, you could buy such products as honey, mushrooms, chestnuts, and *farro*, all of which came from the property, as well as jams and pastries prepared by the kitchen. As we were soon to learn, an ideal Slow Food enterprise.

Two horses tethered at the bottom belonged to some knowledgeable riders who had climbed up the hillside and were enjoying lunch on the terrace. Huge canvas market umbrellas shielded everyone from the sun. There was one other occupied table, and the four men around it were having a hilariously good time. You could tell from their rough dress and the familiar good terms with which they addressed the host, that they were locals, most likely workmen from the village. They had had a good deal of wine, and before their lunch was over they had had a good deal more. We were seated next to them at a large plank table covered with a white tablecloth. We ordered some Chianti and pondered the choices for our meal.

The proprietor, a jolly man who introduced himself as Gabriele Bertucci, the *direttore*, suggested we start with a *farinata*, made with the local *farro*, which had been mixed with frog meat from the river banks, and greens and herbs from the gardens. It was delicious. On his advice, we followed with *tagliatelle al ragu*, cloudlike ribbons of homemade egg pasta bubbling with a rich, meaty sauce. Next, two of us had grilled giant *porcini* mushrooms, the other two a well-seasoned roast of pork. Then there was *insalata mista*, a mixed green salad, all ingredients from the farm, with bottles of oil and vinegar with which to dress it. The exceptional bread, an *integrale* made of *farro* and wheat, and a loaf made of potatoes, were the only things not produced by the farm. They came from a nearby town. Our host cheerfully gave us directions so that we could buy some on our way home. The meal ended with two *semi-freddi*, much like soft ice cream, one of blueberries, the other of apple.

As we were savoring our desserts, the host brought to our neighboring table some *grappa* which he had made, stored in two straw-wrapped demijohns. His friends, more jovial than ever, were still eating—by this time a cheese course—and he poured them each a glass of his brew, followed by a second glass from the other container. Murmurs of approval produced more pours all around and suddenly Signor Bertucci invited us to join in. Immediately fetching glasses from inside, he poured us generous tastes, and stood back to see what we thought. We found that the one in the container covered in green-colored straw was younger, milder, and a lighter, clearer color. The other, in a demijohn covered in natural-colored straw, was a rich amber color, smoother, stronger, and more complex. They both gave a buzz, especially after all the wine we had drunk. Apparently, our appraisals pleased our host. He plunked the two huge containers on our table, fetched himself a glass, and settled in.

He wanted to know all about us: where we were from, where we were staying, and for how long. When he heard we were from California, he asked, as if that state were a small village where everyone knew everyone else, if we happened to know Darrell Corti. We were absolutely amazed! Not only did we know him, but he was a good friend from Sacramento, a second-generation member of a family that for more than half a century had run an extraordinary grocery store and wine emporium called Corti Brothers. After his father's death, Darrell and his sister Illa had taken over. Our host, not surprised in the least by the remarkable coincidence of our knowing Darrell, told us that our friend had recently been to Il Mulino, and he had given a talk on *farro*. The occasion was a dinner, all the dishes of which were based on that ancient grain. Darrell, who knows more about food and wine than anyone I know, had actually been invited to Italy in the first place to talk to a larger group on olives and olive oil production in California.

Signor Bertucci told us that it was not an unusual thing to base a dinner on a single ingredient. Only recently, for example, members from Garfagnana of a group called Slow Food had had an entire dinner based on frogs from the river. He would show us the menu, he said, and was off to search it out. What is Slow Food, we wondered? This was the first time we had ever heard of it, but we were about to learn.

The menu, folded book-style, was blue with a small stylized black snail on each page, the logo of the Slow Food movement, it turned out. The title page announced, "*Il Ranocchio, dall'antipasto al dolce*" or

"The Frog, from antipasto to dessert." With their Prosecco, the diners had had small frogs' legs, marinated before cooking, and some *crostini* covered with a tasty mix of leg meat. That was followed by homemade *tagliolini del Serchio*, light egg noodles with a sauce made of frog meat. A white San Torpé accompanied the pasta. Next there was a *farronata*, spelled as a pun that reflected the grain it was based on, with herbs and greens and shredded frog mixed in, the same dish we had just found so delicious. Rosé Balza went with it. There were two main courses: small stewed frogs served with green beans, and larger frogs, fried and garnished with potatoes. These were washed down by a Chianti Classico, Consorzio Gallonero. It is hard to imagine a frog dessert, but they had one, a *dolce ranato*. I have no idea what that is, but perhaps, instead of something with frog meat in it, it was a pastry like *buccellato*, a specialty from nearby Lucca, baked in the shape of a frog. It came with an accompanying dessert wine, Dolcetto Balan. On the back of the menu was the date, time, and place of the dinner, and the local Slow Food chapter with its address.

When it was clear that we couldn't eat or drink another thing, our host suggested a tour of the property. Walking sounded appealing and we were curious to see the old mill, so we readily agreed. Literally on the banks of the river, the stone building that housed the mill had arched openings to give ready access to the water. The ground floor, where the milling took place, was divided into four large binlike sections, one for storing and grinding *farro*, another for corn, one for wheat, and the fourth for chestnuts. The massive stone wheels, once used to pulverize the grain, remained in place, making it possible to visualize the mill at work. Chestnut flour is used in Tuscany for cakes and special pancakes called *necci*. Sometimes you could find them in Florence on the second and third Sunday of the month in the flea market in Piazza Santo Spirito. Lucia Andreotti and Giorgio Maffucci, who made them, owned an organic farm in Piteglio near Pistoia, with two rooms to rent. They often prepared *necci* for their guests.

Before we departed, our host handed us a colorful brochure that included a membership application for Slow Food. Written in Italian, it gave descriptions of the many activities that being a member encompassed. We were intrigued. The pamphlet, obviously designed for future Italian members (Italy, we later learned, was where the movement started) also emphasized the international character of the organization. Quoting from the brochure, Slow Food was inspired by such rationales for slowing down as "pleasure, conviviality, knowledge, solidarity, and tolerance." We were determined to find out more about this organization and its branches in the United States. We did, and it's a compelling story.

The movement took root late in 1985 when McDonald's planned to open a restaurant in Rome at the very foot of the Spanish Steps in the Piazza di Spagna. Carlo Petrini, a young man from Bra in the Piedmont area, had a fervent interest in things artisanal and agricultural, as well as theatrical, musical, and left-wing political. He was outraged. For several years, as a way of educating others, he had used both radio and journalism to express his views on the pleasures and inestimable importance derived from good food and wine, and how they were in danger of disappearing. He and a group of his friends, who shared strong sensuous beliefs in preserving and enjoying traditional gastronomic values, found that McDonald's and its fast food was the antithesis of all they believed in.

By the summer of 1986, these compatriots had formed a nonprofit organization devoted to their principles, and elected Carlo Petrini their president. They called it Arcigola, after an innovative magazine, *La Gola*, whose concepts they admired. They published an evaluative wine review as a removable section of the daily journal

Il Manifesto. Within a year, the wine review was printed as a separate guide, *Il Gambero Rosso*, which soon became, and still is, the preferred reference for wine lovers and professionals alike. Based on that success, a critical restaurant guide *Osterie d'Italia* followed, emphasizing genuine, traditional eateries. The group was the first to picket the Rome McDonald's, before it was even built. Their efforts got the establishment to eliminate the golden arches, preserving the dignity and sanctity of the Piazza di Spagna, but not, alas, the restaurant itself and its emphasis on fast food.

Clearly something more than protesting had to be done. Backed by a strong constituency of likeminded sympathizers—subscribers to the guides, for example—Arcigola, by 1989, had formulated a manifesto, had convened a meeting in Paris involving delegates from twenty countries, had adopted the name Slow Food, had agreed on a snail as the organization's logo, and had set up shop as a nonprofit international movement. Among its fundamental precepts, the manifesto declares that capitulating to speed has forced us into a lifestyle which, besides eroding our habits and invading our privacy, entails giving up civilized dining in favor of fast food; that if we don't watch out, we'll become at risk for extinction; that we should not "mistake frenzy for efficiency"; that real culture is about "developing taste rather than demeaning it"; and that "quiet, material pleasure," and "doses of . . . sensual pleasure and slow, long-lasting enjoyment," are our salvation.

Slow Food now has more than 75,000 members in over 50 countries. Its local chapters, called *convivia*, alluding to the underlying commitment to conviviality, now number over 600. The goals have expanded from the preservation of our food heritage to searching out and protecting those animals and foodstuffs in danger of extinction. Efforts at biodiversity and ecology insure a responsible use of the land and its products. Publications include *Slow*, a first-rate journal published in English, Italian, French, Spanish, and German, and handsomely designed with full-color photographs and illustrations. The articles, many of them on unusual subjects encompassing global gastronomic interests, are written by well-known writers and experts from around the world. The issues are sent to all members at least quarterly, as is *Snail*, the members' newsletter. There is also an informative Web site and various relevant books on such topics as cheese or wine.

In 2002, a small California publisher, Chronicle Books, put out an extremely handsome volume—a luscious color photo practically on every other page—giving a detailed account of the history of Slow Food, profiles of typical food artisans at work around the world, and a section of traditional recipes that underline the basic concepts of the organization. The book, by a well-known journalist, Corby Kummer, persuasively portrays the power of the ideals that created the movement.

Several years ago, Mr. Kummer, for a long time a recognized voice in the food world and for more than thirty years a senior editor of *Atlantic Monthly*, received an invitation to the Salone del Gusto in Turin, one of many projects that Slow Food has conceived. A grand exhibition devoted to the culture of food, the Salone provides regional foods, tastes, and flavors; offers meals prepared by leading chefs from around the world; addresses such topics as bionics, genetic engineering, and other important contemporary issues; and conducts educational seminars leading to a better understanding of how authenticity can result in better food and a better lifestyle. All this, set among the cultural treasures of Piedmont (the Regional Authority of Piedmont is a collaborator), has given the Salone the pleasurable status of one of the great international food events.

Corby's invitation came to him from Patrick Martins, a young and energetic Slow Food enthusiast from New York, who had spent several years in Italy working with Carlo Petrini in the headquarters in Bra. With his Italian wife, he returned some years ago to this country as the hardworking president of Slow Food USA. When he issued the invitation to Corby Kummer, journalist, he surely had in mind Corby's writing about the charismatic Carlo Petrini and his seductive ideas. But Slow Food was based on ideals so convincing to the editor that, besides writing about them for his magazine, he spent the next five years exploring the concepts through study, research, and travel. Then he got a phone call from a publisher interested in expanding the article into a book, and that is how *The Pleasures of Slow Food: Celebrating Authentic Traditions, Flavors, and Recipes*, was born.

Among its credits, Slow Food has kept from extinction everything from lentils from the Abruzzi region of Italy to Sun Crest peaches grown near Fresno, California. Saving good old-fashioned turkeys is one of the most successful projects in the United States. Heritage turkeys, five endangered breeds that, unlike the overbred, broad-breasted, mostly white-meated fowl that we've become accustomed to, are phenomenally juicy, have more dark meat, are succulent and rich, and can even fly. By supporting a market for them, Slow Food promised the original twenty farmers who agreed to raise them that they could sell them at worthwhile prices. One could even order turkeys in advance for the Thanksgiving table. When Marion Burros, who wrote an extremely informative piece about them in the *New York Times*, roasted several of the endangered breeds, she found them incomparably delicious.

Another success story involves the nearly extinct white wine called Chachetra, vinified solely in the Italian region of Cinque Terre. Anyone who has been to that area knows that the incredible landscape—vast, steep, terraced hillsides overhanging the sea—makes the idea of growing grapes seem mind-bogglingly impossible. Even the promise of such breathtaking views doesn't persuade most people to drive there (foolhardily, we did). Many of the narrow winding roads are literally dangerous cliffhangers. Several winters ago portions of the roadway actually collapsed or were rendered impassable because of mudslides. The majority of visitors either hike, if they are rugged, or take the train wending its way along the bottom of the hills. It makes stops at the five small fishing hamlets, storybook-charming, that are the only villages of the Cinque Terre. In this unlikely place, Chachetra has been produced since the middle ages. Only in recent times had the wine become increasingly unprofitable for the three remaining producers. Slow Food got together a consortium of interested private and public backers who helped buy one and a half acres of vineyard. Now the winemakers, owning the land without cost, can afford workers to help, thus preserving the rare wine, and perhaps even increasing its eventual production.

In 2001, Carlo Petrini published his own volume, *Slow Food*, printed on permanent and durable acid-free paper. It is slim but definitive. The latest enterprise is the University of Gastronomic Sciences, with two campuses in Pollenzo-Bra and Colorno, near Parma in Emilgia-Romagna. It proclaims the validity of gastronomy as a true part of academia through both research projects and teaching. Additional opportunities for students to travel in Italy and experience first-hand its sources of foods and wines will be called "stages." The Pollenzo campus opened in October 2004 with the program on gastronomy; the Colorno campus, devoted to Agro-ecology, is scheduled to open sometime later.

Since our accidental introduction in Garfagnana, for some years now we have actually been bona fide members of the Slow Food movement. We have two small gold snail pins to prove it. We are confident that among other genuine things, *farro* will be around for our grandchildren to enjoy—slowly.

CHAPTER THIRTEEN

The Pharmacy of Santa Maria Novella and Other Tuscan Adventures

The historic Farmacia of Santa Maria Novella in Florence dates back to 1221. Although it is no longer a monastic enterprise, the laymen who took it over have largely preserved its earliest furnishings and original appearance. To enter there is like stepping back into another age. The vast heights of the room, the decorated arches, the ceiling frescoes, the rose window, the bronze and wooden statuary, the glass-fronted Gothic cabinets with old bottles of colored elixirs, truly immerse you in an earlier time. Immediately, as you pass the portal and enter the corridor that leads to the pharmacy, there is a perfume in the air, unusual scents of wild flowers and herbs, that wafts over and almost overwhelms you. You can't help but be transported.

It all began in the mid-thirteenth century with a group of Dominican brothers who had been assigned to the church of Santa Maria Novella (it was then called Santa Maria Fra le Vigne, or Santa Maria

Among the Vineyards). Devoted to charity, which encompassed the care of the sick, they established an infirmary for the ill friars among them, and were soon treating them with herbal pharmaceuticals. There is a written record of the sale of rosewater through the church infirmary as early as 1381. It was then used both as medicine and antiseptic. Many purchasers thought the scented water to be efficacious against the plague.

For years, the dispensing of medicinals was an informal, though continuous, adjunct of the order. By the mid-sixteenth century, the brothers were gathering their own herbs and plants, the sources of their remedies and other products, which had by this time become widely famous. Physicians began directing their patients to purchase prescribed medicines at Santa Maria because of their superior quality. Further, the enlarged pharmacy continuously multiplied its production of unguents and creams, perfumes and soaps, all based on the scents of herbs and flowers.

Santa Maria also employed alchemy to yield such therapies as a curative potion of drinkable gold. Along with its other products, it was dispensed to buyers worldwide, including some in China. By the eighteenth century, the pharmacy was compounding theriac, a complicated medicinal, whose formula contained the flesh of vipers. The chief pharmacist created alkermes, a liqueur which purchasers believed was not only a relaxant (perhaps alcohol-laced like some modern tonics we know of) but had a wide range of healing properties as well. In a pharmacy recipe book, dated 1734, there are exact directions (then called receipts) for *Alchermes Liquida*. On the same page is a recipe for Anti-hysteria Water, *Acqua Antisterica*, which used to be one of my favorite purchases. It made a great gift. The reason I say "used to" is because several years ago, much to my chagrin, they changed the name to *Acqua di S.M. Novella*. No doubt it is just as effective as a medicine, but it is no longer gift-worthy. All of this production brought in a considerable income which, over the years, contributed in part to the prosperity of the monastery, and in part to the enlargement, rebuilding, and beautification of the church, including the installation of many works of art.

Both the popularity and the number of products kept increasing, and with them the profits. With the burgeoning traffic and the small space, it seemed more and more necessary to create a larger sales-room. The former Chapel of San Niccolò, which had fallen into disuse and serious disrepair as the result of various religious suppressions and government edicts, seemed to have the perfect location and size. Profits from the sale of pharmaceuticals paid for an elegant and complete restoration and conversion in the 1840s. Outside of the big vertical neon sign announcing SANTA MARIA NOVELLA, not much else—this room, its furnishings, art, windows, or frescoes—has been replaced or altered since its nineteenth-century restoration. The only augmentation is to the list of products.

Although the pharmacists have dropped *l'Acqua della Regina*, an essence created when Catherine of Medici became queen of France, nowadays you can find honeys, vinegars, candles, sachets, after-shave lotions, perfumes, toilet waters, creams and unguents for the body, powders, oils, dentifrices, shampoos, and more than a dozen different soaps. It takes some thought to decide among the specific formulas for delicate skin, for dry skin, for oily skin, without per-fume, perfumed with gardenia, almond, Iris, mint, lavender, rose, patchouli, vetiver, gardenia, verbena, violet, pot pourri, or pome-granate, to give an incomplete example. There are even soaps for weekend visitors and hand-painted ceramic soap dishes to put them in.

The current list of products also includes remedies for curing whatever ails your hands and feet; potions and creams that provide hygiene for the hair, scalp, and skin; and preventatives for sunburn as well as emollients in case you didn't use them. Some products are created especially for children—vitamin oil, protective skin cream, shampoo, bubble bath, each perfumed differently for boys and girls. Everything smells wonderful. But, unless you have made a decision beforehand and know exactly what you want, this is not a place for hurried shoppers.

You can still visit the old rooms of the original pharmacy, the first of which, the *erboristeria*, opens onto the garden. Adjoining the first room, the old dispensary is much smaller than the new one, but equally grand with its furbelowed multicolored stucco ceiling, elaborate wood carvings swirling above the glass-fronted wooden cabinets, a crystal chandelier, and a fascinating collection of substances that had been created by the pharmacy, as well as a selection of museum-quality antique pharmaceutical tools once used in their production.

The ancient equipment includes old balance scales, bronze and marble mortars and pestles, various seventeenth-century ceramic jars made and strikingly decorated in Montelupo, and classic white lidded vessels made by the still revered firm of Ginori, already notable for its porcelains in the 1800s. Two extraordinary glass thermometers, dating from the seventeenth century, have no resemblance to their modern successors, looking more like fanciful Christmas tree ornaments. One of them is tall and delicate, the other spiraled and shorter, both partly colored by the pink ethyl alcohol that runs through their glass veins and makes them function.

Charles and I marveled at a remarkable collection of ancient editions. One of the most important tomes, a seventeenth-century edition of the *Ricettario Fiorentino*, was first published in 1498 at the behest of local authorities. It remains the earliest public recording of the medical products and their recipes then permitted for sale in Florentine pharmacies.

The cabinets also contain a collection of handsome fifteenth- and sixteenth-century clear glass stills. One, a small alembic type, too large to fit on the shelves, resembles a conical dunce's cap of tin and copper, its spout pointing down like an elephant's tail. Larger alembics, very much in evidence in a faded photograph of the distillery, were relied on in earlier days for refining the ingredients of some of the products of the pharmacy.

Since its beginnings, all of the pharmaceuticals and preparations of the *Officina Profumo Farmaceutica de Santa Maria Novella* have been based on natural components of the highest quality, cultivated using natural methods, and never tested on animals. In short, organic. Early organic. Astoundingly, today you can obtain many of the products in small branches of the pharmacy in Rome, Milan, Paris, London, and a few other cities, and occasionally a very limited number of soaps and unguents in fancy shops like Gump's in San Francisco. But no recent offshoot can ever compare to the long history and mystique of the original premises.

Although Florence responds to the latest trends, such as the mixing of Asian and Western cultures—an example would be the extremely modern and aptly named Fusion Bar and Shozan Gallery—it is hard not to be reminded at every turn, including such visits as one to the Pharmacy of Santa Maria Novella, of that city's deep historical and cultural roots. One thinks of old monuments such as the Ponte Vecchio as unchanged from its medieval origins, yet at one time it had in its middle a thriving piazza where crowds could socialize, the remnants of which are there today. From shops along its sides, butchers and greengrocers sold their wares, and artisans and repairmen provided their services. There wasn't a jeweler among them. It was only at the turn of the sixteenth century that goldsmiths replaced the tradesmen, as well as the entire food market.

Restaurants often reflect history as well, if only tangentially. For example, Omero, where they serve such Tuscan classics as *crostini* and *bistecca*, is right across the street from Galileo's house, which gives one pause. Sostanza, which serves many of the same specialties, remains one of the disappearing examples of an old Florentine custom, a restaurant that is attached to a small food store: entering the dining room, one passes a counter selling foodstuffs before getting to the table.

Perhaps the restaurant Cibrèo makes the most significant connection to the past with its menu of old Tuscan dishes modified slightly for the modern palate. They will even make the classic Renaissance dish of *cibrèo*, after which the restaurant took its name, with a few days prior notice. The reason for the advance timing is that the recipe calls for such hard-to-find chicken parts as unlaid eggs, wattles, crests, and sometimes testicles (in an old Italian cookbook, I've seen a list of ingredients calling for same). It is possible to make a modern-day version using just the giblets and liver of the fowl, which are also called for, but why bother? Here is the recipe (without the testicles):

𝕽 𝕽

Boil ¼ lb. chicken wattles and combs for 5 minutes. Refresh under cold water.

Drain.

In a skillet, heat 3 tbsp. butter until bubbly. Mix in about 1 tbsp. flour, stirring until smooth.

Add 1 small onion finely minced with several branches of parsley (preferably broad leafed or Italian).

When the onion is translucent, add 1 lb. chicken livers, ½ lb. veal kidneys, and the parboiled wattles and combs, cut in two or three sections. Turn heat down and simmer for about 6 minutes or until kidneys are tender.

Add ½ cup dry white wine and ½ cup chicken stock and cook until the gravy is thickened.

Mix the juice of a small lemon with 1 egg yolk and slowly add 2 tbsp. of the gravy, stirring well until smooth. Blend slowly with the skillet mixture, stirring to prevent lumps.

Add salt and pepper to taste.

Add the unlaid eggs (no number specified). Simmer briefly until everything is tender.

Serve immediately while piping hot.

I can't truthfully give the number of servings, but let me say that one portion gave four of us more than ample tastes. I don't think any of us could have eaten a full plate. It is such a rich main course that, according to legend, Catherine de' Medici, one of whose favorites it was, nearly expired after she ate too much of it. On the other hand, there are very old Italian texts, like Artusi's *l'Arte di Mangiar Bene*, that praise its simplicity as a delicate and gentle stew, beneficial for convalescents and for those with queasy stomachs. Along with many other things, our taste in food has obviously changed for the lighter.

Cibrèo, which was founded in 1979, has always been an expensive and somewhat fancy dining room, its menu based largely on traditional old regional recipes. The pricey dishes range from such simple standbys as *farinata col cavolo nero*, polenta topped with black cabbage (dinosaur kale), to *polpettine di ricotta e vitella*, ricotta and veal croquettes, "one of the dishes most frequently requested by our customers," according to Benedetta Vitali, formerly one of the chef-owners, now moved on to Zibibbo. The restaurant enhances the *farinata*, basically cornmeal mush topped with sautéed kale, garlic, and a little olive oil, by adding lots of grated parmesan cheese, much more oil, and a great deal of style. In another glorified variation of polenta, they incorporate traditional herbs like sage and rosemary, together with marinated green peppers, grated cheese, and lots of butter. It is typical to serve sophisticated versions of basically humble dishes like *sformati*, flans, based on such things as spinach, or more complex combinations using meats such as tongue. Tripe often appears on the menu, frequently in a salad. Shellfish as well. Two pounds of squid, cooked with chili peppers, red wine, various aromatics, and a surprising two pounds of spinach, becomes *calamari in inzimino*. There are the usual boiled meats including tongues and tails, and a most wonderful puréed yellow pepper soup.

A dozen years ago, those in the know went around to the back where an unmarked entrance led into a small rustic room with a few wooden tables. There, at less then half the price, one could order, from a slightly abridged dining room menu, the same dishes that had been cooked in the same, shared kitchen. Since there was no restroom in the back, if you needed to use the bathroom you had to pass through the kitchen to get to the facility located in the front. I seem to remember that in the early days there was a sign over the back entry that said OLIO ET VINO, which must have been relevant before the premises became the secret "back door" restaurant. Alas, that eating place no longer exists. The former doorway to it is simply a rear entrance to Cibrèo's kitchen.

For a time, Benedetta also ran a separate shop on the property which sold her baked goods and such remarkable foodstuffs as raisins preserved in grape leaves. Across the street from the restaurant, a bar and café, also owned by Cibrèo, serves an assortment of extremely tasty snacks along with your glass of wine. It was especially handy, we discovered, when we went to the new trattoria, Vinerina Cibrèino. In the same building as the original restaurant, it is the latest enterprise of Fabbio Picchi, Benedetta's former husband, now the sole owner of all the Cibrèo enterprises. Like the former unmarked back room, it doesn't take reservations. However, if your name is on the waiting list, you can settle in at the bar across the way, whiling away the time with some delicious wine and tasty hôrs d'oeuvre. When your table is ready, someone will come across to fetch you. The food is both excellent and original. It has become one of our favorite Florentine restaurants.

Preserving, serving, and partaking of old recipes is one experience that connects to culinary history, but staying on a working farm gives a different historical perspective. Agricultural estates have been around for a long time, and in the last many years, a number of them, all over the country, have begun to take in lodgers. This movement, called *agriturismo*, enables tourists to experience a connection to the environment, albeit in rather comfortable surroundings.

Charles, Ora, Tanya, and I stayed a few years ago in one of the *agriturismo* farms, the Antica Fattoria La Parrina. The estate dates back to the first years of the nineteenth century when it was the residence of newly wedded descendents of two noble Florentine families. The old farm, most beautifully preserved, grows on its thousand acres a variety of fruits and vegetables, makes its own olive oil, produces sheep's, goat's, and cow's milk cheeses from its own animals, as well as an assortment of yogurts, and gathers flowers and herbs from its abundant gardens. It uses old methods (but modern equipment) to produce unusual honeys, including one, made only in the Maremma area of Tuscany, from *paluiris spina Christi*, a particularly spiny wild hawthorne bush that grows in those parts.

The Fattoria also makes some half-dozen fine wines under the Parrina label. Vines have been cultivated in this region perhaps since Etruscan times, but were certainly thriving by the time of Spanish control. In fact, the Spanish word for grapevine, *parra*, is the origin of the name Parrina. Because they are close to the coast, the vineyards are blessed by sea breezes, and a climate and rainfall that are favorable to grape cultivation. Besides wine, the other products of the estate, including its flowers and herbs, are for sale in the farm store. Many of the shoppers come from far around the neighborhood.

All of the farm animals have spirited names—one pony is called Gaio, for example, and one of the sheep is Vespa—and the store has a chalk board which tells you when each animal is due for milking. There are also specific signs marked on the internal roadway, such as the one pointing to Exit, or *Uscita*, a designated right turn for people and another route indicated for animals.

The main villa, with rooms for the paying guests, consists of a grand historic house with an enormous shaded veranda surrounded by spacious gardens. Its large yet intimate lounges are decorated with fine paintings and furnishings, and the property also contains a private church, above which are several fully equipped rental apartments. If guests wish to have dinner on the farm, there is an elegant small dining room. The night we ate there, the service was extremely cordial and the various dishes beautifully cooked. It was a luxurious experience for the four of us, and unlike the modern propensity for a noisy, bustling ambience, this was remarkably serene, allowing, for a change, a camaraderie based on conversation.

An even more remarkable experience is visiting an entire restored village. In Charles's and my case, it was the medieval hamlet, the Borgo of San Felice, in Castelnuovo Berardenga. A sparkling hill town not far from Siena, the tiny village radiates like a sunny day, reflecting the uniformly light golden stone with which it is built. Several small dwellings house the townsfolk, mostly people who now work in the winery or olive oil factory or staff the local hotel. A member of the Relais & Châteaux affiliation, the deluxe hostelry accommodates some seventy or more lucky people. Set among immaculately manicured gardens, the hotel includes a shimmering blue swimming pool and a handsome restaurant, whose tables, set with white linens, flowers, crystal, and delicate china, presage an elegant experience.

We learned about the village several years ago in California when a mutual friend, who knew of our interest in wine and Italy, introduced us to Gianfranco Campione, a visitor who happened to be the marketing director of the San Felice project. He was a charming and erudite man and we became instant friends. During the course of his stay, he told us all about the Tuscan village, its history, and its current developments.

As far back as the beginning of the eighth century, when the fertile soil was already producing successful crops of olives, grapes, and grains, it had become a prize over which feuding local factions warred continuously. By medieval times, it was a walled hilltop village. In recent, modern days, a big Italian insurance company bought the whole property, including some 1800 acres of vineyards, and the olive groves and oak forests that surrounded it. Their aim was to restore the primitive habitat to the original stone architecture typical of rural Tuscany, to build the San Felice winery and a grand hotel, to modernize the production of olive oil, and to engage in a scientific investigation of various grapes relevant to winemaking. Gianfranco suggested that we should come and see for ourselves on our next visit to Italy.

We have now been to San Felice several times, enjoyed extensive tours of the village, its vineyards and winery, the olive oil facility, and the neighboring Ricasoli estate, where the baron of that name first formulated the classical Chianti blend: prescribed percentages of red Sangiovese, red Canaiolo, white Trebbiano, and white Malvasia. After 1967, anyone who deviated from the formula could not use the official label designation of *Denominazione di Origine Controllata*, or D.O.C. To depart from such rigid prescriptions has been part of the recent movement to modernize Italian winemaking.

The Agricola San Felice winery, in the center of town, besides producing some 130,000 cases of fine wine each year, is involved in research dedicated to preserving the authentic traditions of Chianti while at the same time pursuing innovative oenological experiments, many of them in association with the Universities of Florence, Siena, and Piacenza. Perhaps its most important collaborative project, done in partnership with the University of Florence, is the search for and conservation of *viziati:* old vines, among them lesser known Tuscan varieties, as well as those that lost popularity after growers adopted the official formula for Chianti wine. The researchers amazingly traced some 260 *viziati*, with such names as Palle di Gatto, or Cat's Balls; Boggiolè, the Italian version of Beaujolais; and Pisciancione, literally pale red wine resembling urine. The old vines came from broad areas of Tuscany, and now grow on the seven-plus acres that San Felice donated for them. Affiliated with this experiment into the past, San Felice undertook a search for the best clonal variety of Sangiovese, the principal grape used in making Chianti. They planted it in a small, artisanally farmed plot. When they harvested it, the grapes produced an exceptional wine, Poggio Rosso, a traditional Chianti Classico Riserva, made in the traditional way.

Also in the pursuit of making better wine, they planted extraterritorial grapes, that is, Italian ones that came from outside the region, as well as several European varieties, to see how they would fare in the microclimate and soil of Tuscany. By the late sixties and into the seventies, San Felice was cultivating acres of Chardonnay, Pinot Blanc, Riesling, and Cabernet Sauvignon. One of the products, a fine San Felice wine called Vigorello, the first Chianti made entirely of red grapes, incorporates Cabernet Sauvignon and Sangiovese Grosso with the traditional fruit. Italian wines began appearing under the labels of the European varietals from which they were made and winemakers discovered that foreign grapes, mixed with more traditional Tuscan types, lent them subtleties and complexities, elevating the quality of Chianti.

In the late eighties we first sampled some of these wines—very much a reflection of the new trends in Tuscan winemaking—when Gianfranco arranged a special tasting for us. We tried blends of European grapes with standard Tuscan ones, among them an '82 Predicato di Biturica, an '82 Brunello di Montalcino (made on a property owned by San Felice in nearby Campogiovanni), and an '82 Vigorello. Others, like the deep red '83 Grigio di San Felice, with the typical rose and violet nose of a Chianti Classico, had spent an untraditional two years in Yugoslavian oak. We even sipped a floral and perfumy 100 percent Chardonnay, a fresh young varietal that had prospered on the experimental acres that the winery had dedicated to it.

Besides the primary production of table wines, a Vin Santo Santuccio dessert wine is processed in the traditional way, including slow fermentation in small oak casks. *Grappa*, made in a small distillery on the San Felice property, makes use of the lees of Chianti Classico.

The extra virgin olive oil production, another mainstay of the property, had a tremendous setback during the terrible freeze in the winter of 1985. Following the freeze, many of the old trees succumbed, as they did in much of Tuscany, and processing was reduced to a minimum. Although there is some regeneration, it will still be several years before the olive cultivars regain their previous abundance. The San Felice label has long been considered one of the exceptional oils of the region. Several of the finest varieties of olives go into it. Hand picking, though time consuming, lessens bruising. A single crushing done with huge granite millstones from the Alps relies on an ancient method that least alters the quality. The final step, after the sediment is separated, is a period of settling in large clay vessels. Only then is it time to bottle.

CHAPTER FOURTEEN

Truffles

I t was by pure coincidence that we met Paolo and Margherita Urbani in, of all unexpected places, Trenton, New Jersey. It was in the early sixties, at a time when my mother also lived in Trenton. Knowing that the Urbanis had originally come from Italy, she gave them a book I had written on the various regions that were represented by the cooking and restaurants of Rome. It was their fascination with my writing about Italian cuisine that brought us together. We had no idea when we met that they had any connection to food, let alone to luxurious truffles, but it turned out that they were the sole importers and ran the United States branch of Urbani truffles from Scheggino di Spoleto. In fact, Paolo's Uncle Carlo, who owned the firm—the world's largest producer and distributor of that rare form of fungus—was the foremost truffle entrepreneur in Italy. Although it was our mutual interest in good food that cemented our friendship, we didn't realize how fortunate our meeting would actually turn out to be.

For one thing, since truffles at that time were sold mostly to fancy restaurants and upscale hotels and were difficult to locate in stores, we got to order them directly through Margaret and Paul. In those days, according to an old bill I kept, one-quarter of a pound of white truffles came to $85, and three-quarters of a pound of black "diamonds" came to $165, air special delivery from New York included. During the last few years, truffles have cost as much as $3,000 a pound.

Another unforeseen blessing that derived from knowing Margaret and Paul was the unforgettable visit they arranged for us to meet the Urbani family in Italy. They notified the heads of the clan, Uncle Carlo and Aunt Olga, that we were coming, and gave us their telephone number in Scheggino. They filled us in on relevant information so that we would be aware that Carlo's sons, Bruno and Paolo, were sharing much of the work those days. Also by way of preparation, they cautioned us that the family spoke French and Italian, but no English. They drew us a map showing the location of Scheggino, a village in Umbria about eighty miles north of Rome, midway between Spoleto and Terni. They even mentioned that all the roads and highways leading to the village were very good. When we received a cordial telegram from the Italian Urbanis telling us that as soon as we arrived in Italy we should telephone them to arrange our visit to Scheggino, the trip became a reality.

When we arrived in the village, following the excellent directions by telephone, we found Olga and Carlo's home without difficulty. The entire family had assembled to greet us: Paolo, the older son; Bruno, then the mayor of Scheggino; daughter Sandra, who lived fifteen miles away in nearby Terni; daughter-in-law Ada; and two grandchildren, both handsomely dressed up for the occasion. As we talked over glasses of Campari and vermouth in the living room, we learned that Mayor Bruno lived in a restored twelfth-century walled monastery, of which he used perhaps forty of the hundred-odd rooms. A generous and civic-minded man like his father, he got credit for many improvements in Scheggino. The new apartments and homes, the new bridges, the improved street lighting, a refurbished town plaza, had come about at his behest. His father had long been known for the support he gave of his workers, among other things providing them with affordable housing. His generous contributions to schools and medical facilities benefited the whole community.

As we chatted, Carlo referred to truffles as "the perfume of nature." When we asked how to define that elusive perfume, that taste, Bruno pointed out that black and white truffles have different flavors, both impossible to pinpoint. He quoted Brillat-Savarin: "The flavor is simply the flavor of a truffle." But according to his writings, that author had also detected a hint of garlic in white truffles. And he did say that they were "the diamond in the art of cooking." High praise, but hardly descriptive. A number of other connoisseurs have taken a stab at defining the indefinable, using such adjectives as earthy, pungent, inexplicable, smoky, nutty, musky, dank, mushroomy, funky, decadent, and—only for white truffles—akin to overripe cheese. If they smell of ammonia, they are overripe and are going downhill.

We learned that the Greeks wrote appreciatively about them and that the Romans thought so highly of truffles that they dedicated them to Venus. Apicius, even in his early days as a cookbook writer, gave several recipes for truffles. Except for a period of disdain during the Middle Ages, when they were known as "witches' spit" because of their pungent aroma, truffles have always been prestigious, costly, and suspected of having aphrodisiac qualities. Napoleon supposedly sired his only son after a meal of truffles, and promptly promoted his chef. There may be something to it. Studies by German researchers have isolated chemical pheromones in the fungus that are common also to boar and human testes, human male perspiration, and sometimes women's urine. Secreted through the salivary glands of the male boar, they make the female pigs go ga-ga. There is relatively twice as much of the stuff in a truffle.

Carlo, talking about his own background, told us that he was born into a poor peasant family. His lifelong involvement with the mysterious fungus began in his youth when he started helping his father with his small truffle business in Scheggino, where the current firm still has its headquarters. Paolo interceded. Carlo's rags-to-riches success, he told us, is only part of the story. It also goes the other way. "The money that the rich pay for truffles finds its way back to the truffle hunters, poor people. This is the spirit of the whole operation. I think also of the old man who can no longer walk without great difficulty but still he can depend on his dog to run 200 meters and find the truffles for him. I really find this is beautiful."

In describing the philosophy behind the firm, Carlo explained that, "although we have built a great and modern factory, unique in the world, we haven't employed peculiar or complicated techniques. Truffles are virgin, pure, uncontaminated, genuine—in a word, natural things. What we do is extremely simple. Picking—done by the farmer with the help of a dog in the woods; washing—done in tanks with fresh water; sterilization and sorting." Carlo promised us a tour of the factory after we had dined.

The meal we were about to eat came entirely from the family farms, with one exception. The dessert was baked in Terni, in a shop famous for its pastries. When we got to the dining room, the large table, covered with an elegant white banquet cloth of lace and linen, held place settings that shimmered with silver and glistened with crystal. What was surprising to us, for we had never seen it before, was a stack of colorful ceramic plates at each place. Piled one on top of the other for each of the successive courses, they ranged from the largest on bottom to the smallest on top. The dessert, cut into individual portions, was served separately. Throughout the meal, the staff poured generous glasses of red wine from faceted crystal decanters. Of course, the grapes had been grown and the wine made on the property.

Almost every dish of the meal that followed was, not surprisingly, lavishly slathered with truffles. We began with an antipasto of canapés, toasted squares of rough-textured homemade bread from the Urbanis' wood-burning ovens, abundantly spread with chopped black truffles. This was accompanied by a platter of prosciutto, made from their own pigs. The excellent bread that had been grilled for the canapés was served throughout the meal. Next came an indescribable salad: generous amounts of sliced fresh black and white truffles tossed with gruyère, prosciutto, raw mushrooms, olive oil, lemon juice, a scattering of salt, and a good grind of black pepper. *Lumache, al dente* snail-shaped pasta, became the perfect foil for a rich brown sauce of puréed fresh trout from their own streams, first cooked over an open fire and filleted, then mixed with a huge amount of chopped truffles. The main course, *vitella dorata*, showed off portions of buttery young veal from the farm's herds. Stuffed with mozzarella and copious amounts of black truffles, it was sautéed in butter, then garnished with slivers of prosciutto and just-picked peas sweet from the farm's garden.

The Saint-Honoré dessert from Terni, a combination of thin

crisp layers of puff pastry with creamy custard filling and creampuffs oozing with vanilla and chocolate creams, confirmed the town's reputation for excellent pastries. The accompaniment was a refreshing salad made from ripe fruits grown on the farm. The meal ended with port and coffee. As we complimented our hosts on the extraordinary meal, they told us that the family had always attributed their longevity—Carlo's father had lived to ninety and his grandfather to one hundred—to their diet.

Bathed in the amber light peculiar to that province of northern Italy, we made our way to the factory past road signs to Orvieto, Assisi, Perugia, and Spoleto, none of which was far distant. The Festival of Two Worlds had already made Spoleto world famous as a mecca of international culture. It did not surprise us to learn that Gian-Carlo Menotti, its director, was an old friend of the Urbanis. Although its proper name, Scheggino di Spoleto, acknowledged its proximity to the more famous town, the fame of the little village derived entirely at that time from the new truffle factory, an up-to-date, startlingly untraditional plant on the main road into town.

Led by Carlo and his sons, we toured around the plant, each operation that we saw bringing forth an explanation or comment from one of them or the other. They informed us first off that when the truffles reached the plant after harvest, they were packed in one of the several substances used to conserve them: either sand, wax, sawdust, ashes, bran, or rice. The best way to clean fresh truffles, Paolo told us, is to plunge them in tepid water, removing any soil with a soft brush. We watched the process, a gentle cleaning by machine, then an equally gentle brushing by hand. Some were peeled, all sorted by size. Carlo added that it wasn't necessary to peel truffles, except if they were going into a pâté. The tubers that were headed for immediate storage were packed in air-tight containers and submitted to a brief sterilization. Others underwent drying and preserving under oil, a method then popular in France. Some were canned or preserved in bottles, the best quality undergoing a brief cooking. That reminded Bruno to tell us that, whenever possible, truffles should be added over the top of a dish or stirred in just before serving. Long cooking extinguishes their pungent flavor.

Next we went to "Fort Knox," the name for the three floors of subterranean storage vaults, the destination of the truffles that we had seen being packed in air tight containers, reserved for future shipping or processing. The air-conditioned cellars had six-foot-thick poured concrete walls and a reassuring closed circuit television security system. I had never seen so many truffles in my life—in the monetary value of that time, three or four million dollars worth.

Carlo told us that as a very young man he had traveled to France, studied their techniques, and brought back a process for preserving truffles. Later he developed a method of canning, using truffle juice instead of brine, that most successfully preserved the pungent flavor. Paolo added that his father had been a pioneer in truffle cultivation and reforestation, having planted, over the years and with reasonable success, some 30,000 oaks together with their surrounding soil or with earth that had been scientifically inoculated (oaks are the favorite trees for the fungus to colonize beneath). A year before our visit, the firm had opened three large narrow greenhouses one-half mile from the factory. There they had potted six different species of oaks that were between four and eight inches in size. The plan was to inoculate the total of a million seedlings for the purpose of planting or selling to other countries.

Besides the new factory in Scheggino, the family had some 3,700 acres spread over two farms, one in their own village, the other in Orte. At that time the firm employed sixty full-time workers locally, supplemented during the harvest by 2,000 gatherers. The plant also canned the truffle peelings and pieces, made a truffle purée and a cream of thrush and truffles.

To our surprise, their biggest enterprise involved exporting to France. Many an Urbani truffle has ended up under a French label. At the beginning of the twentieth century, France was harvesting 2,000 tons of truffles annually. But subsequent loss of agricultural sites and workers to urbanization, widespread chemical impact on the ecology, a number of severe summer droughts, and two world wars brought a sharp decline in truffle growth over several decades. For years, the French supply depended on an ever-increasing Italian contribution. Carlo told us that Urbani had quietly been shipping fresh truffles to France since 1915. Once bottled or canned in France, they could, and still do, legally pass as a product of that country and bear a French label. Italy recognized Carlo for his efforts, made him a *Cavaliere della Corona*, and heaped awards and honors on his firm.

In France, we learned, female pigs, smelling that musky phero-mone, were commonly used to root out truffles, but often they ate the prize before the human gatherers could stop them. Although in some parts of France pigs were still employed by traditionalists, the trained dogs used in Italy increasingly took over, being schooled in trading the truffle that they had located for a biscuit or a piece of bread. Their training began by giving hungry puppies a good whiff of truffle, then burying it for the pup to find. If it did, it was rewarded with bread or biscuits. The idea was for the animal to associate the scent of truffles with food. Finally the dog learned to sniff the ground until it smelled the aroma associated with the fun-gus, then to dig with its paws until it unearthed the treasure, and once retrieved, to carry it to the hunter. Sometimes the gatherer helped in the final stages of digging with his truffle spade. The customary cube of bread rewarded the truffle hound's skill and allayed its hunger. There was not much danger in the animal's swallowing the prize. Dogs, not prone to the same pheromones as pigs, much preferred bread to truffles anyway.

The dogs were usually mongrels, the Urbanis told us. Even so, their lack of breed was not an obstacle. Truffle hounds, when rigorously trained by professionals, fetched huge amounts of money. A truffle hunter, called a *tartufaio* in Italian, *trifolao* in dialect, usually owned at least two dogs, oftentimes many more. Customarily foraging at night to avoid poachers, a constant threat, the hunters also secretly guarded any locations where they had found tubers, sometimes places that had yielded finds for older generations of their family. On occasion, tiny yellowish flies, responding to a faint odor escaping through a fissure, swarmed over a cache of harvestable truffles as a potential food source for ready-to-deposit larvae, but such pointers were exceedingly rare.

When we wrote to the Urbanis to thank them for the grand day that they had devoted to us, we got a response from Olga, whose meal, as we had mentioned in the letter, we had found incredible. In her reply, she gave us the recipes for all of the dishes that we had had, except for the dessert from Terni, commenting that actually "my very favorite of all is really the simplest, an omelette of truffles." Although we didn't have that at the dinner, she threw in the recipe for that one, too.

She included some cooking tips: Contain the perfume of a truffle under a lid or inside a pâté. Well covered, truffles can be refrigerated for up to five weeks. Wrapped in foil, they freeze perfectly and can be grated or sliced as needed. To double their use, put one in the refrigerator for a day or two sealed in a plastic bag with whole eggs in the shell. The truffle will be usable in other dishes and the eggs will make an exquisite omelette or truffle-flavored scramble. The aroma of truffles tucked into rice will permeate the grains. The taste and smell are so invasive, a little is a lot. Juices, peelings, pieces, and purées can serve well in recipes calling for truffles. A few slivers or pieces slipped under the skin of a turkey or other bird or sliced over fettuccine will turn them into very special dishes. Flavored with bits of truffle, a classic brown sauce becomes a sauce Périgordine, a treat over roasted or broiled beef.

If you have a fresh truffle, of course use it in the following recipes. Otherwise you will get affordable and excellent results by substituting peelings, purées, slices, or pieces.

Olga's Omeletta al Tartufo Bianco
White Truffle Omelette
For each portion:
   3 eggs
   salt and pepper
   1 tbsp. butter
   ½ white truffle, finely sliced

Beat the eggs with the salt and pepper. Melt the butter in an omelette pan. Add a few truffle slices and cook for just an instant or two, only enough to flavor the butter. Remove them with a slotted spoon and add to the rest of the truffle slices. Turn the beaten eggs into the hot butter, stir a time or two, continuously allowing the liquid portion to run over the mixture at the edge as it sets. When the omelette is beginning to become firm, sprinkle a few slices of truffle in the still runny center. Fold the near edge partially over the center, and by tilting the pan and moving it back and forth, slide the omelette, unfolded side forward, to the edge of the pan. Tilt the pan over a plate and roll the omelette over onto it so that the seam side is underneath. Cover with remaining slices of truffle and serve immediately.

INSALATA DI FUNGHI E TARTUFI
Mushroom and Truffle Salad
   ½ cup olive oil
   juice of 1 lemon
   salt and pepper
   ½ lb. firm, white mushrooms (the Italians use *ovali bianchi*)
   6 stalks celery, cut in thin matchstick slices
   ½ lb. Gruyère cheese, cut in thin matchstick slices
   2 slices prosciutto, cut in thin matchstick slices
   1 white truffle (if using canned, reserve the juice)

Mix olive oil, lemon juice, salt and pepper in the bottom of a salad bowl. If using canned truffle, add the juice. Clean the mushrooms with a brush or damp sponge, keeping them as dry as possible. Slice them razor thin. Add to the salad bowl along with the julienned celery, gruyère, and prosciutto. Toss until dressing and ingredients are well mixed. Slice the white truffle thinly over the top. Serves six.

LUMACHE ALLA URBANI
   1 cooked trout, skinned and boned (about ¾ lb. or 2 cups)
   1 black truffle or ½ ounce or more of pieces or peelings
        and the juices
   2 filets of anchovies
   1 clove of garlic
   salt and pepper
   1 cup olive oil
   juice of 1 lemon

2 or 3 tbsp. veal or chicken stock, broth or gravy

1 lb. *lumache*, spaghetti, or other pasta

In a blender, food processor, or large mortar and pestle, coarsely mix together the trout, truffle pieces and their juices, the anchovies, garlic, salt and pepper, olive oil, lemon juice, and stock, broth, or gravy. It should have the consistency of a very thick sauce. Serve over 1 pound of well-drained lumache or spaghetti cooked just until firm (*al dente*). Serves four to six.

CUSCINETTI AL TARTUFO NERO
also known as Vitella Dorata (Stuffed Veal Cushions)

For each portion:

1 large or 2 small slices of veal, pounded thin
(about 4 ounces per portion)

salt and pepper

1 slice gruyère or mozzarella cheese for each slice of meat

1 or 2 very thin slices of black truffle

For cooking:

beaten egg (1 egg will serve for six portions)

flour for coating

butter

olive oil

white wine

For garnish:

1 cup cooked green peas

chopped parsley

Spread veal pieces flat and sprinkle with salt and pepper. Place 1 slice of gruyère or mozzarella on half of each and top with 1 or 2 slices of truffle. Fold the meat so that the plain side covers the cheese side, enclosing it envelope fashion. Skewer the edges closed with toothpicks. Put flour in one bowl, beaten eggs in another. Dust each piece of veal in the flour, dip in beaten egg, and coat again with flour. While preparing the veal, start to melt the butter together with a little olive oil in a heavy skillet (about 3 tbsp. butter and 1 tbsp. olive oil for six portions). When it is sizzling hot, add the veal "sandwiches," turning once so that each side is golden brown. Remove to a warm serving platter. Add 2 or 3 tbsp. white wine and any juice from the truffles. Cook a minute or two over high heat, scraping the brown particles into the gravy, and pour over the meat. Garnish with 1 cup cooked green peas, reheated for a second in the skillet, then scattered over the top, and with a sprinkling of chopped parsley.

ℜ ℜ

A traditional dish of fondue shows off white truffles perfectly, and although Olga didn't send that recipe, I can't resist including it below. Finally there is a recipe for a favorite of mine, which I actually learned in France. It is a potato dish from the Sarlat area in the Périgord, where all the best French truffles hail from, but who knows if they are not actually Italian tubers, shipped to France by Urbani.

ℜ ℜ

Fonduta con Tartufi Bianchi
Fondue with White Truffles

> 1 lb. Italian fontina cheese
> 4 cups milk
> salt
> 3 tbsp. butter, melted
> 4 egg yolks, beaten
> 1 white truffle

Grate fontina cheese or cut into very small cubes, cover with milk and let it soak for at least two hours. Melt the butter in a large saucepan. Add the cheese and milk and stir gently until the cheese has melted and the mixture is smooth. Slowly add the eggs one at a time over very low heat and stir continuously until they are well blended and the mixture has thickened. For each portion, slice half of the truffles on individual warmed plates, spoon the fondue on each plate, and add the remainder of the sliced truffles on top. Serve immediately while still warm. Serves four to six.

Pommes Sarladaises
Potatoes Sarladaise-Style

> 6 medium potatoes (russet type)
> ¼ lb. butter
> oil
> 1 black truffle, sliced, or 1 oz. black truffle pieces or peelings
> salt and pepper

Preheat the oven to 425°F. Butter well a round cake pan or an oven-proof heavy frying pan, preferably with a non-stick surface and set aside. If you are lucky enough to have a *pommes Anna* mold, use that.

Peel the potatoes and slice into ⅛ inch disks, about the thickness of a fifty-cent piece. Melt the butter with a few drops of oil in another frying pan. Add the potatoes in two batches and cook each for five minutes without allowing them to color. Move them about so that they will not stick. Season with salt and pepper.

Arrange the cooked slices in a spiral overlapping pattern, starting from the center, in the bottom of the reserved pan or mold and make a row or upright border against the edge. Mix the truffle slices into the remaining potatoes until they are distributed evenly throughout. Turn them onto the arranged slices in the pan, it doesn't matter which way, and fill to the top edge. Pour in any remaining melted butter. Bake covered for about 20 minutes.

Remove the lid. Using a flat knife or spatula, turn the tops of any protruding edges to flatten them down, folding them over just slightly toward the center. The top of the potato mixture should now be even and flat across. Cook uncovered for about 25 minutes longer or until done when tested with the tip of a knife. The outside edges should be golden brown.

To unmold, loosen all around with the edge of a knife. If the potato cake sticks, a small amount of butter drizzled down the sides and over the top, and a lid to cover it for a minute or two, will help to free it. After removing the lid, invert a serving platter over the top and turn upside down so that the pan is inverted over the platter. Tap the bottom well all over and lift the pan off. If any potato pieces have stuck, remove them with a knife and replace them on the unmolded potatoes. Serves six. Difficult but yummy.

Our fascinating introduction to the world of truffles spurred us on to find out more. Among the things we learned are these: It turns out that there are some three hundred varieties of truffles in the world, not all of them edible or particularly tasty. They are fungi, related to morel mushrooms, molds, yeasts, mildews, and *huitlacoche*, the black fungus that grows on ears of corn and is sometimes called the Mexican truffle. Unlike their relatives, they grow exclusively underground. The savory ones come primarily from Italy, France, and Spain. In the latter country, a Basque farmer named Salvador Arotzarena is harvesting a bountiful crop, making him the Urbani-like truffle king of his region.

They were eaten by the Romans, who considered them aphrodisiacs, and by the Arabs, whose desert truffles were known in ancient Rome. In more modern times, the French writer Colette was a proclaimed afficionado. In *The Oxford Companion to Food*, Alan Davidson tells us that some of the influential ways to help reestablish a formerly productive truffle orchard include doing such improbable things as working on the land or adjacent to it by building things like a roadway, particularly if it requires using bulldozers, or, even more improbably, having a neighborhood basketball team adopt the ground as their playing field. He is serious.

The white truffle, *Tuber magnatum pico*, the one the cognoscenti admire and pay the most for, grows only in Italy, particularly around Alba in Piedmont, but also in other regions, most notably in Tuscany, Romagna, and the Marche, the last producing a very high-quality tuber, which some think is the best of all. Connoisseurs of course prize the more plentiful black truffle, *Tuber melanosporum*, harvested largely in central Italy, in Spain, and in the Périgord region of France, but none of them would turn down one of the other varieties gathered commercially, such as a coarser-skinned *Tuber brumale*, a midwinter truffle; or a *Tuber aestivum*, otherwise known as a summer truffle; or even a *Tuber albidum*, which is a lesser variety of white truffle, harvested from January to March, somewhat sharper than its big brother, but good enough, especially when mixed with a butter or oil flavored with the real thing.

Usually somewhere between the size of a pea and a golf ball, truffles can grow as large as six inches across. Blacks can weigh in at a pound or more, whites at as much as two pounds. A Roman businessman bought the largest truffle ever recorded (four pounds), found near Alba, with the intention of presenting it to the then president of the United States, Harry Truman. Besides growing larger, whites have that unique, slightly decadent odor. A truffle is about three-quarters water, ten percent protein, fifteen percent carbohydrate, contains small traces of minerals, and practically no fat. One ounce has only 30 calories. Black truffles mature from deep red to black with a coarse, pocked skin faceted like a diamond. White truffles are really grayish tan and are always eaten unpeeled since their skin provides the most intense flavor.

Propagated by spores which produce a network of microscopic threadlike sprouts called hyphae, the fungus enlarges, branches out, invades and grows around the roots of certain trees, most commonly oaks, particularly *Quercus pubescens* and *Quercus ilex*, and sometimes filberts, *Corylus avellana*. Poplars, elms, beech, chestnuts, "lime" trees *(tigli)*, willows, and even some pines, occasionally also become hosts. The growing tissues or filaments, the vegetative or fruiting part of the future truffle, is called the mycelium, and it develops a symbiotic exchange of nutrients with the tree. When mature, the enlarged mass, called a mycorrhiza, produces new colonies of mycelia. The "fruit" or truffle is the final result. Its seeds, in this case spores, are in pockets called asci.

Truffles require good drainage, a moderately hilly terrain, and a soil with adequate calcium. A balance of warmth and summer rainfall is essential for a good harvest. The season for collecting white truffles is September to December; for premium blacks, November to March; and for summer blacks, June to December. Since the truffle grows anywhere from a few inches to three feet underground, random digging for it would destroy its whole reproductive network. For a long time, a Professor Batista Monchiero of Piedmont had the only training school for truffle hounds. His graduates cost in the thousands. Both the French and Americans were working on a machine that could detect the tubers by responding to a molecule present only in ripe truffles. The last I heard, pigs and hounds were still filling the employment rolls.

There are several edible native American species of truffles, including *Tuber californicum*, which has been identified in California, and *Tuber gibbosum*, which grows at the base of Douglas firs in the Pacific Northwest. It is also known as the Oregon white truffle. It got its Latin name because of its camel-like bumps, *gibbosum* meaning "humpy." Both the North American Truffling Society and Dr. James Trappe, a mycologist of the Forestry Sciences Laboratory in Corvallis, Oregon, have undertaken a variety of scientific studies of native species, in the course of which Dr. Trappe has identified more than 100 of them in that region alone, but few are edible outside the *gibbosum* family. Oregonians at one point have also had a hand in cultivating inoculated trees in Texas, where the climate for truffle raising is favorable.

Harvested in Oregon since the fall of 1982, the *gibbosum* is sold in a few specialty food shops. It has a faintly turpentine or piney taste, almost pitchy, and although as pungent, it is not nearly as complex as the *magnatum* or the *melanosporum*. Some tasters have described the flavor as more vertical, with none of the mixed high notes of the European species, perhaps because the *gibbosum* has fewer of the sulfur components that provide, among other things, the pungent garlicky or oniony smell peculiar to its European cousins. The beige color of the *gibbosum* and its near twin, the *geopora*, misled a few early discoverers into thinking that they had found the Alba-type white truffle. The season, much the same as for forest mushrooms, is from late September to the end of January. Heavy rain or freezing temperatures destroy both forms of fungi. Signs of red-backed voles and deer, the nature of the forest floor, and the appearance of certain mushrooms usually indicate the presence of *gibbosum*. However, since most trainable animals are not attracted to them, people must search them out and perform the harvest themselves.

In November of 1975, J. Ralph Stone and Harvey Trione, bankers from Santa Rosa, California, after a visit to the Urbanis in Italy, acquired the rights to several thousand California acres, imported two Italian-schooled truffle hounds, and tried unsuccessfully to find native truffles. Among other things, one of the dogs was pregnant and motherhood proved to be a stronger draw then sniffing out fungi.

For hundreds of years, the exotic tubers have managed to elude cultivation, but a few successful scientific processes under controlled conditions inspired new attempts to grow them commercially. Based on work at the French National Institute of Agronomic Research (*l'Institut National de la Recherche Agronomique* or INRA) in Claremont-Ferrand, the firm of Agri-Truffe, a nursery licensed by the French government, began in 1972 producing as many as 100,000 inoculated trees yearly for sale to potential farmers. Each mycorrhized tree came, and still does, with a numbered guarantee of quality from Agri-Truffe-INRA.

In the United States, there have been continuous attempts to farm or to cultivate truffles on a commercial scale. Inspired by Agri-Truffe, an American affiliate, Agri-Truffle, under the direction of François Picart, a Frenchman, had similar farms near Austin, Texas, and Santa Rosa, California, from 1981 until 1985. They offered potential buyers oaks and filberts inoculated with *Tuber melanosporum*, as well as detailed advice on how and where to farm them. The expected cost per an acre planted to 250 trees, at that time $6,000, included soil preservation, maintenance, and irrigation. There were possible tax advantages. Agri-Truffle told its prospective clients that with a projected 80 percent success rate and a wait of ten years, the time needed until the first harvest, an acre would yield about 100 pounds of truffles that would fetch $500 a pound retail.

The French Agri-Truffe is still going strong, but has not been affiliated with Agri-Truffle since 1985. Soon after that, the American firm was dissolved. According to Pierre-Jean Averseng of Agri-Truffe in

France, Monsieur Picart has moved back to France and has a big company called Buffalo Grill, a chain of steak restaurants, the shares of which are quoted on the French stock exchange. When I first heard of Monsieur Picart long ago in California, he hadn't yet become involved with truffles. He was then canning snails, California *Petits Gris*, the common escargots you find in your garden, preserving their flavor in an original and highly successful way. He gave that up because Taiwanese snail purveyors were able to undersell him.

Besides numerous attempts to discover the clue to the cultivation of truffles, as well as to develop a mechanical harvester, there have been a variety of schemes and pursuits, sometimes fraudulent, connected with the rare fungus. Among the honest efforts that have come to my attention is a mail request that I received in the early nineties, a solicitation to invest in a Mendocino, California orchard of five thousand mychorrhized hazelnut trees that would produce *Tuber melanosporum* in five years, thereby doubling my money (*"magari,"* as they say in Italy, "God willing"). Although I thought it was legit, I questioned the five-year maturation date, and I passed it up. A dozen years ago, I saw an ad in a trade magazine offering golden truffles from Africa's Kalahari desert, "unique, delicate, aromatic [at] only a fraction of the price of their black or white European cousins," though it didn't mention the actual cost. They came frozen whole, dried in slices, or made into a paste. Apparently the native bushmen are unique in being able to locate truffles by scanning the forest floor by eye. (I didn't order any of the Kalahari fungi either.) A few years back, a farmer in North Carolina reported success in his efforts to find truffles under some of the 500 hazelnut trees that he had planted for that purpose a dozen years before. Since his yield brought a better profit than farming tobacco on the same acreage, he got a sizeable federal grant to study better ways to produce truffles as an alternative crop to tobacco.

There are also many ways to cheat. Poaching is so feared that there is great secrecy among the gatherers. In fact, secrecy invades all aspects of truffle dealing, including locked doors and sales for cash only. Some buyers carry such large sums of money that they employ bodyguards. Cheaters also show amazing ingenuity. Jacques Pébèyre, a respected French truffle processor and supplier, has seen his share of inventive fraud. He has a case full of black rocks which were mistakenly purchased from unscrupulous but skillful "truffle" sellers. His collection includes various metals that were fraudulently inserted into tubers to increase their weight, then sold at the market to buyers who paid truffle prices for a bit of lead or a heavy nail. If the truffle is not properly cleaned of the dirt that naturally clings to it—sometimes as much as 20 percent of its weight—the buyer pays extravagant prices for plain old soil.

Another prevalent scheme is substitution of a lesser fungus for a superior one. The far less expensive summer truffle is neither as desirable, as complex, or as pungent as the *melanosporum*. Yet it is sometimes sold as the higher priced tuber because of its strong resemblance. Pébèyre tells of one such swindler who paid a $5,000 fine (at 1980 prices) and served six months in jail for doing just that. A French processor earned an even larger fine for dyeing lowly and inferior pale truffles black, then labeling and selling quantities of them as the real black diamond, canned whole, scattered through pâtés, or generously sliced in foie grâs. Paul Bonnet, from a multigenerational truffle family in Carpentras in southern France, reported that chefs in one of the local villages were even stirring the faux black truffles into their omelettes.

On the positive side, there are such traditions as the annual Truffle Mass, held in southern France in the twelfth-century village church of Richerenche. Members of the truffle fraternity always wear their official robes; at the conclusion of the celebration, instead of the customary monetary tithes, the whole congregation donates money-raising truffles to the collection plate. A hundred years ago, in Sorges in the Dordogne region of France, there was a thriving truffle market, drawing people from the whole area. Today, lacking the once abundant supply that made it a hub, the town has a modern reminiscence of the past commerce, the Maison de la Truffe, a museum devoted to the accoutrements associated with truffles. Exhibits include such things as old tools and gadgets, some of them adapted to the purposes of harvesting the fruit, others that prevented it from being consumed by a greedy sow. There is also a modest array of truffle-related gifts such as cookbooks dedicated to recipes for the tuber. Another similar commemorative institution, the Musée de la Truffe, is in Vaucluse in southern France. And in Paris, in the Place de la Madeleine, is an entire shop dedicated to the tuber, La Maison de la Truffe. For sale is a glorious array of *melanosporum* and a large selection of other truffle products. We have sometimes bought truffles there for transport back to the United States.

Alongside the display of artifacts in museums, the scholarly investigation of the tuber has burgeoned. In July of 1998, the first international meeting on the "Ecology, Physiology and Cultivation of Edible Mycorrhizal Mushrooms," including many sections devoted to the latest studies on truffles, took place in the Swedish University of Agricultural Sciences in Uppsala. But the fungus basically still remains a mystery. No matter that specialists now know the ideal climate and location where it may prosper, no one can say with certainty whether a mycorrhized tree will produce or whether it won't.

An altogether different approach, to create truffles in the laboratory, a feat that various experts in Europe and the United States have been experimenting with for years, was finally accomplished in 1989 in Woodland, California. It began when the scientist Moshe Shifrine went to Kenya in the 1960s to study cattle diseases. On his trip, he observed the natives gathering truffles from the Kalahari Desert in South Africa (the same ones that I more recently turned down), and came away obsessed. His efforts to cultivate truffles in captivity started with the spores of purchased French *melanosporum*, subjecting them, in Petri dishes, to the same climatic and nutritional conditions that they would get in the wild. But he didn't give up his day job as professor at the University of California at Davis until 1987, when he finally succeeded, after thirty years of trying, to produce a cultured black truffle. In fact, lots of them. But they were quite different in appearance from the wild ones, resembling more a lumpy carpet made of small individual bumps, each one a tiny fruit of the prized species. I have heard its appearance compared to "slabs of beef jerky," or perhaps more kindly, in a left-handed compliment sort of way, to "black carpeting."

Shifrine realized that although he could now produce the favored black truffle, he couldn't cultivate it in a marketable quantity. However, he had met Randy Dorian, also a microbiologist and professor, at a technical laboratory when both were doing work there. It seemed that with Dorian's expertise in mass cell production, they would be able to adapt Shifrine's formula to a process that yielded truffles on a commercial scale. They did just that. Shifrine then formed a company and made Dorian vice president. They obtained enough money from friends and family to start a laboratory in a former warehouse near Sacramento, dedicated solely to cultivating and marketing homegrown truffles.

In keeping with his associates abroad, Shifrine maintained the utmost secrecy, even installing burglar alarms and sensors. He revealed little of the growing process to anyone, except whatever he had to tell the government office to apply for a patent. In an interview for a newspaper, he repeated the known fact that the chemicals involved in giving truffles their mysterious aroma were still unidentified. He told little other than that his procedure involved duplicating the familiar wild environment in a sterile laboratory. No exact temperature, no clue as to the nutrients, no key to the amount of light or humidity or whether they were changed or remained constant. About all that he admitted is that the truffles, once activated, were transferred to very large growing trays and harvested after a year, which meant that, being youthful, they didn't develop the propagating spores that their older wild brethren did. To maintain their production, Dorian and Shifrine had to cultivate their truffle spores in the laboratory once a week.

Shifrine introduced his laboratory-produced truffles at the International Food Show in San Francisco in March of 1990. A reporter for the San Francisco Chronicle reported the event, complete with a confrontation between a Frenchman from Perigord and his wild truffles and Shifrine with his slablike home-grown wonders. The Frenchman vociferously claimed that Shrifine's tubers were not truffles and the American entrepreneur, equally adamant, claimed that they were. The standoff was never resolved.

The American partners produced a wide range of truffle products, many of them dehydrated or dried. These included powders, flakes, pastes, extracts, and oils, which the company recommended for imparting flavor to dishes like the ravioli that the team offered at the fancy food show. Top gourmet markets and specialty food stores began to stock their products. The secretive laboratory fungus is now part of the lore about the still mysterious *melanosporum*, the best of the black truffles.

The truffle markets, particularly the one in Alba, are yet another aspect that has grown up around the harvest of the underground tuber. Although many communities in the region have markets devoted to the local fungus, Alba is certainly the most famous, and one that we have been to several times. We have never attended the national festival in mid-October, a spirited affair we are told, replete with ancient costumes, music, colorful shields, flags and banners, and processions that wend through the streets.

The first time we attended the market, it was an incidental adjunct to a tour of Piedmont wineries that happened to coincide with the early truffle harvest. Carlo and Ora Cipollas's friend, Renato Ratti, a late renowned winemaker of the Piedmont area, set up a program for the four of us that included visits to some of the leading winemakers — Angelo Gaja in Barbaresco, Fontanafredda in Fontanafredda, Ratti himself in l'Annunziata di La Morra, Aldo Conterno in Bussia di Monforte, G. Borgogno in Barolo, Elvio Cogno in La Morra, Paolo Cordero di Montezemelo in l'Annunziata di La Morra, Prunotto in San Cassiano Alba, and Cinzano in San Vittoria d'Alba. Ratti had set aside time in the program for a visit in Alba to the cathedral, the church of San Giovanni, and the Museum Federico Eusebio, as well as a visit to the truffle market then taking place. He had also made reservations for lunches and dinners at restaurants in the area, but included one delicious evening meal, cooked by his wife, on the protected balcony of the Ratti's home. All of this took place over four days.

In the wineries, we tasted Barbarescos, Barolos, Nebbiolos, Barberas, various Dolcettos, Caremas, Grignolinos, Freisas, Pinots, Arneis, and Moscatos. Some tastings were formal with the proper tasting sheets to fill out. In one case, after we had been given a grand tour and sampled the wines, the owner invited us back after dinner to taste some really old, library Barolos. We found them strange to our taste, almost oxidized, but that quality, to the Italian winemaker's palate, is most desirable. When we later discussed this with Maynard Amerine, the great wine expert from the University of California at Davis, he shared our opinion about older Barolos.

Before our scheduled visit to Angelo Gaja, we were having lunch at a restaurant that specialized in simple local dishes made from traditional recipes. Suddenly, a man who had spotted us approached our table with the warmest possible greetings for Carlo, who, it turned out, had been his economics professor some years before in the university. It was, of course, Angelo Gaja himself, who insisted on treating us to lunch, then proceeded to give us a memorable tour of his winery and local vineyard properties.

Years later, I was reminded of this coincidence in another Piedmont restaurant, da Felicin, in Monforte d'Alba, where we had, among many other delicious dishes, a pâté made of white truffles. As we ate, my husband and I noticed a table of English speakers, who ended up seated next to us when the host moved us to lounge chairs for our after-dinner coffee. When we had exchanged the ritualistic where-are-you-from and what-do-you-do, it turned out that one of the four Englishmen was Mark Savage, whom I had never met, but had corresponded with at length because he was writing on the Zinfandel Club of London for a book on California wine that I was currently working on for the University of California Press and Sotheby.

A second coincidence concerning Angelo Gaja himself occurred many years after our chance meeting with him in Piedmont. I was with the Berkeley Wine and Food Society for a tasting of Otard cognacs in a private room of the now defunct Square One restaurant in San Francisco. Unbeknownst to us, a group of visiting Italian winemakers were having dinner in the main dining room, which a waiter, knowing that we were interested in wine, happened to mention to us. Sure enough, Gaja was among them, and when the waiter told him about us, he came to our room, huggingly remembered our cordial meeting in Piedmont, and graciously met and talked about the latest developments in Italian wines to the members of my group.

On our first trip to Piedmont, our interest in the annual truffle market was increasingly whetted by the sumptuous dishes that we ate in the various local restaurants. We had such simple things as an omelette slathered with white truffles; *carpaccio*, raw veal sliced thin, or better yet, seasoned uncooked veal chopped like a tartare, both dishes with an abundance of white truffle shavings; and many dishes of truffled *risotto* (although the rice dish at Belevedere in La Morra made with barolo but no truffles was pretty spectacular). Perhaps best of all was *tajarin*, the Piedmontese term for *tagliatelle*, the famous egg noodles, over which truffles were shaved until you told the server to stop. To determine the price, the truffles, kept in a huge domed receptacle, were usually weighed before shaving, on a wonderfully old-fashioned brass balance scale, and again afterward. Each time the proprietor lifted the lid of the truffle container, the strong aroma of the fungus pervaded the entire room.

For us, the epitome of the noodle dish was served at Locanda Contea in Neive, owned by Elisa, Tonino and Claudia Verro. Claudia, the chef, uses thirty egg yolks to a little over two pounds of flour, to make her *tajarin*. Ethereal! The only thing to match it in my memory is the first course of a birthday dinner my husband treated me to in Paris at Le Petit Bedon, *les truffes sous le cendre*, golf ball-sized black truffles anointed in goose fat, wrapped in white cooking paper, then set to bake under the ashes of a wood fire. Ours came in a flaky puff pastry, so they had to be baked first and then finished wrapped in kitchen paper covered with ashes. Escoffier's recipe calls for seasoning with salt and pepper and a sprinkle of brandy, then wrapping in *pâte à choux*, the type of pastry usually used for cream puffs. His instructions are for baking in an oven for a half hour, no cinders in sight. (*Sous le cendre?*) *Larousse Gastronomique*, oddly enough, calls for first seasoning the truffle with salt and pepper and spices (unspecified), plus a splash of brandy. Before enclosing in kitchen paper hermitically sealed with a mixture of flour and the white of an egg, the tuber is wrapped in a very thin sheet of fatty bacon. The cooking is done, for an inexcusable forty-five minutes, in an aluminum pan covered with both hot ash and "glowing" embers.

The truffle market in Alba takes place in the old section of town, off the Via Vittorio Emmanuele, nowadays closed to traffic to allow the shoppers full access to stores full of refreshments, edibles, and clothing. Off to one side is an entrance to a courtyard in which is erected, solely for the occasion, a large white canvas tent housing the truffle market. Outside the tent there are many questionable characters who stealthily bring forth their bulbous handkerchiefs wrapped around tubers that they offer you for much less than the going price. Beware! Some of these may be the real thing, but often they are less valuable fungi. Inside the tent are a dazzling array of truffles set out on tables, and a number of displays exhibiting such truffle products as oils and pastes. Serious buyers were sniffing away before making a decision. The aroma was overwhelming.

On one of our visits to the market, a Japanese television crew making a film on the unique Alba white fungus, mistaking us for Italians, photographed us at length smelling the truffles (knowledgeably), discussing the attributes with each seller (in our limited Italian), but never being able to make up our minds as to which we were going to buy (none). We never saw the TV program when it aired in Japan, but we were most happy to help out, bogus though we were.

A couple of years ago, we decided to revisit the Urbanis. Carlo and Olga had long since passed on, and Bruno and Paolo had taken over. Bruno was no longer mayor of Scheggino, but his administrative duties at Urbani were now supplemented instead by being president of the Banco Populare d'Umbria. Paolo's daughter, Olga, named after her grandmother, was the young child who, long ago, dressed in her fancy clothes, had been at our introductory dinner in Scheggino di Spoleto. Since 1985, she had been working in the firm in the design area and in management. When we met with her, she turned out to have grown into a stunning young woman, dark-haired, highly intelligent, with alert eyes, and makeup so subtle it made it seem as if she wasn't wearing any. In short, she was vibrant and stylish, casually dressed in chic pants and shirt, in that informal way that is, no matter how hard one tries to emulate it, only and absolutely Italian. She made us feel instantly as if we were old friends, and our conversation flowed with the ease that is usually reserved for close acquaintances.

She brought us up-to-date on the company. Her father, Paolo, as we well remembered, had had a charisma that attracted people to him. For example, he was so loved by the truffle hunters, they had become so attached and loyal, that they sold their tubers to him instead of to other buyers. That may help to explain why 70 percent of the truffles in the world still are Urbani.

He also showed ingenuity. Once, faced with a poor harvest, he had thought up a new line of products that infused the truffle flavor where dishes called for it but where the real thing was unobtainable. These first items were so successful that they had become part of the ever-expanding line, which now included oils impregnated with white or black truffle essence; a *salsa* of black *melanosporum*; truffled *tagliatelle* and *tortellini*; a butter with white truffle flavors, *crema di burro con tartufo*, that was especially good in making risotto; various purées of white, black, and summer truffles; as well as a fondue of cheese, a cream of olives and hazelnuts as well as of wild mushrooms, and even boxes of chocolates—all impregnated with truffle flavors. Jars of flour, strongly intensified by white truffles, needed only a meager pinchful mixed into regular flour to give an aromatic flavor to béchamel sauce or fresh-made pasta.

Beyond the various types of fresh truffles, now also sold frozen, the products incorporated olive oils, mélanges of truffles put up in glass jars, truffled pâtés, frozen *porcini* mushrooms, and a variety of truffle slicers, gift baskets, elaborate silver bowls, and ceramics from Deruta, all encompassing an assortment of Urbani products. The company had certainly expanded beyond our original introduction to "Fort Knox" and its millions of truffles in storage.

Olga told us that Paolo and Margherita Urbani, who used to direct the United States interests of the Italian firm, and who first got us interested in truffles, had retired. The now independent distributorship, operating out of a loft in SoHo in New York City, is owned by Rosario and Andrew Safina, whose family had been very close to the Urbanis. Although the firm obtained both the right to use the Urbani name and to offer their products, Urbani Truffles USA no longer has a formal connection to the business in Italy.

One of the recent and potentially troublesome problems for the Italian firm is a Chinese truffle which has made its appearance on the world market, usually impersonating the great black truffle, _Tuber melanosporum_. The Chinese imposter, _Tuber indicum_, or as Olga called it, _T. hynalaiensys_, is identical in looks but lacks the taste and aroma of its European relative. Whereas the Italian black truffle might sell for $500.00, the Chinese fungus goes for around $25.00, so the easy substitution has dire financial consequences. The Italian NASA, our equivalent of the FDA, is looking into it.

At the end of our visit, Olga supplied us with all sorts of handsomely designed books and notebooks on Urbani Tartufi, as well as a promise to show us the updated factory in Scheggino, plus a private telephone number for reaching her. Although we hadn't expected such a warm and hospitable welcome, she was carrying on in great style the generosity and friendship of her family. Looking at her background, that didn't surprise us. It was only the truffle, the cause of our meeting, that still remains, in spite of all the technological advances and scientific research, absolutely mysterious.

CHAPTER FIFTEEN

From Sardegna to Dozza

Traveling from place to place in Italy, it sometimes seems as if you are passing from one completely different country to another. To add to the mystique, there is a continuous overlapping of the remnants of prehistoric times with the marvels of the ultramodern. Given the comforts of tradition and older ways, some villages resist modernity, while others, although embracing more recent ways of doing things, still recall their ancestry as often as possible. The country abounds in archeological wonders, layers upon layers of history, remote regions that remain removed from the enticements and frenzy of modern life. Occasionally you even stumble upon an ancient village that hasn't changed its long-ago costumes, let alone its older habits. Numerous feast days, festivals, celebrations, carnivals, and contests, most of them splendid in ancient dress, are annual events all through the country: the horse-back races in Siena and Asti; the chess game in the piazza of

Marostica, with costumed people playing the pieces; the decorated boats and masked participants during Carnival in Venice; the innumerable celebrations of wine, particularly its harvest; and the endless festivals dedicated to foods from boar to fish to gnocchi to polenta to wild strawberries.

The most outrageous and chaotic of all food events must be the battle of the oranges in Ivrea, a town in Piedmont. Each year, as part of the observance of Carnival, the citizens of the community, too far north to grow citrus themselves, send for a whole trainload of blood oranges from Sicily, and then proceed to spend days pelting each other with them. No one would even consider eating them; they serve as wicked munitions only. The hundreds of heavily fortified combatants, wearing strategic padding, masks, and helmets and mostly on horse carts, engage in this violence, covering each other and the city's streets and buildings with brilliant red juice and copious remnants of orange peels. In the end, one of the teams of horse-cart warriors is declared the winner, but the fun for the throwers is really in hitting their targets, being drenched in juice, and in general participating in the wanton destruction and chaos that result throughout the city. I would not like to be on the clean-up crew.

From ancient past to modern present, such historical juxtaposition is clearly prevalent in Mediterranean Sardegna, which we know as Sardinia, the second largest island after Sicily off the coast of Italy. We once spent a couple of weeks there on vacation, and managed, without even trying, to see everything from traditional shepherds' villages high in the mountainous hills of the Barbagia, where some still wore their ancient dress, to the mysterious *nuraghi*, rudimentary prehistoric stone dwellings that dotted the landscape everywhere. Thank heavens we didn't encounter any of the bandits or kidnappers reputed to be lurking in the remote regions of the interior. Only flocks of sheep, herds of goats, and the occasional shepherds who tend them, now and then an olive grove or a vineyard, but mostly wild terrain, infrequent villages, and uninhabited stretches of mountains. I am told, although we didn't come across any of them ourselves, that there are even villages where they speak Genovese dialect or Catalan, reflecting the language of the settlers in those regions.

At the absolute other extreme, we stayed at the Hotel Pitrizza, one of the modern luxury resorts developed by the Aga Khan on the Costa Smeralda, and visited another, his Gaudíesque Hotel Cala di Volpe, with its amoeba-like offset windows in brilliant colors of glass. Both were fantastic, but as unreal as movie sets. (We much preferred the smaller Pitrizza, with its thatched roofs and massive stone walls, private patios and beaches, and edgeless swimming pool.) Our stay was memorable, but the hotel could have been any-where that had a gorgeous beach setting and a staff trained to pam-per the guests. Nothing particularly Sardinian about it.

We encountered another aspect of today's culture, not a pleasant one, as we drove along much of the perimeter of the island. We were alarmed by the ubiquitous sudsy foam on all of the streams and waterways and the sheer numbers of discarded plastic containers tossed everywhere, modern pollution at its worst. Clearly, the islanders hadn't yet embraced filtration systems or trash cans.

The basic food of Sardegna is based on the peasant food cooked by the women in the villages or by the numerous shepherds during their long nomadic periods of isolation. During our visit, that simple cuisine was in noteworthy contrast to what was served in such mod-ern resorts as Pitrizza. There we ate more universally Italian dishes than Sardinian, user-friendly, luxurious, and utterly delicious to be sure, but hardly typical fare of the land. Even in restaurants that had spruced up their decors, some going as far as installing dance bands and bars, you could still find a cuisine based on traditional specialties.

When we dined at Pitrizza, one of our favorite dishes was rock lobster, which we assumed was in bountiful supply because this was a land surrounded by the sea. I was surprised to read many years later in Joseph Bastianich's and David Lynch's fine book, *Vino Italiano*, that eating creatures from the ocean was only a recent culinary innovation in Sardinia. According to the authors, islanders used to stay away from the regions abutting the sea both because of the dangers of foreign invaders, of which there were many, and the prevalence of malaria. That makes good sense. But, fortunately, nowadays you find both numerous fishing boats and the villages that launch them, as well as widespread offerings of seafood on restaurant menus.

Perhaps the most famous dish of the island is *porceddu*, wild spit-roasted suckling pig. Perfumed by the juniper, myrtle, wild sage, and olive woods, among the many aromatic fuels found in abundance, the meat takes on a unique savory quality. Spit-roasting, here perfected to an art, includes frequent basting of the skewered piglet, which results in an incredibly crunchy mahogany skin yielding to succulent morsels of flesh. Kid is also prepared this way, as are innards and sausages. Tripe, undulating on its skewer, is often cooked over the coals. Game, including wild boar, bear, and various birds, makes up a large part of the diet, a food source available to the hunter as well as the shepherd, who must often spend months at a time in remote regions. *Carraxiu* or *carrargiu* is the name for cooking a buried pig or other animal, first decked out with assorted herbs and aromatics, in a fire pit dug in the ground. When the coals are ashen, the pig is put in place, covered with earth, with a gentle fire set over it. Then it is roasted very, very slowly, which produces a pork that is both toothsome and tender.

"Recent culinary innovation" or not, many dishes based on fresh products of the sea were in abundant supply when we were there: baked mussels, grilled eels, baby octopus and squid (sometimes stuffed), large lobsters, and a bounteous fish stew, *cassòla*, spiced with chili peppers and made from whatever fish and shellfish made up the day's catch. We once had a delicious fish, I know not what, cooked in Vernaccia, a wine that in Sardinia is made in a sherrylike style. It is also sometimes served as an aperitif. Others that are prominent among the island's vinous specialties are a white Vermentino and a red Cannonau, the island's name for Grenache.

There is pasta, of course, such dishes as ravioli stuffed with spinach or ricotta, various uncomplicated preparations of spaghetti, and *fregola*, rather large-sized couscous, boiled instead of steamed, then served with a sauce like regular pasta or as an addition to soup. *pecorino* cheese, made from the prevalent ewe's milk, is widely acknowledged as one of the best of its kind in Italy. Fiore Sardo, a less famous but very good version of *pecorino*, sometimes incorporates cow's milk. I tasted some recently at a San Francisco restaurant as part of the cheese plate, but it didn't have the slightly smoky overtones of the cheese that we ate in Sardinia. We once had a *pecorino* on the island, topped by a bitter honey unlike anything else we had tasted, but one we could never find on the mainland. Although we didn't get to try it, a spreadable cheese called *callu de cabreddu* is matured in a pouch made from a slaughtered young goat's stomach. Goats have several tummies and I've read that it is always the fourth that is used for cheesemaking.

Just as the cheeses were, and often still are, made by the shepherds, the bread-making role fell to the peasant women. Their most famous creation is *carasau*, also called *carta di musica* or *foglia di musica*. The large discs of crackling bread, at least a foot in diameter and much thinner than a pancake, are so called because they resemble sheet music. Dry and not readily spoilable, they are perfect for the shepherds to take along on their extended mountainous sojourns.

Once we traveled in Apulia (Puglia in Italian), the heel of the

Italian boot, where we found mysterious *trulli*, built later and kept in much better shape, but still reminiscent of the Sardinian *nuraghi*. Whitewashed dwellings of native limestone with primitive conical stone roofs that end in pointy whitewashed cupolas, they, like their Sardinian counterparts, seem to be put together without mortar. The most recent structures are at least centuries old, despite their well-kept appearance, and although the original houses were built even before the Romans, they are not prehistoric, as the enigmatic stone piles of Sardinia are. Their origins, however, remain equally unknown. With domed interior ceilings, they are mostly used for housing, historically and presently. Currently inhabited wherever they appear, in the village of Alberobello there are over a thousand occupied *trulli*, as well as one that is used as a church. Elsewhere they pepper the terrain, sometimes in bee-hive clusters, particularly in the southern section of the province, an archaic, omnipresent addition to the landscape. They look like the homes of elves, and it takes one aback to see real people emerge through their doors.

Compared to the west coast of Italy, we found Puglia's beach front along the Adriatic, the longest in Italy, mostly less picturesque, consisting of straight stretches of sand dotted with modest hotels and unadorned rental cabins. It was off season when we were there, so there was a certain unspruced look to everything, repairs and paint jobs still needed before the hoard of tourists would arrive. Most of the beach towns were, in fact, deserted. Judging by the ubiquitous signs on the rentals, ZIMMER FREI, or vacancies, the majority of tourists must have come from Germany.

In a few areas, particularly up north around the Promontorio di Gargano, the coast is more scenic, sometimes clifflike, with more attractive beach facilities and picturesque rocky beaches. Further south, about a half hour from Bari, the Castellana Grotte are the most extensive and famous of the grottos in Puglia. A fantastic and seemingly inexhaustible series of subterranean caves, they consist of chambers filled with endless icicle-like protrusions from the ceilings, columnlike formations crowding the floors, splendid colors, and stupefying shapes and crenellations.

Several resorts have hot springs, hydrothermal spas, and good bathing. Some of the towns have their charms, such as the Arabic whitewashed Ostuni climbing up its hill. Like many places in Italy, there are old medieval quarters in some villages that are more picturesque than the newer and more nondescript parts that surround them. Off the highways there are enticing small country roads, many lined with crude stone walls, that are quite appealing.

The major Pugliese attractions seem to be historic reminiscences reflecting the various civilizations that once lived there. These range from bronze age dolmens to Italy's oldest Greek fountain in Gallipoli, and include remnants of Roman amphitheaters and columns. In the cathedral in Otranto, there is a huge mosaic pavement dating from 1165, the colors of which are vivid enough to have been cast today. Vibrant with figures and symbols, it depicts the story of human life. Perhaps the high point of things historical is the well-preserved octagonal castle of Frederick II, with its echoing eight octagonal towers, perched atop a hilly mound in Castel del Monte, where it was built in the thirteenth century as a summer home.

But mostly, except for the Murghe Hills, the peninsular Promontorio del Gargano, and a few other sections of coastline, Puglia consists of uninterrupted plains, flat and fertile, land used for agriculture and pasture. The production of such staples as wine, olive oil, and wheat make Puglia an agricultural leader, at least in crop quantities. The large amount of wheat available established a widespread skill in bread baking, for which the region became famous, particularly since it relied on homemade starters for the fermentation. Commercial production, with its packaged yeasts, was beginning to take over from the characteristic country loaves, even by the time that we were there.

In certain areas, while some of the mountains in the background were snow-capped, on the plains below we drove past stands of Queen Anne's lace, bridle bush, yellow scotch broom, and cistus. In some places in the Caserta area, grape vines were trellised between poplar trees, a technique, also used elsewhere, to shield the vines from the ravages of the hot climate. There were many groves of olives, and the vegetation changed to drifts of wild fennel, lavender, and mustard. We even spotted cactus and bamboo, pine forests, cypress, and eucalyptus trees. There were still occasional World War II gun embankments, and in Porto di Badisco we saw graffiti urging "*rivoluzione.*" Plastic sheets covered many dormant fields. When it rained, motorcyclists often hoisted umbrellas for protection. Still abundantly used for transportation when we were passing through, horse carts had huge wheels and enormous double yokes. In Taranto on the gulf, we stopped in a restaurant where I was the only woman present. We ate delicious oysters, for which the region is famous.

On the road, there was a hazardous disregard for driving rules, even noticeable in reckless Italy, and in a country where everyone seemed to be exceptionally friendly, we experienced a highly unusual rudeness in some hotels and restaurants, an impatience that we had never experienced before. In that southern, poverty-stricken land, the changes taking place were obviously coming about too quickly for some people to absorb. Accompanying modern progress was the detritus of industrial development: plastic debris on the roads, among the pines, in the camp grounds, on the beaches, in the streams. Abandoned wrecked cars were epidemic, ubiquitous billboards rose at the sides of roads, and some pretty dreadful modernistic architecture stood out among the buildings. It was a relief to come across an old-fashioned butcher who offered goat, lamb, and pork, *pecorino* and prosciutto, and *carne alla brace*, or spit-roasted meats, in his *macelleria*.

Puglia is known for the quality and abundance of its vegetables and for its semolina specialty, *orecchiette*, little ear-shaped pastas, more often dressed with broccoli, cauliflower, rapini, broccoli rabe, or other greens than with tomato sauce. Sometimes, the veggies are mixed together with the tomato base, red-white-and-green like the Italian flag; many times they are a primary addition to a meat-based sauce. *Orecchiette* turned out not to be our favorite pasta, a bit thick and chewy for our taste. The dough, first formed into a long thick roll, is then sliced into smaller portions, which are pressed by the thumb into little ears, more or less anatomically correct, leaving some parts thicker than others, which may explain our lack of enthusiasm. Fortunately, the freshness of the vegetables in the sauce made up for the lack of delicacy in the pasta. Cabbages, eggplants, artichokes, turnip greens, and all sorts of other veggies often turn up in the sauces or are cooked as dishes by themselves, a good cuisine for vegetarians. Obviously, the Pugliese prefer pasta with some substance, although they do eat lasagne and all of the usual noodles. They make little gnocchi of pasta dough, heavier than the usual potato, semolina, or ricotta base used elsewhere.

With a coastline as long as Puglia's, much of the provender comes fresh from the sea: all kinds of fish, eels, and shellfish, wonderful mussels, and those fantastic oysters from the Gulf of Taranto. There the babies start their life in one inlet, then are moved to deeper water in another sheltered lagoon where they mature. Because of the nature of the Gulf and its lagoons, the oysters are exposed to a mixture of salt and fresh water, a combination that, when they are harvested two years later, makes them something quite special. I am told that the production is large enough—several million mollusks —to accommodate many restaurants outside of Puglia. First-rate mussels are also raised the same way in Taranto. Besides being served on their own, they sometimes join other fish and shellfish in soups or stews, common fare along the coast, as are the ubiquitous octopus and bountiful squid. No bigger than a thumbnail, the best octopi that we ever had were in a coastside restaurant in Puglia.

Inland there is mutton, but along the coast the meat choices are usually lamb or kid. Less costly innards have a role in the cooking, but vegetables and pasta are the true base of the cuisine. The Pugliese make several cheeses, drawing about equally on the milk of ewes, cows, and goats. The standout is *burrata*, a type of mozzarella unique to that area. Nowadays, you can get it outside of Puglia, but like others of its type that travel poorly, it is a far cry from eating it where it is made, and seductively delicious when it's fresh. The outer casing is made the traditional way and looks like a large unbaked biscuit. But surprisingly the cheese has an utterly delectable filling of mozzarella stretched into long fettucine-like strings mixed with a creamy, almost buttery liquid made from the whey. It more than makes up for those chewy pastas.

Puglia is a very large wine producer. Much of the output is used for blending, but there are a number of bottled wines, many with D.O.C. (*Denominazione di Origine Controllata*) certification, some of which we have happily been drinking for years in the United States. Among these are Taurino's Salice Salentino, made from the Negroamaro grape, widely planted in the southeast; and his Notarpanaro, a blend based on that same robust red grape. At home we also have drunk a lot of A-Mano and other wines made from the Primitivo grape, which brings up a recently solved mystery.

California is noted for its Zinfandel, the origins of which, for the century and a half since its introduction to the state, have been a mystery. It first appeared in this country early in the nineteenth century on Long Island, then was grown in New England, from whence it came to California by 1850. Although the first importation to the eastern United States is traced to Austria, more recent thinking suspected that the origin of the grape was actually Puglia, because the Primitivo there bore a striking resemblance to Zinfandel, as it was known in the States. (There are two principal varieties, Primitivo di Gioia and Primitivo di Manduria, named after the places from which they come.) Several years ago, Italian clones of Primitivo were imported to California, but the resulting wines were somewhat different from Zinfandel. Mike Grgich, a California vintner of Croatian decent, campaigned for the Plavac Mali grape from Croatia as the possible source, even going so far as to experiment with a vineyard in that country. Finally, Carole Meredith, a professor at the University of California at Davis, and two Croatian scientists, solved the mystery through DNA testing.

The classic wine grape, the European *vitus vinifera*, has remained virtually unchanged through the centuries except for natural cross-pollination, which resulted in varieties. Nowadays new grapes are created deliberately. Cross-pollination resembles human reproduction in that it requires two "parents" who each contribute half of the genetic markers. Before DNA testing, the resemblance of leaf and berry to family relatives often led to false presumptions. That was what led Mike Grgich, the California winemaker, to think that Plavic Mali was Zinfandel. He was close. As it turned out, it was one of its parents. (The other was Dobricic.)

Genetically, both Primitivo and Zinfandel turn out to be the same fruit as the unpronounceable and almost extinct Croatian grape, Crljenak Kastelanski. It seems to have been exported long ago from Croatia to both Puglia and to the United States, assuming different names in the process (thank heavens). Carole Meredith theorizes that the then prevalent phylloxeria and other debilitating causes nearly wiped it out, but not before it had produced a much more hardy relative, Plavic Mali, now one of the most highly respected red wine grapes in Croatia. Meredith also supposes that it was probably monks, emigrating from the Dalmatian coast to close-by Puglia to escape religious persecution in the eighteenth century, who probably introduced the grape to Italy, where it became known as Primitivo.

How it got to Austria is yet another mystery. Perhaps it made its way into the nursery specimens of the Emporer Franz Josef, an avid collector. His Austro-Hungarian domain also encompassed Croatia. The distinct styles of growing, harvesting, and producing, the variation in climates and soils, and family clones probably account for the differences in the wines. Probably. But in any case, a toast to DNA, Carole Meredith, Ivan Pejic, and Edi Maletic, those two Croatian scientists from the University of Zagreb. *Salute!* A raised glass of Zinfandel to all.

Just west of the border between Puglia and Basilicata, on the other side of a large ravine backed by the eastern Murghe Hills, is the town of Matera. It is home to the strangest conglomeration of prehistoric cave dwellings, or *sassi*—over 3,000 of them—that one can possibly imagine. Climbing up two hillsides crowned by the cathedral, they make the landscape look like a huge beehive or honeycomb. The excavated caves date from Paleolithic times when the inhabitants of nearby grottos, naturally formed in the rock, realized that they could dig out the soft rock or tufa on the jagged cliff to make better places to live. The labyrinth includes an ancient water system, dug into the limestone, made up of cisterns to collect and store rainwater. It was the only source of the precious liquid for hundreds of years; in recent times, both plumbing and electricity have been installed.

At one time home to some 20,000 inhabitants and covering over seventy acres, the *sassi* became a national shame after the publication of Carlo Levi's book in 1948, *Christ Stopped at Eboli*. More than ten years before that, Mussolini had Levi detained near Matera for his anti-fascist activities. During his year in that impoverished southern region, he was shocked by the crude and primal state of the inhabitants' existence there, as if Christ and his blessing had stopped in Eboli, a town just below Naples. Ten years later, the local proverb "Christ stopped at Eboli" gave Levi the title of his book. His vivid account of the extreme poverty and ancient ways of Basilicata turned the country's focus on that area, a heartfelt condemnation so severe that there were even movements, though never realized, to demolish the *sassi*. But by the early 1950s, people had left the cave dwellings in droves until the old town was nearly uninhabited. Some thirty years later, newly written laws supported builders who went about refurbishing the deserted homes, and in the nineties Unesco decreed the site to be of World Heritage status. Now a thriving population lives in the renovated houses, complete with modern accoutrements, and the rebuilding goes on.

Thanks to their hillside configuration, the roofs of one set of *sassi* become the roadways for the dwellings above them. Although we found the going rough underfoot, it was possible to climb around the various levels and even enter some of the unoccupied dwellings. Nowadays I understand that an official guide is, if not mandatory, at least a good idea. The most remarkable thing in this unbelievable city is the series of 150 underground churches, the *chiesi rupestri*, most of them dug out of the rock by Benedictine monks in the middle ages. Some of them, originally separate churches, monasteries, and convents, have at some point been combined to make larger places of worship. Although a few still occasionally conduct services, and others are not in use at all, we found that the subterranean churches make excellent galleries for the display of art, at least judging by the first-rate sculpture exhibit that we saw. Many of the underground premises have remnants of early frescoes dating back to the tenth century, some in fairly good states of preservation.

From our hotel window in the Albergo Italia we had an incredible view out over the *sassi* and the countryside beyond. The middle-aged *signora* who ran it was welcoming, naturally kind, and extremely generous with her suggestions about the best way to get into the complex of cave dwellings. We felt that we had met an invaluable friend. It was she who told us about the sculpture exhibit in the underground church and that it was worth visiting the extensive quarry that wasn't mentioned in any of the guide books; she also told us about Da Mario and the Trattoria Lucana, where we could find traditional dishes at dinner. Among other things, we sampled stuffed artichokes, *bruschette* with wild arugula, a vegetable mélange resembling the French *ratatouille* of eggplant, peppers, tomatoes and zucchini, a pasta shaped a bit like *orecchiette*, sauced with meaty *ragù* and two kinds of cheeses (*pecorino* and smoky *scamorza*), roasted lamb and potatoes, veal *osso buco*, and wild fennel sausages. All of this was accompanied by the local red wine, Aglianico. We had, indeed, found a knowledgeable and trusted friend in the innkeeper.

The monochrome beige color of the *sassi*, the extraordinary quality of light, and the scale, all make Matera a likely stand-in for the increasingly dangerous city of Jerusalem. Or so filmmakers have discovered. The latest one, Mel Gibson, has used it as a setting for his controversial movie, *The Passion*, about the final twelve hours of the life of Jesus, which actually took place, of course, in old Jerusalem. Before that, Richard Gere, playing the role of the main character, filmed *King David*, substituting Matera for Jerusalem. Even before that, way back in the 1960s, Pier Paolo Pasolini, the famous Italian master, realizing the similarity between the two cities, made *The Gospel According to St. Matthew* in Matera instead of the Middle East. In the latest shoot, the Gibson film, some 1,500 townspeople were hired as extras, growing beards, donning sandals, robes, and armor, and looking very much like denizens of Jerusalem in the time of Jesus.

In a completely different, more modern vein, yet in its way equally intriguing, is a wonderful village called Dozza, where artists gather every other year to paint elaborate scenes on the *outsides* of the houses. Some twenty miles from Bologna, in the more prosperous north, the town is tiny, picturesque, and hilly, with narrow cobbled streets, several with archways over them, and inset loggias to guard against the weather. Most of the windows have plant boxes with cascading flowers, which like the shutters, do not deter the painters in the least. It seems that every surface is covered with elaborate scenes, some of which have definitely modern configurations and bright colors.

When we were there, a painting that especially caught our eye was a scene of five scantily clad women, each with different colored hair and wearing a different colored shift, performing the various chores of the harvest, from grape picking to stomping the grapes. The vines were as high as trees, and an orange-clad redhead was about to ascend a ladder to reach the fruit, while three of her companions had wicker containers heaped high with clusters. Off to the right of the damsel who was stomping, a brunette in a brown dress, there appeared a wine press, at the ready for the time when the fermentation was over.

The paintings, all of them extremely well crafted, lent an altogether charming air to the village. One of the more realistic frescoes depicted a huge wall, obviously a kitchen setting. On it, hanging by a heavy string affixed to a nail, a fish was suspended—about the size of a sturdy trout—and on the floor below were some boots, obviously recently worn, judging by their lumpiness and the state of their laces. An old chair with a well-worn rush seat fraying over the edges stood next to a kitchen table with an open drawer. On its top, under the fish, appeared a life-size empty wine bottle, a glass, a piece of fruit, a knife, an opener, and various other necessities.

Some murals were semiphotographic, such as a guitar player, one of several figures set between the tops of the loggia and the windows and flower boxes a foot or two above them. Others looked like the best museum-quality abstract paintings or mightily modernized folk art. Although most were extremely complicated, serious works of art, a great deal of humor was incorporated, and the overall effect was colorful and joyous. Some large walls were decorated by two or three different artists, one over the other, going up three stories. The most remarkable thing was how the renderings simply skirted the windows, adapted to the archways and hanging flower baskets, and filled the town, like some high-class gallery, with an incomparable art show. It was an experience like nothing that we had ever seen, let alone imagined.

While we were in Dozza, we went one day to the handsome brick fortress with its two round towers, the larger of which has an ancient angular tower in its middle, the smaller of which has slots which were used for pouring hot oil on approaching enemies. Not very nice, but those were the customs in those days. A working draw-bridge and a courtyard building once used by the families' marks-men, more our kind of thing, offered further protection against hostile invaders.

The well-refurbished fortress was once home to two related families, the Campeggi and the Malvezzi, who, true to their times, maintained prisons and torture chambers, with remnants of chains, trap doors, and instruments of torture, for all to see. Some inscriptions, made by the prisoners incarcerated there, remain on the walls. The families also maintained a private chapel, but true to their adherence to the mores of the time, it opened on a deep well, with razorlike projections, presumably to spike those thrown into it.

A sizeable kitchen with a quadrated stone floor contained a very large wood-burning stove with numerous ovens and cooking surfaces, grand copper pots, ceramic jugs and casseroles, all sorts of instruments and accoutrements for use in cooking and fire building, as well as porcelain-looking white dinnerware, vases, and serving vessels. Miscellaneous kitchen furniture included what I assumed was a rudimentary, hand-operated dumbwaiter, going I know not where.

In what were formerly some of the dungeons of the fortress, a huge space now refurbished—renewed vaulted brick ceilings, up-to-date indirect lighting splashing over the walls, and handsome modern wood cabinetry and shelving—turns out to be the Emilia Romagna Wine Cellar. An extensive collection of regional D.O.C. and D.O.C.G. wines, on display in a vast modernized space, manages to remove you far from the dungeons of the past into an ironic setting for public wine tasting that could not be more contemporary. It is the kind of typically Italian renovation that makes old forms into breathtakingly new ones and magically manages to transform a space without giving up its past. But knowing that past, and judging from the size of the place, they sure took a lot of prisoners in those days.

Among the many rooms on the visit, everything from grand bedrooms, reception areas, tapestry displays, antechambers, laundries, and pantries, perhaps the most significant in terms of the village is the display of the painted wall: some of the original murals from the houses of Dozza. In glass display cases, by way of historic documentation, are also photographs of the frescoes. Fortresses in Italy, even ones that have been restored as well as this one has been, are not unusual. But an art gallery encompassing the outside walls of all the buildings of the village is a fascinating spectacle that we were lucky enough to see.

From the *nuraghi* of Sardinia and the *trulli* of Puglia to the *sassi* of Basilicata, and even the more modern custom of painting the outsides of the houses in Dozza, Italy offers in a small geographic space some of the most vivid, kaleidoscopic glimpses into its history. This juxtaposition of ancient and modern is not special to the country, but the beguiling Italianate way, elucidating and at the same time charming, must certainly be unique.

CHAPTER SIXTEEN

Venice

As incredible as your first sight of Venice is, it doesn't seem any less overwhelming no matter how many times you see it. It reminds me of the time in 1948 when our architect, claiming that we would never use it, tried to discourage us from putting a deck on the west side of our house. (We persuaded him otherwise only because it was there anyway, as the roof over the carport.) Now, having lived in our home for over fifty-five years, our constant pleasure in that outdoor space doesn't seem to diminish. We use it all the time. We often have alfresco meals there, entertain our friends there—everything from serving drinks and hôrs d'oeuvre to a few to hosting very large parties. There are ever-changing views and mind-blowing scenes at twilight. Although one sunset is similar to the next, like the varied snowflake, there is never the same one twice.

It's the same sort of tingling excitement that we experience when we return to Venice. There is something indescribably thrilling about the views of a city strung together by an infinite series of waterways, something remarkable about entering a villa in a gondola, something awesome about having every police transport, fire engine, garbage collector, and ambulance, every taxi and bus, every funeral procession and hearse, waterborne.

When we first went to Venice, staying in a *pensione* with our two small children, the city proved to be so fascinating and mysterious that we were hooked forever. The inescapable intrigue in the air, the voluptuous color in the paintings, the constant hint of the city's former eminence, and above all the bubbly celebration of life, are so seductive that returning frequently is irresistible. And each time, amid favorite old places and treasured new discoveries, we learn a little more of the complicated history of this city of canals.

Built on more than one hundred islands connected by lagoons and an endless complexity of waterways, Venice went from the ninth-century settlement of its founders, who were fleeing from their enemies, to a prosperous and gaudy empire in the mid-1400s. Rich in jewels and eastern spices, the province acquired more and more far-flung territories and an enviable trading position. It was a time of unprecedented wealth and power. The city's gradual decline began in the latter half of the fifteenth century. Yet it still echoes its past. There is an abundance of festivals and celebrations, many with elaborate costumes and masks. There is still the joie de vivre at every turn: Architectural marvels from the past and museums filled with old masters exist amidst smart new shops, and there is the undeniable physical presence of all that water.

Nowadays, Venice worries about the rising waters, which could overwhelm and finally conquer this unique place. There are constant schemes to build seawalls and otherwise protect the city from the floods and destruction that already overwhelm it. So far, there seems to be no agreed-upon solution. Until there is, wooden sidewalks provide passage for rain-booted Venetians whenever Piazza San Marco is inundated by heavy rains and rising tides.

On our frequent visits, we have stayed in various neighborhoods. Before the Fenice opera house burned in a horrible fire, we often booked into the adjacent hotel, La Fenice et des Artistes. For several years after the fire, we could not stay there. It was too sad. Our friend Elena, who was for many years the Italian coach for the San Francisco Opera, requested that her friends, in lieu of gifts to her for an important birthday, give to the fund that was instrumental in preserving world monuments, specifying La Fenice. (Thanks to such efforts, the opera house is now rebuilt.)

In the old days, when we could afford it, we stayed at the Hotel Royal Danieli, by preference in the old wing, a fourteenth-century palazzo, with its enormous rooms, high ceilings, palatial luxuries, up-to-date marble bathrooms, flocked wall paper, and excellent beds. When our friend Florence arrived for her first visit to Italy, Charles stayed in Rome to represent the family at Barbara and Piero's church wedding, while I took Florence to Venice and to the illustrious Danieli. We had a splendid room overlooking the lagoon, where we enjoyed our room service breakfasts with that very special Venetian light accenting the view. The roof-top restaurant and terrace, although its menu was expensive and the cooking somewhat under-seasoned and internationalized, was well worth going to for the incomparable panorama.

We traveled everywhere by *vaporetto*, a water bus propelled by steam. When we felt flush we used a *motoscafo*, a motorboat taxi. Since everyone has to ride once in a gondola, we did that, too, making sure we had the advice of the hotel as to how much we should pay and settling the fare before boarding. The ride includes being sung to by the gondolier at the same time that he skillfully poles the boat in sometimes close maneuvers. To cross a canal from one bank to the other, one uses a ferry called a *traghetto*. And cross the banks we did, to see all the wonders, from Ca' d'Oro, a beautiful palace-museum on the Grand Canal, to the Accademia with its far reaching display of Venetian painters, to the Ca' Rezzonico, a museum of eighteenth-century Venice. We viewed the Doge's Palace and the Basilica, with its remarkable façade and its golden mosaics and altar, in the Piazza San Marco. When we got tired, we sat at one of the outdoor tables at the Café Florian, enjoying a refreshment and listening to the music provided by the house orchestra. Many people in the enormous square were either feeding the blizzard of pigeons or posing for pictures with them perched on their shoulders or whirring in flight. Only later did we learn from our friend Tanya that you could save an immeasurable number of *lire* if, at the same establishment, you sat at a tiny bar indoors to order your drink.

We also had adventures. One of them was going to the hairdresser. According to the hotel, whose advice we sought, the salon was the very best in town. We came out so pouffed, in spite of our protests, that we seemed to be wearing eighteenth-century wigs, but the hairdresser proudly assured us that we were sporting the very latest in hairstyles. Very self-consciously we made our way to the Taverna La Fenice, a first-class, handsome restaurant near the opera house, where we had reserved for dinner.

After we had been graciously seated and our orders taken, a table of gentlemen was seated right next to us, obviously friends of the proprietor. He was most cordial to them, laughing and joking, and took their orders himself. Assuming that we were non-Italian-speaking tourists and wouldn't understand a word of what was said, one of the men, glancing over and smiling at us, ordered prosciutto and figs. In Italian, figs have one word for the fruit, and by a simple change in gender, another for the female part which it is supposed to resemble. He used the latter, all the while glancing at us. The table and proprietor laughed uproariously at their little joke and we became increasingly uncomfortable, particularly because our hair-dos made us feel like tarts anyway. They continued to discuss us and, although the food was delicious, we didn't much enjoy our dinner. By the time they brought the bill, we felt we had to mention that we had understood everything and didn't enjoy their hilarity.

The proprietor swore not only on the Virgin Mary, but on his mother's head and those of his children, that no such thing had gone on. It was simply a misunderstanding, they were simply admiring our style, and certainly they had never mentioned "prosciutto and figs." But it was the first time those words had come into the conversation, for our general complaint hadn't mentioned them or any other specifics. The proprietor was by this time raising his voice in pitying tones, flailing his arms, and beseeching us to believe him. Do I simply imagine that he shed a tear or two? Tables nearby were staring at us. We desperately wanted out of there and paid our bill as quickly as possible. Looking over our receipt later, we realized that, in all the bluster, the restaurant had included things we had not ordered nor received. Added to everything else, we had overpaid.

Venice above all, is a city of extravagance. In the mid-fifteenth century, at the height of its exuberance, the wealth of Venice came from the importation of exotic goods and the other profits of conquest, which also contributed in large part to the glorious art and architecture and a cityscape gilded in true Byzantine fashion. Gondolas, their hulls painted elaborately and their lavish trimmings done up in luxurious fabrics manufactured in the city itself, transported an equally colorful population, many of them artists and intellectuals. As an outgrowth of their profuse use of silk, Venetians planted a large crop of mulberry trees to grow their own silk worms, which fed on the leaves. It turned into a thriving industry.

Venetian society, frequently elaborately costumed and masked, still revels in its festivals. There are even claims, although it is no longer the case, that one of the favorites, the celebration called *Carnevale*—usually at the end of February preceding Lent—lasted as long as six months in its heyday. The *Festa del Redentore*, held originally in July of 1575 to signal the end of a horrible plague in Venice, like the *Carnevale*, has become an annual event, culminating in spectacular fireworks on the Grand Canal. Palladio, the famous architect, designed Il Redentore church on the island of the Giudecca to mark the first festival. In September there is a colorful Regatta on the Grand Canal. First there is a procession of historic boats peopled by revelers in medieval costumes. Then there is the race. The competing rowers are wildly encouraged to gain the championship by the rousing cheers of the crowds on the banks. All of this is to mark the end of the summer, the shift of Venetian vacationers from their country retreats back to the city. (The Italians can, and do, find any excuse for a celebration!) Two more recent events, the Biennale, held in even years to exhibit contemporary art from around the world, and the annual showing of international films on the Lido, draw worldwide attention to modern culture.

The extravagance of Venice is also well-displayed in its cuisine. It developed as an ethnic east-west mix, derived historically in part from the influences of the invaders and the conquered, and in part from the prosperous and widespread maritime trade. The foreigners introduced and perpetuated many of their food preferences, while the traders introduced the city to such near eastern exotics as pepper, ginger, cloves, and cinnamon. Rice from Spain became a staple, appearing in such venerable dishes as risotto and the Venetian trademark *risi e bisi*, creamy rice cooked with the freshest new peas of springtime. It is traditionally served at yet another celebration, the Festa of San Marco in April, a commemoration of Venice's patron saint. Polenta, now also a standard, is made from corn that came originally from America, although in this city white corn is as common as yellow. Both types are more finely ground here and gnocchi are often made from polenta. Perhaps this was the first real fusion cuisine. Less speculatively, it is certain that Venice introduced the world to forks and most probably to glassware; it was being blown on the island of Murano, now famous for its glass, by the late thirteenth century.

Festivals always include sumptuous feasts, many eaten aboard boats festooned with lights and flowers and bobbing on the water. *Sfogi in saor*, sole in a piquant sauce, is a traditional nourishment on the *Festa del Redentore* and a favorite Venetian dish, which happens to meld east and west. The gently fried sole is marinated in a sauce consisting of sautéed onion slices, vinegar, wine, cinnamon, cloves, pepper, bay leaves, pine nuts, Malaga raisins, and sometimes tiny pieces of candied lemon peel. In restaurants, sardines are often substituted for the larger fish.

Venetians eat a brilliant array of seafood and shellfish, which are in abundant supply from the waters surrounding the city. The bounty includes infinite varieties that you have never before seen, let alone heard of, most of them local species of more familiar creatures. There is octopus, baby octopus no bigger than an inch across, and every size in between; small calamari, large calamari, all types and sizes of squid, various scampi, prawns and shrimp, *gamberetti di mare*, sea crabs, soft-shell crabs from Murano, eels, razor clams, scallops big and small and the tiny ones called *canestrelli*, sea dates, mussels, and a plenitude of other mollusks, as well as an endless assortment of fresh fish from the ocean and the lagoons. *Brodetto* (in local dialect, *broeto*) is fish soup; depending on what is fresh from the purveyor, its well-seasoned broth contains generous chunks of sea creatures and an abundance of crustaceans.

Mantis shrimp or *squilla*, often prepared in garlic and oil, appear on menus as *schile agio e ogio* in Venetian dialect, which tends to leave out or not pronounce the letter "l." Sardines, besides their frequent pickling in that sweet and sour sauce, are often cooked *scotadeo* (also dialect), so piping hot that they are likely to burn your fingers. Anchovies are cooked that way, too, although in much of Italy it's baby lamb chops on the bone that are prepared *scotta ditto*. When you pick them up, they scorch your fingers, hence the name, which means just that. In Venice *bottarga*, the pressed eggs of fish, is usually made from tuna. *Baccalà*, air-dried cod, which possibly made its way originally from Spain (although being air-dried rather than salted, it more resembles *stoccafisso* from Scandinavia), is usually prepared *mantecato*—that is, by soaking it, boiling it in milk, and whipping the flakes to a froth with good olive oil and garlic until it resembles fluffy mashed potatoes.

According to an article by our friend Johnny Apple, published in the *New York Times* early in March of 2004, all is not so rosy, however, with the native seafood being replaced by other species or by farmed or frozen products (although not often accurately labeled as such). More and more, there are added chemicals and preservatives, poisonous and polluted waters, and such substitutions as the less tasty, faster growing Manilla clam (planted and grown locally for several years now) for *vongole veraci*, without which you can't make a decent clam sauce. According to Johnny, it's not news that canny restaurateurs have been taking advantage of unwary tourists for centuries, but with advances in technology and transportation creating endless international supplies, the situation has become very much worse. Reputable restaurants, however, still serve exceptionally fresh local products, expensive as they may be, instead of gross imported substitutions, so beware of touristy places! Our friend writes that when you taste them you will find that the local Venetian sea creatures are "sublime — small, delicately textured and incomparably sweet . . ."

When they're not eating fish, whether at home or in a restaurant, Venetians also eat quantities of *bovoleti*, small snails gathered from the fields, and teal, mallard ducks, and other water fowl that make their homes in the lagoons. Among the favorite pastas are *bigoli*, a kind of enlarged, dark wheat noodle made on a special instrument called a *bigolaro*, and often sauced with a hefty ragu made from the duck. Venetians are also fond of a rice dish called *risotto all'onda*, or wavy rice. On occasion, we have eaten a most wonderful Venetian invention, *sopa caoda*, a soup concocted from toasted bread and pigeons, the birds' origin never specified, but judging from the enormous avian population in St. Mark's Square alone, they must be locals. The small pigeons known as *torresani* are from the neighborhood and usually spit-roasted, but maybe they are also the source of the soup.

The city contains numerous markets but nothing compares to the amazing and endless Rialto stalls near the Rialto Bridge. There, in the *Pescheria*, or fish market, you can find every fish and shellfish imaginable, always decorously arranged like still-life paintings. Nearby displays feature vast assortments of seasonable fruits, vegetables, and mushrooms like *porcini*. Although you see local variations of artichokes all over Italy—purple, green, chokeless, large, small, elliptical, round—only in Venice, and only in the latter half of April, do they grow the bitter *castraure*, or "castrated" first sprouts. From April into May there are also *botoli*, smaller, less bitter, less expensive, and with more harvestable blooms to each plant. *Canarini* sport a bright yellow coloration, hence the name "canaries," and come from the island of Sant'Erasmo. Besides the highly prized *castraure*, there are artichokes grown in the Malamocco gardens on the Lido that are colored a lighter yellow. All of these varieties, however brief and rare their existence, can be found in the vegetable stalls of the Rialto Market.

In the last few years, specialty stores in the United States have begun to carry some of the varieties of radicchio that come from the Veneto area of Italy. Elongated like a head of romaine but usually resembling tighter heads of endive, the radicchio of Treviso (the area is often dubbed the garden of Venice) looks more red than white, and has the bitter taste of the chicory family. Excellent as a salad ingredient, it is also often baked slowly with a drizzle of olive oil, but it is especially delicious when grilled. The radicchio from Castelfranco, on the other hand, is a rounder, tighter head, although sometimes it has little ruffles at the edge of the outer leaves. It has the mottled colors of Italy, red, white, and green, and is a very colorful and crisp addition to a salad. The Berkeley Bowl, my market at home, has been carrying it recently, but they have had the Treviso for a long time. The radicchio from Chiogga, the fishing village at the end of the Venice lagoon, is more traditionally red and round. It's the type most widely available in stateside produce markets.

In the restaurants of Venice we have, over the years, sampled a good many of the specialties of the city. Two of them were at the famous Harry's Bar, now run by Arrigo Cipriani, whose father Giuseppe (but always called the *Commendatore*) founded the place over fifty years ago. We had our first Bellini cocktail there, an invention of Papa. It is a delicious drink made of local puréed fresh white peaches and Prosecco, the Italian sparkling wine that comes from the Veneto. Italians more usually drink the bubbly straight as a champagne-like aperitif. We also had a dish there that the restaurant is often credited with inventing: *carpaccio*, razor-thin slices of raw beef with a mustardy-mayonnaisy sauce dribbled on top. It is an excellent way to begin a meal. Although there is no doubt whatsoever that Harry's Bar invented the Bellini, and possibly the *carpaccio*, it certainly named them both, each one after a Venetian painter.

Da Montin, a rather simple trattoria, served us our first sauce for *bigoli* made with anchovies and onions, as much a favorite of the locals as that made from duck. One of their specialties, and also our first time to try it, was *coda di rospo*, the succulent grilled tail of an anglerfish, which is seldom cooked with its ugly froglike head attached. At Ristorante Fiaschetteria Toscana their menu consists of classic Venetian dishes in spite of its name (a *fiaschetteria* is a glass flask in which beans are cooked in Tuscany, and as far as I can tell, neither that, nor any other Tuscan dish, is on the menu). Among the many local favorites was a *frittura della Serenissima*, mixed fried seafood in the style of the city (la Serenissima is another name for Venice), which incidentally earned us one of those *Ristoranti di Buon Ricordo* plates. We also sampled a risotto made with the wild greens called *carletti*, a first for us, but it didn't earn us a plate.

At the trattoria Da Ivo, it is hard to pass up the huge Tuscan-style steaks, but we often did in favor of local dishes like calves liver. In Venice, where it is as much a specialty as fish and shellfish, they slice it small and very thin. Cooked quickly and perfumed with onions, it becomes an absolutely delectable dish. This is the restaurant where we first ate wild strawberries with balsamic vinegar and pepper. In the spring, the menu features large white asparagus from the nearby town of Bassano.

That village is also famous for its *grappa*, so famous, in fact, that its official name is Bassano del Grappa. The walled fourteenth-century medieval center is also famous for its life-size game of chess, played every other September in the Piazza Castello. Dressed in fifteenth-century costumes, the participants who play the various "pieces" continue a tradition begun by one group of knights challenging another.

On a visit there one time, in order to learn more about the distillate, we went through the Poli museum and distillery. It is near a covered wooden bridge, the Ponte Vecchio, which crosses the

Brenta river, and was constructed after a design by Palladio. We have a couple of restaurant plates that depict it, although each one features a different food specialty. The museum, located in the fifteenth-century house of a nobleman, proved to be as fascinating as it was educational. We learned that the Poli distillery uses a traditional, very old copper still with twelve steam-run cauldrons to make the "*cotta*," or base eau-de-vie, out of the grape pressings. In the old days, Titta, the great-grandfather of Jacopo Poli, the master *grappaiolo* at the time of our visit, used to distill, illegally, grape pomaces for the city's inhabitants in a still that he had built himself. He got around the neighborhoods by propelling it house to house on a cart. His more law-abiding son, Giobatta, who modified a steam engine from a locomotive to create his still, founded the Poli distillery as a legal business in 1898.

As a memento of our visit, we bought some official *grappa* glasses. They are colorless, tulip-shaped vessels with long stems and a protruding ring that prevents the hand from straying up to the bowl and warming the liquid. They also direct the *grappa*, by the flare of the lip, to the front part of the tongue, where the taste buds are receptive to "sweetness," which is part of the complexity of the drink. These were being hand-blown long before the twentieth-century invention by Georg Riedel of a different wine glass for each variety, the result of the recent trend of designs meant to send the contents to the right part of the mouth.

In Venice, it is a pleasure to broaden one's knowledge of local dishes at the restaurant Al Covo, one of our favorite places. For example, we have often had their *fritto misto*, a platter of various shellfish, including soft-shell crab when it's in season. To our surprise, it sometimes incorporates a wedge of lightly battered and deep-fried raddichio from Treviso. We frequently finish our meal with their fine zabaglione, a popular dessert in the city ever since the importation of Marsala from Sicily. The owners, Cesare Benelli, a very good-looking, white-haired Italian, and Diane, his svelte and handsome wife, couldn't be more cordial. In spite of her trim figure, she makes most of the desserts. Obviously, she doesn't overindulge in them. And unlikely as it seems, she originally hails from Texas.

Several years ago, we were telling Diane that Johnny Apple, who then lived in Washington, had once told us that he thought highly of Al Covo. The American couple seated at a table next to us couldn't help but overhear "Washington," because they lived there, too. We began to chat. When we revealed we had a daughter who also lived in D.C., of course they asked her name. The woman couldn't believe our answer. She told us she was a professional photographer named Leslie Cashen who specialized in children's portraits. Every year since they were little, she had taken our grandkids' pictures, and still does, and one time when we were visiting, she took ours, too. Suddenly we all realized that there was a reason we all looked familiar. We remembered with delight our visits to the photography studio in their house. Somehow, we hadn't expected to renew our acquaintance with the Cashens at a table next to us in far away Venice.

One of the best ways to eat well in a foreign city is to follow recommendations from locals or nonresident Italians who spend a lot of time there. Sandro Rossi, who comes from Italy, has for many years run the wonderful Café 1870 in Oakland, California. When he learned that we were about to go to Venice, he suggested one day at lunch that we try a non-chic, out-of-the-way trattoria, Altanella, on the island of Giudecca. It turned out to be a comfortable place with excellent food, well-worn menus, and a Venetian clientele. There were no large villas in this working-class neighborhood. Instead, the canals were lined with three- or four-story houses, and the waters were crowded with numerous fishing boats, some with sails, and some moored with an enormous number of large floating wicker baskets tied to them. We thought they must be crab or lobster traps. Several men were maneuvering their boats by poling them standing upright, the way gondoliers do. At Altanella, we ate very well including our first try of *bacalà alla Visentina*, a more complex version of the air-dried cod that we were familiar with, in this case flavored with onions, garlic, and anchovies. The grilled *branzino*, or sea bass, served with polenta, was memorable, the simplicity of its preparation, a hallmark of Venetian cooking, bringing out the pristine flavors.

Because we share mutual friends, we once called Marcella and Victor Hazan, who teach and write about food and wine, for advice about where we should eat. They had lived in Venice for years but before Marcella could give a proper answer she peppered us with appropriate questions—meat or fish? fancy or simple?—that sort of thing. She settled on Ai Barbacani in Castello-San Lio, which turned out to be a perfect choice. Among other things we had a *carpaccio* made of razor-thin slices of fish (bream, I think), not the meat that is universally used in that dish.

Most wonderful of all, to accompany our desserts at the end of the meal, the waiter poured us a wine we hadn't ordered, tasting intensely of the wild strawberries from which it was made. Or so we thought. But our waiter informed us that the wine, Fragolino, was actually made from a grape named Uva Fragola, for its strawberry-like flavor. Although it is a popular drink in Venice, we probably would never have ordered it. If it were not for recommendations from friends, we might have missed out on such other treats as a salad of the special Adriatic crab called *granceola*, served in its shell; or a sumptuous dish of baked eel wrapped in bay leaves; or wild duck from the lagoon; or grilled wedges of white, not yellow, cornmeal polenta.

There are two Cipriani hotels whose restaurants are remarkable in different ways, one of them on the Giudecca and one on the island of Torcello. Also on the Giudecca, Harry's Dolci, run by Arrigo Cipriani of Harry's Bar fame, is another delightful spot founded by a member of the tribe. Neither of Arrigo's places is now connected to the hotels, nor to the deluxe Cipriani hotel in Asolo, where we have also once ventured. I understand that the hotel on the Giudecca no longer belongs to the family, but the one on Torcello is managed by Bonifacio Brass, whose mother Carla, the sister of Arrigo, was the daughter of Giuseppe Cipriani, the founder of it all.

If you are headed for the hotel in Venice, there is a private launch which takes you from St. Mark's Square across the lagoon to the resort on the Giudecca. When the weather is good, it is the most pleasant experience imaginable to eat lunch outdoors on the terrace. Everything seems to taste better when you're bathed in sunshine. Besides the sheer joy of luxuriating in the surroundings, there is picture-perfect food. The extravagantly sized swimming pool has nothing on the basketball-like cantaloupe that I consumed one day dining with friends. We have a snapshot to prove it. The chocolate *gelato*, although we didn't manage to photograph it, with its chocolate gondola wedged across the top and its pool of bitter orange sauce, is sensational to look at, and absolutely scrumptious to eat.

Most people select from a bountiful buffet which offers such things as pastas, salads, and a variety of hot dishes, including fish that is truly local. For the à la carte types, handsomely arranged plates arrive from the kitchens. The cooking is well prepared—on the simple side rather than three-star lavish—but it's the whole experience that is memorable. One could just spend the day people watching. It was not unexpected, for example, that one afternoon, lunching on the terrace, we were suddenly aware of a familiar-looking couple seated nearby, he stylishly chic but casual, and she encompassed in an organza-like, ethereal cloud of yellow. They were the restaurateur Wolfgang Puck and designer Barbara Lazarus on their honeymoon.

It takes almost forty-five minutes by *vaporetto* from Venice's Fondamenta Nuova to the island of Torcello, where the Locanda Cipriani is tucked away. In the old days, to get to the inn from the boat entailed a long walk along a battered path next to a small canal. We often detoured before lunch to see the Cathedral of Santa Maria Assunta or the even simpler church of Santa Fosca. Going back to the seventh century, altered in the ninth, and again in the eleventh century, the cathedral is not so grandiose and gigantic as many that were built later, more in scale with the small piazza that houses it. Some intricate Byzantine mosaics were probably reset or added to the walls in the twelfth and thirteenth centuries and others, in the latter period, to the apse and some of the vaults. But I find that the octagonal church of Santa Fosca, built in the tenth century and next to the Locanda, is even more appealing, and I visit it every time we go to Torcello. Although more and more visitors are crowding in, it still conveys a calm that few places can offer these days.

Unfortunately, in the last several years the rambling path from the dock has been enlarged and finished over, so that the original meandering quality is all but forsaken. There are two or three *osterie* and restaurants, souvenir stands, occasional houses, work being done on the canal, and even a charge to go on a tour of the cathedral. Although there is no trouble finding your way to the Locanda, some of the remote quality that appealed to the honeymooners who stayed there has been lost. Considering that there has been a settlement on Torcello since the seventh century, modernization, no matter how inevitable, still seems a pity.

Once at the Locanda you can opt for lunch indoors or out. Weather permitting, we prefer the well-shaded outdoor patio. At one time, an adjacent organic vegetable garden supplied the kitchen, but Bonifacio Brassi told me that they had to give it up because in the winter it was water-logged, requiring chemicals to remove the salt, thereby making it no longer organic. The thing to eat in this lovely spot—and they will cook it for you whether it's on the menu or not—is the black *risotto* made with squid ink. It's absolutely delectable.

Although Torcello can be a leisurely full day's excursion, those whose time is limited can stop off on the same trip to see the lace making on the picturesque island of Burano, or to visit the glass factories on Murano. A school for lace making, founded in the little fishing village of Burano in the 1870s, acknowledged its importance as the center of the Venetian industry. On Murano you can witness glass blowing in the establishments that produce en masse, although the more exclusive manufacturers like Venini and Cenedese are not open to the public. However, exceptions are sometimes made for customers who have purchased items in the shops that are the factories' retail outlets in the city.

It takes a much shorter ride to get to the informal Harry's Dolci. Once landed, in order to find the restaurant, you must make your way to the west end of the Giudecca between the Church of Sant'Eufemia and the sizeable old Molino Stucky warehouse. I confess that we have never eaten indoors in the restaurant proper, although curiosity has led us inside to inspect the place. (It strikes me as handsome enough, in a laid-back sort of way.) Instead we've opted for dining outside, the only feasible option for a lazy afternoon. Overlooking the Canale della Giudecca with the buildings of Venice on the other side, the shaded tables, draped in white and fanned by gentle breezes, have as a more immediate backdrop the traffic of boats that constantly glide to and fro. It provides a good antidote for the bustling crowds of the city.

A dapper Signor Cipriani meanders seamlessly among the tables, chatting with his guests, making sure that everyone is eating well and having a good time. With appealingly simple food and gracious service, you can't help but enjoy. On a hot summer afternoon you can eat lightly, perhaps starting off with a salad of mixed seafood or marinated baby artichokes. Along with the customary follow-ups, there are several appealing sandwiches on the menu. For dessert eaters, the chocolate cake is world-class, made in the nearby bakery that Cipriani also owns. The well-prepared food is uncomplicated and delicious, but it's the whole experience that delights you.

One of the more pleasant local traditions for residents is to have a glass or two of wine at one of the *bacari*, or wine bars, accompanied by a vast and savory array of tapaslike snacks called *cicchetti*. But it is also a way for foreigners to sample the genuine foods of Venice, including many that you can't find in a regular restaurant. The *bacari* derive their name from Bacchus, the frolicsome god of wine, and in his spirit they are festive, convivial gathering places. Although they may be strangers to each other, members of the crowd often indulge in animated conversation while they snack on the bar food and sip a glass of wine.

Before there were wine bars, gondoliers seeking shade from the intense summer sun used to take shelter under the shadow of the Campanile in San Marco Square and drink a glass of wine to refresh themselves. Because in Italian the word *ombra* means shade, it soon attached itself to the wine, so in Venice the common word for a glass of wine became *ombra*, or its diminutive *ombretta*. *Di bianco* means "white," *di rosso* means "red." The birth of the wine bar came about when the custom of taking a refreshment gradually spread from San Marco to the indoor counter. Now the city is dotted with *bacari* and many of them have put in tables and expanded into *osterie* or regular restaurants.

Our favorite is called Al Mascaron. Although there are now tables in two smallish rooms where you can eat *osteria*-style, and a few tables in the bar itself, crowds still gather around the counter for a stand-up glass of wine and the smorgasbord of snacks that is offered. The last time we were there, we sat at a table and had the most wonderful pasta with assorted sea creatures, as well as an assortment of *cicchetti*, which we picked out at the counter ahead of time. Another place that we go back to often is Vino Vino near the Fenice theater, the food provided for by the excellent restaurant Antico Martini. Although they didn't take credit cards the last time we visited, they did accept reservations through the parent restaurant, an exception to the rules that usually apply to wine bars.

Another notable difference is the quality of wine among the *bacari*. Most often the wine in Venice is *beverino*, that is, pleasantly drinkable, refreshing, fruity, and unsophisticated. But at Vino Vino, as well as at several wine bars and many restaurants, you can get a choice of excellent wines from all over the country.

Cicchetti usually include a vast display of local fish and seafood; small filled rolls or triangular sandwiches called *tramezzini;* various cold cuts—everything from the more familiar prosciutto and salami to one made out of a pig's snout; braised or fried meatballs; tiny land snails; marinated, braised, or grilled vegetables, including, in May, those bitter castrated artichoke buds called *castraure;* many types of sausages; hard-boiled eggs, sometimes draped with anchovies; whipped and garlicky dried cod; tripe; spleen; and *nervetti* (marinated calf's foot). At some bars you can even get small portions of gnocchi, pasta, or risotto. One of the most addictive choices is olives, always fried and often stuffed. Another is *frico,* a flat tidbit of melted cheese, which in its finished stage resembles somewhat a very crunchy cracker.

Adventures are not lacking in this city of canals. Often a friend clues us in to something that we hadn't heard of before. Ora's daughter Tanya, for example, in her capacity as an official guide, discovered that the Church of Zaccaria had the most wonderful Bellini painting. When she told us about it and how to find it, we followed her instructions: From the Riva degli Schiavoni, near the Danielli Hotel, you go through a *portico* or passageway called Sottoportico San Zaccaria. On the right-hand side there stands the church, and inside, its remarkable painting.

Another discovery was the number of shops selling paper made by local artisans. Besides rolls of patterned paper for wrapping, you can find boxes, stationery, note papers, all sizes of books for all kinds of uses, picture frames, carnival masks, whimsical animals, and other *objets,* all covered with fanciful papers. One chooses with care and deliberation because these treasures are not inexpensive. But it's a delightful and instructive way to spend some time browsing.

Sometimes, you happen upon an event that turns out to be more of an adventure than you had ever imagined. For instance, more than fifteen years ago, in the company of Charles's brother Len and his wife Draselle, we happened to be strolling past the old church La Chiesa di Vivaldi di Venezia when we noticed that I Virtuosi dell'Ensemble di Venezia would be giving a series of concerts, featuring the famous composer for whom the church was named. Since we all liked Vivaldi, we enthusiastically agreed to get tickets, anticipating a pleasant way to spend an evening. To our surprise, the performance turned out to be one of the most enthralling musical events any of us had ever attended. Thinking about it later, we agreed that it was due in part to the intimacy of the small church and its fine acoustics; in part to the stalwart musicians who played extravagantly well; and in part to the stellar program they chose—several of Vivaldi's concerti. What we thought was a small local group, the Ensemble, although permanently attached to the Church of Vivaldi, has performed all over the world and made numerous recordings, one of which, of course, we now own. Their conductor, Giovanni Guglielmo, also violin soloist for the group, had first distinguished himself as founder and principal soloist for I Solisti Veneti, and for ten years before that played first chair with the orchestra of La Fenice. For me, it is always an exciting experience to hear the seventeenth-century music of Antonio Vivaldi. But the fact that he was Venetian and that we heard the concert in his hometown, not to mention the church bearing his name, made it even more memorable. It turned an anticipated pleasant evening of music into something special.

Perhaps the ultimate adventure for a traveler is the chance to live in a house rather than a hotel, to shop in the markets and prepare the food as the locals do, in short to experience the life of a resident rather than that of a tourist. We had lived for long periods in Rome and Tuscany, but in Venice we had always been tourists staying in hotels. All that changed several years ago when my friend and agent, Robert Lescher, told us about the house that his family had rented in the Cannaregio district. He and Susan and daughter Susannah had tried it out for a month. They liked it so much that every summer they went back. They gave us the address so that we could see if it was suitable for us.

To reach the *villetta*, according to their instructions, we had to take the *vaporetto* #52, which goes up to Fondamenta Nuova and skips the Grand Canal, and is therefore less crowded. Our stop, Tre Archi, was the next one after the Ponte Guglie, the first bridge on the Cannaregio Canal. Once off the boat and the short wooden rampway, we faced a small bar with a few tables out front, permanently occupied by the old men of the neighborhood enjoying their cigarettes and espressos. To the right of the bar stood an arched entry to a cobbled walkway, the Calle Ferau, although the last time we were there, no street signs were in evidence. Past a small field-stone courtyard on the left, it was only a few feet to reach the house. Number 916 and the owners' names were on the door. Painted pale salmon with contrasting dark green shutters, the little house stood unattached. From the corner of the second floor a street lamp projected on the diagonal by means of a bracketed metal arm. Rigged by a pulley, two or three lines for drying clothes ran beneath the windows of the upper story. Altogether, it looked charming, like an over-sized doll house.

To see the interior we had to go to the bar to fetch the key. The barkeep, a friendly chap, hauled out a large ring with dozens of keys attached. Clearly he had access to the entire neighborhood. He amiably accompanied us and tried one key after another until he had exhausted them all without success. Not to worry, he told us, he had an equal number of different keys back in the bar and we would try those. So we traipsed back to his building, exchanged the key ring, and began trying the new set. Halfway through, the door opened.

Immediately in the entryway were several pairs of rain boots, a necessity when heavy precipitation made lakes out of passageways. The small living room had several bookshelves crammed with regional tomes, guides to Paris, several art and history volumes, and various machines for making music, their cords wired together and plugged into the modern outlet in the best Rube Goldberg style. The furnishings consisted of a striped velour loveseat in a wooden frame, modern wall sconces to give light, small end tables, a blue canvas director's chair, and a shaggy dark area rug partially covering the checkerboard parquet floor. A floor-to-ceiling mirror in a wooden frame leaned against one wall, making the room look twice as large. Besides framed artwork, there were handsome ceramic vases, a Byzantine wall hanging, and gauzy drapes covering the windows. A round bronze shield, probably ancient and about three feet in diameter—the kind of thing a Roman warrior would have carried —stood against the modern hatched radiator cover under one of the bookshelves. In spite of some of the older decorations, the fresh white paint gave the room a cheerful, contemporary look.

The wall behind the loveseat, with a portion cut out and framed like a window, gave an open view of the kitchen, at the same time serving as another device for making the small living room seem larger. The kitchen itself became my favorite room, combining modern appliances and contemporary wooden cabinetry with handsome brick walls. Centered in one of them was a great raised fireplace for use in cooler weather. Presumably it was also one you could cook in, judging by the various hanging tools and those placed on the copious workspace that extended hearthlike in front of the fire. An abundance of assorted copper pots shined from hooks behind the cooking top set into the marble counter. At right angles, a few feet from the fireplace, the black face of the separate oven punctuated the brick and wood surrounding it. There was a pantry for storing grocery items, a wine rack, a fine wooden chest with a dozen tiny drawers for spices, numerous canisters, flasks, espresso pots, knives in a wooden block, all sorts of kitchen tools, and even a large mortar and pestle. For eating breakfast, lunch, and dinner, there was a round wooden table with black leather director's chairs nestled under the wall with the opening to the other room. When we stayed in the house, we would put our customary vase of flowers on the table. Thanks to the large cutaway, it cheered the living room as well.

To gain access to the second floor, there was a handsome marble stairway with a simple polished brass handrail. Indented in the wall at the bottom, a lighted display showed off precious *objets*. Upstairs a master bedroom let in light through the same gauzy curtains. The giant wooden wardrobe stashed hanging clothes, and a multidrawered chest provided for all the rest. A double bed with a fine wooden headboard, its pillows and quilted cover in stark navy blue, contrasted with the white walls and the curlicued Venetian glass chandelier hanging above it. There were swinging reading lamps attached to the wall on each side of the bed, a small miracle in Italy. In many hotels, if they have them at all, the lamps contain bulbs so dim as to be virtually useless.

Also on the second floor was the study, white with the same breezy curtains, furnished with an off-white couch that turned into a bed for extra family or guests. Against one wall, a handsomely grained wooden cabinet metamorphosed into a desk when you lowered the large hinged door. A sizeable drying rack, which took up the rest of the space, turned out to be doubly fortunate. When we later rented the house and Ora came to visit us, she used to hang and store her clothes there. Unfortunately, there were no closets or dressers in the room. Mini houses have some drawbacks.

The one other room upstairs, a modern bathroom, contained a shower, a toilet, a bidet and, blessed be, a washer-dryer. Delicate garments that wouldn't prosper from machine drying explained the need for the drying rack. When Ora was there, we hung such items on the clotheslines strung for that purpose outside the second floor windows. Completely tiled, the bathroom was a handsome cornflower blue for the floor and, except for a blue band running waist high around the middle, white for the walls. The towels and bathmats were all dark blue. Very harmonious.

To rent the house turned out to be a fine decision. It was quite different from our usual experience in Venice. For one thing, we loved walking through *our* neighborhood, especially along the canal. There you never saw hordes of foreigners, only local, hardworking, cheerful people going about their chores. We admired the occasional window boxes brimming with colorful flowers, delighted in shopping in the bakery and from the stands in the market, and enjoyed occasionally stopping at an informal café for lunch at the water's edge. Every so often there were red, green, and striped flags fluttering colorfully across the boat traffic, on lines strung from the second stories of houses on opposite sides of the canal. It was an animated scene, vessels scurrying to deliver everything from lumber for building to boxes of goods for the sprinkling of shops tucked here and there. There was even a working backhoe afloat on its barge, with an accompanying scow for depositing the muck it dredged up. The occasional small restaurant or bar was very casual, including the unlikely Chinese place with its bright red lanterns and its red and white sign in three languages: RISTORANTE CINESE in Italian; and (indecipherable to me) some Chinese characters which presumably said the same thing; then CHINA TOWN, which may, in fact, have been, instead of a bad translation, the proprietor's idea of a chic English name.

Perhaps the most moving and revealing experience that we had, however, was exploring the nearby ghetto in all its detail, right smack in our own neighborhood. Years before, we had gone to, and found overwhelming, the old Jewish cemetery near the church of San Nicolò on the Lido. I wouldn't be surprised if that emotional event were not the inspiration for our serious in-depth interest in the ghetto. Just getting to the inaccessible cemetery had been a time-consuming adventure. One had to take the *vaporetto* #1 from San Zaccaria, and then walk about fifteen minutes north from the boat dock, quite a trek in the summer heat of Venice. (There were buses for the weary.)

Because the cemetery had been in disuse and long closed to the public, we could only peer through the metal spokes of the portals to see a part of the disheveled burial grounds. Surrounded by high walls, full of weeds and tumbled tombstones, it was a sign of the long neglect the land had suffered. Yet we could feel the age and significance of this ancient place. By a few years, its oldest identifiable tombstone outdated the earliest marker in the Jewish cemetery in Prague, making it one of the first burial sites in Europe for members of that faith.

Once owned by the Benedictines, the land was set aside in 1386 by the Venetian state as a place for the city's Jews to be interred. Everybody else was buried on the more illustrious Island of San Michele. In 1770, the Jewish cemetery's operation ceased; from 1774 up until the present time, burials have taken place in a new but still segregated cemetery, on a parcel of land nearby. The tombstones in the old location reflected the history of the Jews' migration to Venice—from the first Ashkenazis from eastern and central Europe to the later Sephardics from Spain and Portugal.

The earlier Ashkenazi grave markers were simple rectangular slabs with engraved Hebrew lettering. By the time of the Sephardics, who came to Venice later, after their expulsion from Spain in the late fifteenth century, the stones became much more ornate, reflecting the Spaniards' somewhat rococo taste. Families boasted heraldic coats of arms, which often decorated their headstones along with portraits, garlands, cherubs, human figures, and all sorts of flora and fauna. Some individuals had horizontal markers elaborately carved like sarcophogi covering the entire gravesite. In the nineteenth century, when the first grounds had long since been abandoned and were in distinctly bad shape, they were a favorite place for Lord Byron and Percy Bysshe Shelley to ride their horses. Apparently, the desolation appealed to them.

Though the cemetery was still in disrepair and closed to the public when we were there, since that time, international efforts, under the guidance of a committee from Venice, have acknowledged its importance and successfully refurbished the historic site. While draining the sunken, swamplike portion, workmen discovered more than one hundred tombstones that had completely disappeared under the earth. They repaired, photographed, and catalogued them. Landscaping consisted of thoroughly clearing and thinning the rampant vegetation; rebuilding peripheral walls repaired the centuries-old damage; and righting, repairing, reinstalling, and documenting the rest of the grave markers and other monuments completed the restoration. Designated a cultural public monument in the winter of 2000, the cemetery now offers official tours. Anyone interested in history would agree that such recognition was long overdue.

It is uncertain when the first Jews came to Venice. Whether some of them were there by the tenth century is not clear, but a reported edict forbidding ships to discharge merchants of that persuasion suggests that they were at least trying to take up residency. From early on, Jewish welfare consistently vacillated with the condition of the state, and the faithful were subjected to alternate tolerance and oppression. When the city needed municipal funds, often fiercely depleted through territorial wars, Jewish moneylenders were invited to ply their trade (although restricted in the amount of interest they could charge, sometimes below the going rate). If municipal times were good, intolerance took over, and they were kicked out.

During the middle ages, Venetian Jews had to wear yellow star-shaped patches, and later yellow hats (although for a time travelers were exempted because, if identified, they might be subjected to serious attacks elsewhere). During the Inquisition, Spain and Portugal demanded forced conversions to Christianity, calling the converts *"Marranos,"* an insulting word meaning "pigs" in those languages. *Marranos* secretly never gave up their Judaism, embracing it in private, but without leadership or the guidance of community. A survivalist first and foremost, a *Marrano*, therefore, became a combative person of uncertain or distorted faith, sometimes had to rely on a kind of protective camouflage in his dealings, and was often perceived as either wavering or outright untrustworthy—all of which made him suspect and mistrusted by both Jews and Venetians. But a significant number of converted *Marranos* became practicing Jews again when they migrated to Venice.

Never accepted as true Venetians, people of Jewish faith could not own houses or land but could rent for long terms without difficulty (although their rental payments were more than that of a Christian lessee). They were limited to such occupations as banking, moneylending, and pawn brokering, selling used clothing, outfitting ships, being merchants, or much-in-demand physicians. At one point, they were permitted to bear arms to insure their safety, and some even enjoyed a certain freedom, affluence, and status in the community. In Venice, to be sure, their situation was more favorable than in most places. But even in times of hostility in that city, although there may have been severe restrictions, no physical harm ever came to any of them, an exception to the general practice elsewhere, before and since. Their comparative, but always limited, freedom, however, finally brought out an extreme increase in overt anti-Semitic behavior. The prevailing enmity was such that by the spring of 1516, a municipal decree, roundly defeated only the year before, now ordered the physical segregation of Jews to an enclosed residential quarter, which became famous as the world's first ghetto.

In Italian, the verb *gettare* means "to cast," and the Venetian word for foundry, *geto* or *getto*, is derived from it. It became "ghetto" in Italian, and hence to the rest of the world. The new ordinance declared that the Ghetto Nuovo, an iron foundry that had once made cannons, should henceforth be designated as a separate quarter for those of Jewish faith. High walls were installed, and moatlike canals surrounded it. Sets of entry gates, closed and locked from night until morning, served to separate the population from the rest of the city. Heavy fines and even imprisonment faced those who broke the rules, with one exception: When their non-Jewish clients realized that they couldn't make house calls at night, physicians were exempted. Resident Christian guards made sure that the Jews, who were obliged to pay them for their "services," strictly obeyed the regulations. At all times of the day and night, guard boats patrolled the surrounding canals. The Jews had to pay for them, too. As a final insult, the houses that they occupied, officially emptied of their former residents, cost one-third more rent for the new lessees than the previous tenants had paid. On the more favorable side, the new rentors enjoyed the legal rights to long-term leases, which also could be sold, inherited, or given to another person.

Actually there were three contiguous ghettos. An older iron factory, the Ghetto Vecchio, was the original. It expanded to the area south of it, the Ghetto Nuovo, the one designated to confine the Jewish population. The third, created in 1633 as a space for new Jewish arrivals, was called the Ghetto Nuovissimo. This newest ghetto had neither shops nor *scuole*, as the synagogues were called, but the houses were more handsome and aristocratic, and the population less crowded. It was the density of the Ghetto Nuovo, with its small crammed flats and shared lavatories, that made the authorities favor expanding eastward to an area accessible by a bridge across the canal.

Narrow tunnel-like passages served as entranceways to the Ghetto Nuovo. Unlike houses in most of the other neighborhoods, those in the ghetto were six or seven stories tall, many of them surrounding the sizeable circular plaza, or *campo*, as the Venetians preferred to call it. I once read somewhere that it was probably the only square in Italy that didn't boast a café. Pawn brokers, secondhand clothing shops, three banks, and other small businesses occupied the street level. The residences and synagogues were on the floors above them. Banco Rosso, although now a private house, still has its historic sign over the normal-sized wooden door. The entrance, set back from the square under a timbered, beamed loggia, seems miniscule by today's standards. The Old Ghetto also seems to have contained some small shops that offered produce and kosher meat, and the two Sephardic synagogues, still in use today. In the Ghetto Nuovo, there are nowadays refurbished apartments, cafés, restaurants and shops, and a tour that includes the museum and three synagogues.

In the only surviving bakery that still makes all of the traditional pastries, the clientele can always count on finding a good supply of unleavened matzoh, along with the other breadstuffs. In appearance, it is different from the flat brittle sheets familiar to us. Rectangular like an elongated brick and much thicker than a cracker, it has wider indentations that go all the way through, making it look somewhat like a lattice. According to a sign in its small display window, the bakery's specialty is *dolci ebraici*, or Jewish sweets. At the time that we visited, we met the baker, Giovanni Volpe, who was not a Jew, he told us, but had learned to make all the traditional wares from a baker who was. There were two other signs in the window that reflected more modern tastes, right alongside the old Jewish specialties: *panini imbottiti*, sandwiches, and *pizza napoletana*.

Reflecting the many areas in the world from which the Jews of Venice had originally come, there were five *scuole*, or synagogues, constructed within the sixteenth century. The first, in 1528, was the German School, followed by the Italian and Canton synagogues, all Ashkenazi. The name of the Canton School has nothing to do with geography, as attested to by its congregation, but rather with one of two possibilities: Since in Venetian dialect *"canton"* means corner, the very location of the synagogue may have created the name; but more accepted is the probability that it was named after the family of bankers who helped pay for its erection. The larger and later Levantine School, and the even larger and later Spanish School, were those built in the Ghetto Vecchio. Alongside the Spaniards, in the congregation of the latter, were *Marranos* from Spain.

Because it was the earliest built, we decided to see the German School first. The building inside has a rounded gallery, plush with red cloth behind ornate balustrades. Chandeliers hang from the ceiling, there is much gilding and dark wood, and some of the walls have marble inserts. The gold, elaborately curlicued doors to the ark for the Torah reflect the importance of this sacred scroll. We were astonished at the abundance of rich materials and the extravagance of the decoration in all the synagogues, especially in comparison with the crowding and unpretentiousness of the ghetto itself.

Both the Italian and Canton Schools had high pulpits and stage-like altars, a response to, and derived perhaps from, the sense of theater prevalent in the incredible setting of Venice itself. Rising above the third-floor Canton synagogue, but only partially visible through the crowd of taller buildings around it, was a domed six-sided cupola. A stained-glass window filled each of the angles, more glass than solids. In the daytime, when the light entered, it made the colorful patterns scintillate and the dome itself transparent and airy. A large double window on one wall repeated the theme, but when there was too much sunshine, closed bright red drapes protected the room within.

In the Ghetto Vecchio, the two Sephardic synagogues both conducted Friday night services, one in summer, the other in winter. Both had exteriors slightly reminiscent of Venetian palaces. Because the Spanish School was not open when we were there, we only saw the neo-classic interior of the Levantine School, and found very elaborate wood carving, an extremely high pulpit, and marble that one would expect to find in an important place of worship outside the ghetto. The Baroque Spanish synagogue is supposed to be the grandest, most extravagantly decorated of all. The congregants of both Schools were mostly important merchants, coming directly from Spain or by way of Greece.

Italians often spoke in the dialect of their region, while others reverted to their native tongues. The Ghetto was a place where one was accustomed to hearing a multitude of languages, including Hebrew. No matter their country of origin, all of the Jews were Orthodox in practice. In keeping with their conservative beliefs, they separated the sexes in places of worship. Upstairs, just under the ceiling, and away from the pews for the men, the synagogues had screened galleries for the women worshippers.

One day, we visited the Museo Ebraico, where we found an exquisite collection of articles used in practicing the faith: Torah shields; gold and silver finials used for the sacred scrolls; shofars, or rams' horns; oil lamps, candlesticks, and menorahs; spice boxes and Passover plates; and a thousand other such items. The collection in the museum, along with the latest refurbishing of the synagogues, was one of the attractions that gave tourists a sense of Judaism.

The fall of the Venetian republic, in 1797, also marked the end of the ghetto. The removal and destruction of the gates, which had segregated the Jews since the early sixteenth century, now guaranteed their freedom of passage. Earlier that year, while the state was still fighting a losing battle with Napoleon's forces, the people of the ghetto had offered large quantities of cash and silver to bolster the effort of the Venetian forces. As one of its final acts a month before its collapse, the senate issued a decree of effusive gratitude for the loyalty and attachment of the Jews as demonstrated by their present gift and their generous contributions in the past. Almost one hundred years before that, on the plastered salmon-pink wall of a building just inside the Sottoportico di Ghetto, the authorities had erected a stone slab which still exists, pontifically outlining the numerous rules and regulations of the ghetto.

Under the new freedom, some Jews continued to make their homes in the ghetto until the emergence of Fascism once again turned them into enemies. On December 5, 1943, and again on August 17, 1944, during the Second World War, the Nazis deported a total of 246 individuals to concentration camps. The number included children as young as three, and elderly residents of the Casa Israelitica di Riposo, a rest home built on one side of the Campo in the Ghetto Nuovo. Of that number, eight people (some estimates say four or five) came back. Attached to the walls of the rest home are numerous wreaths and bouquets as well as anonymous banners saying simply, GRAZIE.

There are also other memorials to the holocaust victims. The fine artist Arbit Blatas has created seven powerfully moving sculptures on a wall adjacent to the rest home, their darkened slabs contrasting poignantly with the brick on which they are mounted. On one of the accompanying plaques, the city of Venice remembers the Venetian Jews who were deported to the Nazi concentration camps.

Another chilling commemoration has the power and constraint of a prison wall: horizontal iron bands crossed with larger vertical bands, restraining behind them many long wooden planks with all the victims' names and ages incised on them. The effect is so overwhelming that it is as if the prisoners themselves were behind those metal bands straining to get out. Mounted in front of them on slightly heavier standards is another sculptured plaque, also by Blatas, L'ULTIMO TRENO, THE FINAL TRAIN. It depicts a freight train, its doors ajar, disgorging a constant surge of humanity. Nazi soldiers armed with guns hold back the regurgitated masses, who are surely on their way to the gas chambers.

There is a more cheerful aspect to the rest of the Campo. Besides the Museum of Jewish art, there are small craft shops run by artisans, and others that sell religious articles. In David's Shop, I found postcards with fine photographs of the ghetto. When we were there, the quarter was home to about thirty families, quite in evidence, judging by the laundry fluttering on lines strung from several windows. There is a resurgence of simple markets, crafts, and shops. In spite of prevailing gaiety, the sobering lessons of history, so well memorialized here and a constant reminder of man's culpabilities, should keep us all on the alert.

Epilogue

Little did we know what Italy would mean to us when my husband applied for a Fulbright fellowship to do research in Rome in 1958. We spent an unforgettable year there, allowing him to do his research and the whole family to explore the splendors of that country. We were smitten. Americans, with the exception of the wealthy people who had made "the grand tour," weren't well traveled in those days. For me, Italy, the first foreign country I had ever visited, came as a revelation. What had been a serious awakening of an interest in wine and food when we went from Trenton, New Jersey, where we grew up, to a job in Berkeley, California, now became a deeper and absorbing involvement. In the United States, what had been a window opening on the cultural differences and attitudes from east to west now became a passageway to even greater differences spoken in another language.

Italy changes the lives of most Americans who go there—the

effects of overwhelming friendliness, landscape, sea, Umbrian light everywhere, primary colors, rhythms, music, flowers, markets, an abundance of gratifying food—sensual pleasures that easily overtake the puritan spirit that seems to be part of our baggage. The immersion in ancient history, reflected everywhere in ruins and restorations, made us feel the past in a way more profound than we ever could at home. In Italy, we were inspired. We traveled as much and as widely as we could. We made friends who are still good friends more than forty years later. And we went back as often as possible.

Because we had been something like American postwar pioneers in Italy, we were the source of information for friends and acquaintances who were going on their first trips. The most frequent questions were culinary. One of my friends, an editor who had found our advice useful, suggested putting it, somewhat expanded, into book form. She took the outline to New York with her, and the next thing I knew, I had a call from a publisher.

It took a long time to write in my hesitant Italian to fifty restaurants, representing in Rome the various regional cuisines of the country. Forty-eight restaurateurs wrote back, many of them at length, many of them using both sides of tissue-thin paper, almost all using pen and ink, everyone enclosing recipes, all of which had to be tested.

It was a huge task to write that book, one which spilled over into my husband's next fellowship, this one in Paris. That summer we went back to Rome where Rita Benazzo, my trusted friend and a superb cook, helped me test the recipes. Our apartment there was often festooned with twirls and ribbons of drying pasta. Our only crisis came when we were preparing the recipe for *bollito misto*, mixed boiled meats, which included a calf's head. The delicacy was the eye, which Rita insisted I should have, but which, of course, she coveted. After much polite but insistent argument, she accepted it, much to my relief and her pleasure.

Over the years, we have had many lengthy stays abroad, always enriching, always instructive, and above all, always pleasurable. For me, writing down our adventures in Italy was a way of reliving them; for the reader I hope it conveyed some of the magic of our experiences.

The summer of 2004 we took Sonia, my son's second oldest child, to Europe. First stop was Venice, then Rome, Florence, and a week in Paris. Her favorite was Florence. We had already taken her older sister, Naomi, to Europe, which had noticeably influenced her. When she became a Stanford student, she spent her junior year abroad: first semester Paris, then two semesters in Florence. Although, like her sister, she loved all the destinations, her preference was for Florence. Sam, the youngest, will have his turn in a year or so. My daughters' kids, Wynne, Cole, and Max, got their first taste of Italy this year.

All indications are that this next generation of American travelers will prosper from, learn from, and willingly accept the differences discovered in their new foreign experiences. By total immersion in other people's customs, languages, and history, not to mention their joie de vivre, we hope that our grandchildren, as well as many other voyagers, will be intellectually broadened, and become truly tolerant citizens of the world. It certainly worked for us.